THE SOCIAL NORMS APPROACH TO PREVENTING SCHOOL AND COLLEGE AGE SUBSTANCE ABUSE

THE SOCIAL NORMS APPROACH TO PREVENTING SCHOOL AND COLLEGE AGE SUBSTANCE ABUSE

A Handbook for Educators, Counselors, and Clinicians

H. Wesley Perkins, Editor

JOSSEY-BASS
A Wiley Imprint
www.josseybass.com

Published by Jossey-Bass
A Wiley Imprint
989 Market Street, San Francisco, CA 94103-1741 www.josseybass.com

Jossey-Bass books and products are available through most bookstores. To contact Jossey-Bass directly, call
our Customer Care Department within the U.S. at (800) 956-7739, outside the U.S. at (317) 572-3993, or
fax (317) 572-4002.

Jossey-Bass also publishes its books in a variety of electronic formats. Some content that appears in print
may not be available in electronic books.

Library of Congress Cataloging-in-Publication Data
The social norms approach to preventing school and college age substance
abuse: a handbook for educators, counselors, and clinicians/H. Wesley
Perkins, editor.
    p. cm.
Includes bibliographical references and index.
   ISBN 0-7879-6459-X (alk. paper)
  1. Students—Substance use—Prevention. 2. Youth—Substance
use—Prevention. 3. Substance abuse—Prevention. 4. Social norms. 5.
Peer pressure. I. Perkins, H. Wesley.
   HV4999.Y68.S653 2003
   362.29'083—dc21
                                                      2002155025

Printed in the United States of America
FIRST EDITION
HB Printing   10 9 8 7 6 5 4 3 2 1

CONTENTS

PART THREE: EXPANDING SOCIAL NORMS INTERVENTIONS TO OTHER COLLEGE STUDENT APPLICATIONS 133

PART FOUR: YOUNG ADULTS AND SOCIAL NORMS WORK BEYOND THE CAMPUS 171

TABLES AND FIGURES

Tables

Figures

For my daughters
Jessica and Kiah

PREFACE

In recent years, the social norms approach to preventing risky problem behavior and promoting health has been gaining the attention of an increasing number of researchers, educators, social workers, and counselors who work with adolescents and young adult populations. Starting as a research topic and then growing into a successfully applied strategy for preventing substance abuse and other problem behaviors, it has rightly gained this attention with notable positive effects in populations where the lack of positive change has been apparent with other methods. The approach is fundamentally grounded in the scientific model of discovery. It asks what the reality of social behavior among young people is and contrasts it with their perceptions. It offers a theory predicting behavior based on actual and perceived norms, proposes a model of intervention based on this theory, and considers the empirical evidence of effectiveness when the model is implemented in practical intervention contexts. This science-based accountability is a standard that should be (and increasingly is) called for when a prevention program is supported by schools or local communities.

The chapters in this volume present work by many of the researchers and health education practitioners who have been doing pioneering scientific work on social norms approaches to prevention in higher education and in adolescent school age populations. It has grown out of the various authors' work reported at five consecutive national conferences on the social norms model, beginning in 1998 and 1999 at Big Sky, Montana; in 2000 in Denver; in 2001 in Anaheim, California; and most recently, in 2002, in Philadelphia. We have been fortunate to have so many people gather annually in a conference devoted entirely to examining this health promotion strategy; I have been honored to address the gathering each year and watch the growth of interest in this movement. The enthusiasm exhibited by conference participants has made clear to me the value of getting the information and examples of this strategy and its various applications into print for a larger audience.

I have put together this collection of material to serve three primary purposes. First, readers new to the social norms approach will find that the introductory chapter and discussion in the subsequent case studies lay out the basic principles of the model and formulations of how social norms interventions work. Second, the book aims to present a good deal of scientifically collected evidence supporting the potential for applying the model and its positive effect when evaluated in intervention case studies. Today most educators, counselors, and clinicians are hungry for results. Not only do they want assurance that they are not engaged in a futile strategy squandering time and resources, but they simultaneously need to satisfy funding agencies and community constituencies that increasingly call for programs using approaches that can actually demonstrate positive results. Indeed, I believe the biggest attraction of the approach (in addition to its emphasis on healthy imagery) is the variety of success stories in these case studies where no other approach has been able to produce this kind of result. Third, program educators, school administrators, and other prevention practitioners will find many examples of a variety of intervention messages and strategies that have been tested in this range of case studies. With appropriate modifications, many of these methods and messages can be implemented in other secondary school, college, and community contexts.

I want to thank all of the contributing authors for their encouragement in my efforts to construct this compendium of social norms work in the substance abuse prevention field. Their cooperation in responding to my various requests in developing each chapter was crucial in producing this book. I am also appreciative of the editors at Jossey-Bass, especially Alan Rinzler and Amy Scott, for their initial interest in my proposal; their gentle and constructive criticism, which helped improve various chapters; and their labor in putting the manuscript into its final form. Lastly, I would especially like to express my gratitude to two close associates who are currently part of the Alcohol Education Project team at Hobart and William Smith Colleges. Debbie Herry has served as our project assistant, and David Craig, professor of biochemistry, directs the project along with me. They have been good friends and collaborators in the project's local and national initiatives to promote the social norms approach, and they have given me much needed support as I prepared this book.

January 2003   H. Wesley Perkins
Geneva, New York

PART ONE

INTRODUCTION

CHAPTER ONE

THE EMERGENCE AND EVOLUTION OF THE SOCIAL NORMS APPROACH TO SUBSTANCE ABUSE PREVENTION

H. Wesley Perkins, Ph.D.

The growth in the prevention field of what has now become known as the "social norms approach" has been a long time coming. It began almost twenty years ago with a few surprising research findings about social norms and their misperceptions (Perkins and Berkowitz, 1986) followed by proposals for practical application of these findings (Berkowitz and Perkins, 1987) and a comprehensive theoretical model of the prevention approach (Perkins, 1991, 1997). The strategy suggested by this perspective remained on the margins of prevention literature and practice, however, for quite some time thereafter. Nevertheless, interest grew and a few brave prevention workers branched out to embrace it in the years following these publications. Today, although the approach is by no means dominant in the health promotion field, nor in the programs of primary, secondary, or postsecondary education, it has become a popular topic that prevention specialists are turning to with greater frequency as a positive alternative to traditional methods.

Some administrators, health workers, and educators have reluctantly begun to acknowledge the potential; others have experienced a dramatic conversion to the social norms perspective, with renewed excitement and zeal for potential change. Some people in prevention work have been attracted by the intriguing logic of the approach itself, but much more of the growing popularity has been driven by two related phenomena. First, the failed efforts or lack of improvement using traditional strategies in most youth and young adult target populations has led professionals to look for new methods out of sheer frustration with the stagnant situation. Second, the field of health and safety promotion is recognizing the need to go beyond simply restating problem behaviors or positing what are believed to be good prevention practices, to documenting effective prevention results. Indeed, there is growing recognition that we need to know what works and then move in those directions. The prevention field is finally becoming more serious in demanding science-based evaluation. This demand is making evident the pervasive lack of impact from traditional strategies and the impressive emerging data on reduction in substance abuse and related problem behaviors that has been achieved through social norms strategies.

Looking Back: Transitions in the Prevention Field

The historical trajectory of substance abuse prevention work with adolescents and young adults in recent decades is instructive for understanding current interest in the social norms approach. Traditionally, prevention concentrated on reactive strategies, that is, those waiting for the problem to appear before taking action; they are an attempt to fix something once it is broken. This work has focused on ways to rehabilitate problem users and addicts, or contain their problem behaviors. In secondary schools and colleges, this usually means getting the individual into a counseling program, requiring a workshop on the effects of drugs and risks of abuse, or a punishment such as required community service. If serious rules are broken or the substance abusing individual is a threat to others, we suspend him or her. Some of these interventions may be ultimately necessary at one level to restrain and hopefully change the high-risk individual and his or her destructive behavior. These strategies are labor-intensive and expensive, however, and are mostly "containment" measures for these problem youths. They do not reduce the overall prevalence of the problem among high-risk youth; nor do they reduce the substance abuse that occurs in the larger population of youths who would not necessarily be categorized as addicts or persistent problem users.

The prevention field has moved well beyond that limited approach, of course, toward strategies that for several years now have been called "proactive." These strategies are designed to address potential problems in a target population before they start or before they become highly problematic. Much of that work has used traditional health education models that rely on teaching and advertising about the health risks and pharmacological dangers of substance use. Most would agree that it is a good thing to be more knowledgeable about potential substances one might consume, but unfortunately this knowledge alone has not proven to have much effect in reducing problems, especially in youthful populations that are not particularly concerned about long-term health consequences or mortality. More-over, most advertising directed at inoculating youthful populations takes a nega-tive approach, relying on rational behaviorist assumptions that people inevitably avoid actions that incur punishment or negative consequences for themselves. At-tempts to scare young people straight—to "scare the health into them" by vividly portraying extreme dangers of use—lose credibility, however, as youths dismiss their own chance of such an event, believing it to be relatively improbable (with some accurate statistical basis for that notion, regarding extreme consequences).

More positive proactive strategies attempting to change individuals have often concentrated on changing attitudes with techniques such as values clarification training and self-esteem enhancement exercises. Other strategies seek to create positive "alternative" social events. The idea in each instance is to give students the armor, or at least the social diversion, to avoid alcohol and other drug abuse. Again, however, costs in many of these labor-intensive programs are high and a notable reduction in alcohol or other drug abuse with these methods has not been demonstrated.

In the face of these limitations and failures, prevention work has begun to con-centrate more on the environment and how the larger culture within which stu-dents live may offer the critical focal point for successful prevention. This perspective looks at how phenomena beyond the individual's personality and per-sonal values and interests may be important determinants of the individual's be-havior and to what extent they can be changed. The discussion and research now emanating from this environmental movement takes two directions, although they are by no means necessarily mutually exclusive. The first pursues a public policy strategy: creating legal and institutional policy restrictions in the school environ-ment to reduce access to alcohol, tobacco, and other substances. It institutes puni-tive measures and controls to discourage problem behavior overall. These policies are set up not only as environmental controls on individuals but also as constraints on business and organizations within the community that affect the availability and promotion of alcohol and other substances. In some circumstances, these policies have been effective, to a degree, in reducing problems among adolescents. In col-lege populations, however, creating new restrictive policies as a singular response to problems has not to date produced the desired reduction in problem use.

The Emergence of the Social Norms Approach

Finally, we come to what we call the social norms approach, with its own theories of behavior and strategies for intervention. It can be understood as environmen-tal in that it is not immediately concerned with directly changing an individual's personal attitude. It uses, instead, the revelation of accurate information about the environmental context—in the form of group or population norms—to reduce individual problem behavior and enhance protective behavior. On the surface, the approach may sound a bit nonsensical: using what already exists in terms of normative patterns regarding substance use to change or reduce the problem behavior within those patterns. But there is a simple, perhaps elegant, logic to the approach, as we shall see. What is demanded of prevention specialists and health educators when first encountering the social norms philosophy and strategy is that they be willing to suspend their accustomed notion of how to change behavior and start thinking "outside the box."

The story of the development of the social norms approach begins with research documenting misperceptions about peer norms. The initial systematic research on this topic was conducted several years ago at Hobart and William Smith Colleges (Perkins and Berkowitz, 1986), a small private college in upstate New York. Research on this student population demonstrated a pervasive and continuing pattern of misperception about alcohol norms among student peers. Students generally believed the norm for the frequency and amount of drinking among peers was much higher than the actual norm or average level of consumption, and they believed their peers were much more permissive in personal attitude about substance use than was the true pattern of attitudes. Even though actual levels of consumption in this college population were fairly high as found in many college environments, the misperceptions about the norms for peer attitudes and use still far outpaced the actual norms.

Following this research, similar misperceptions of alcohol norms were found (and reported in unpublished prevention program research) at institutions diverse in region, size, and student characteristics, among them the University of California (Los Angeles), Linfield College (Oregon), Carroll College (Wisconsin), the University of Virginia, and the University of Arizona. Published research demonstrating pervasive misperception of peer drinking norms was subsequently reported from studies at the University of Washington (Baer, Stacy, and Larimer, 1991), Princeton University (Prentice and Miller, 1993), and Northern Illinois University (Haines and Spear, 1996). Among students attending a university in the Northwest, Page, Scanlan, and Gilbert (1999) found that males and females alike overestimated the extent of heavy episodic drinking among their peers of the same and opposite gender. In research conducted on nationwide data from colleges and universities that have participated in the Core Institute Alcohol and Drug Survey, Perkins and others (1999) found most students perceived substantially more use of alcohol among their peers than really occurred at their school in all of the one hundred institutions in the study. This pattern of misperception was the result at each particular institution, regardless of the actual level of use locally. Thus we now know that exaggerated perception of alcohol norms is commonly entrenched in both public and private schools of every size across the country.

Likewise, these patterns of exaggerated perception have been found for all other drug types included in substance use research (Perkins, 1994; Perkins and others, 1999). Misperceived norms also exist across subpopulations of youth—not just among men, not just among women, not just among certain ethnic groups, nor simply among students who are living in residence halls, but also among commuter students, Greek organizations, and independents (cf. Baer, Stacy, and Larimer, 1991; Baer and Carney, 1993; Borsari and Carey, 1999). Various groups may have their own level of actual use, but misperceptions are widely held across most subpopulations. Furthermore, these misperceived norms are not unique to college populations; they can also be found in the high school context (Beck and Treiman, 1996) and statewide populations of young adults (Linkenbach, 1999).

Importantly, none of this research claims that alcohol or other drug abuse is only a minor or inconsequential problem among adolescents and college students. The evidence is clear, for example, that collegiate alcohol abuse in particular presents substantial and fairly widespread consequences that negatively affect the abusing individuals, others around them, and the academic institution with which they are associated (Perkins, 2002b). Rather, the findings of social norms research point out that, regardless of actual problem level, perception of the pervasiveness of these problems far outpaces actuality.

Causes and Consequences of Misperceived Norms

Perkins (1991, 1997, 2002a) put forth a comprehensive theory of the causes and consequences of this phenomenon that was based on attribution theory, social conversation mechanisms, and cultural media predicting that these misperceptions would be found among most students in virtually all peer-intensive environments. First, there is the general social psychological tendency to erroneously attribute observed behaviors of other people to their disposition, and to think the behavior is typical of the individual when the action cannot be explained by the specific context or put into perspective by knowing what the other person usually does most of the time. So when one observes a peer involved in substance abuse, one tends to think it is characteristic of that individual when it cannot be explained as an unusual or rare event by personal knowledge of the context. We simply tend to assume that what we have observed of others on occasion is what they normally do if we have no concrete basis to think otherwise.

Second, the extravagant behavior of an individual or a few people under the influence of alcohol or other drugs is easily noticed and remembered, whether it is a funny scene of uninhibited action, the disgusting circumstance of someone sick from inebriation, or a frightening encounter with a belligerent or violent individual. Youths go home from parties and social gatherings remembering and talking about these incidents and focusing on how drunk or "wasted" some peers were, rather than talking about the less interesting majority who remained abstinent or sober. We simply do not collect information from a cross-section of peers in social gatherings and reflect on it in casual conversation. Instead, the tendency is to recall the most vivid behaviors and then conversation gravitates to the extreme incidents, in the end making them seem more common than is really the case.

Finally, cultural media reaffirm and amplify these exaggerations. Music and film entertainment for youth and young adults frequently depicts and often glamorizes substance use, making it appear to be more common than it is among most youths. Then news media and community forums give headline attention to the problem behaviors among youths, rather than highlighting the healthy majority who are typically not seen as newsworthy. As the news and public discussion concentrate on the problem, the fact that it is a statistical minority gets lost on youths who simply hear the story that many young people are involved with alcohol, tobacco, and other drug use. This story quickly gets translated to "most" and "almost all" youths, as it is passed along in casual conversation. Left unchallenged, the exaggeration will persist over time.

On the basis of social psychological theories of conformity, peer identity formation, and cognitive dissonance, Perkins (1997) has argued that such misperception is likely to have substantial consequences on personal use. Research has long pointed to the dramatic power of peer influence in adolescence and young adulthood, but what has not been adequately considered in previous research and prevention strategy is whether this peer influence comes simply from what other peers actually believe is the right thing to do and how they behave, or from what young people *think* their peers believe is right and how they think most others behave. The social norms model proposes that much of the problem behavior may come from students following "imaginary peers" as they wish to, or feel pressured to, conform to erroneously perceived group patterns. Several studies of college students at large and small schools in various regions have supported this claim by showing that perceived social norms are significantly correlated with students' personal drinking behavior (Clapp and McDonnell, 2000; Nagoshi, 1999; Page, Scanlan, and Gilbert, 1999; Perkins and Berkowitz, 1986; Perkins and Wechsler, 1996; Wood, Nagoshi, and Dennis, 1992). It is a sociological dictum that if a situation is perceived as real, it is real in its consequences; perception of reality can ultimately produce behavior leading to a "self-fulfilling prophecy" (Merton, 1957).

Most adolescents, young adults, and indeed most everyone else are heavily influenced by the norms and expectations of other people. We are social creatures, operating for the most part by what the social group has set out as guidelines and expectations. The problem is that most students do not accurately perceive what the normative guidelines and expectations of their peers really are, and so they are guided, if not controlled, by a "reign of error" (Perkins, 1997). Students who are ambivalent about drinking or using other drugs and prefer to abstain feel pressure to indulge because they erroneously perceive that "everyone" expects it of them. Students who, left to their own inclination, would choose to drink only a moderate amount of alcohol with limited frequency are likewise nudged along to drink more heavily by their mistaken notion of what most other peers expect them to do and what they think most others are doing at parties and other social settings. Thus students with relatively moderate attitudes sometimes take risks with their drinking that they would not otherwise take, thanks to their distorted perception of norms. Finally, students who do have a permissive personal attitude, and who are thus personally prone to frequent heavy drinking or taking risks with other substances, can do so without reservation, naïvely thinking they are part of the majority. Perversely, other students give them the license and encouragement to do so because most other students hold the misperception of what is normative as well, even if their own behavior does not reach the falsely perceived standard. Overt peer opposition to destructive behavior declines in the face of misperception. Students become less willing to speak out against abuse and less willing to intervene when a peer is about to engage in risky behavior because they think they are the only ones who are concerned or uncomfortable with the actions of a peer.

Students with the most permissive personal attitudes are therefore bolstered by the misperception they (and others) hold and articulate, which makes them believe they are in a comfortable (albeit fictitious) majority. If students who are at high risk in terms of their own attitude begin to acquire or hold a more moderate—more accurate—perception of the peer norm for alcohol use, however, they are then placed in a more cognitively dissonant circumstance, which makes heavy drinking more difficult (Perkins and Berkowitz, 1986). Perkins and Wechsler's research (1996) on nationwide data from 140 colleges and universities found that differing personal perceptions of the campus drinking culture have an important impact on students' own use and problems, in addition to the effect of the actual climate at various campuses. It also found that the effect of these perceptions was strongest in accentuating or constraining alcohol abuse among those students with the most permissive personal attitudes.

If youths are pulled in the direction of these exaggerated (misperceived) norms, as the research suggests, then one might wonder why students do not ultimately reach the level of consumption and risk in their actual behavior that they perceive to be the norm among others. Several factors explain why actual norms never rise to meet the level of perceived norms. First, when actual risky behavior among students at a school increases, so does the misperception of group members, through a series of causal dynamics where conversation and memory give attention to extreme behaviors, making them seem normative (as previously described). So misperception continues to outpace reality as the new extreme behavior becomes the object of attention and talk, as if it were normal. But this explanation alone would suggest a continuous inflation of actual and perceived norms, with the implication that a perpetual increase in substance abuse should be rampant. This is not the case, of course, for at least two reasons. First, not all youths are personally affected equally by their misperception of the norm. Biology, religious beliefs, and jobs, for example, exert a constraint on some youths in spite of their exaggerated notion of what others do. If one can not physically tolerate ingestion of alcohol, as is the case for some people, or if one is raised within a belief system of strict abstinence, one is not likely to drink or drink heavily just because one thinks most others do so. If the young person has to work a part-time job that conflicts with social activities where alcohol is readily available, then one has less opportunity regardless of misperception of the social norm. So not all students steadily increase their risk behavior on the basis of their misperception. Nevertheless, even those "protected" youths can still be a problem as "carriers" of the misperception "virus," spreading it to others in conversation who in turn may be personally influenced (Perkins, 1997).

The second reason actual secondary school or college norms of a student population do not noticeably inflate for the group as individuals change behavior in response to their misperception is that we are not observing a static population where students remain forever as one group increasingly conforming to their misperceptions. They move through secondary school and college. Substance use behavior does increase for a cohort as it moves through grades and enters college. Then students graduate and react to new perceived norms of the "real work world," or they drop out of school along the way (not infrequently because of a drug or alcohol abuse problem nudged along by their misperception of norms). So the "pool" of youth in the system responding to misperception is ever changing, as students move through educational institutions. They frequently respond to misperception of the norm for their new grade or new school negatively but ultimately move out of the group they erroneously perceived, all the time creating the illusion of a static level of substance abuse to the observer looking at the aggregate rate. Left unchecked, these taken-for-granted misperceptions of peer norms continue to work perniciously and unnoticed as both students and prevention specialists focus on the problem behaviors.

The Social Norms Model of Substance Abuse Prevention

The strategy of the social norms approach, put simply, is to communicate the truth about peer norms in terms of what the majority of students actually think and do, all on the basis of credible data drawn from the student population that is the target. The message to students is a positive one—the norm is one of safety, responsibility, and moderation or abstinence because that is how the majority of students think and act in most student populations. (Whether the normative message focuses specifically on moderation or on abstinence depends, of course, on the substance involved and the age level of the youthful population.) In some instances or on the basis of some empirical measures, the actual norm may not be ideal, but it will be substantially less problematic than what students believe the norm to be. Therefore, communicating the truth about student norms becomes a constraining intervention on problem behavior, no matter what the actual norms are. As students begin to adhere to a more accurately perceived norm that is relatively moderate, the actual norm becomes even more moderate as the process of misperception leading to problem behavior is reversed (see Figure 1.1).

Any social norms intervention initiative must begin with collecting and assessing credible data identifying misperception and constructing data-based messages to counter them. Then a variety of methods can be employed to deliver the social norms message about accurate positive norms. Strategies have included print media campaigns (posters, billboards, student newspaper articles and ads, and targeted mailings to students), television and radio announcements, computer media communications, and classroom presentations. Peer educator programs have begun to focus their work on delivering messages about accurate positive norms. The approach is even being integrated into brief counseling strategies, where normative feedback is provided to confront misperceptions and help break

FIGURE 1.1. MODEL OF SOCIAL NORMS APPROACH TO PREVENTION.

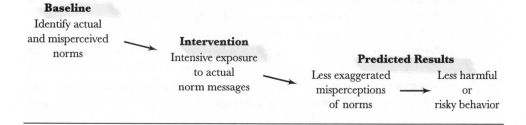

down the denial of students with a problem by letting them see where their behavior falls on the continuum of actual behavior. Several case studies and experiments using a number of these strategies with young and college age students have yielded significant positive results in terms of reduced substance use (Agostinelli and Brown, 1995; Borsari and Carey, 2000; Haines and Spear, 1996; Hansen, 1993; Hansen and Graham, 1991; Jeffrey, 2000; Johannessen, Collins, Mills-Novoa, and Glider, 1999; Perkins and Craig, 2002; Schroeder and Prentice, 1998; Steffian, 1999).

Chapter Contributions to This Book

The methods of collecting data, the choice of particular normative messages, and the means of delivering the credible information vary, of course, across school contexts and age groups. The projects presented in the chapters of this book present examples with further breadth and detail of social norms strategies along with extensive evaluation data providing evidence of the impact of this approach. In the first set of case studies (in Part Two), we find a number of college campuses that have introduced intensive social norms initiatives targeting alcohol abuse, each witnessing a remarkable reduction in high-risk use following introduction of this approach. Their findings are even more remarkable given that several nationwide studies have demonstrated no reduction in the high-risk drinking rate at colleges and universities in general across the nation over the last ten years, when these case studies were being conducted (Johnston, O'Malley, and Bachman, 2001; Wechsler, Lee, and Kuo, 2002).

These applied experiments in college populations are quite important taken together as a set. They make a strong collective statement of the potential power of this approach, for two reasons. First, although any one case study might be criticized for imperfect methodology in some regard—be it a low survey response rate, a limited set of empirical measures, or the limited ability to control other events in the immediate campus environment occurring during the experimental period—the potential weakness of any particular study is far overshadowed by the consistent positive result achieved by all experiments conducted with diverse methodologies. Second, this consistent positive result was found across a range of schools representing academic institutions in the eastern, midwestern, southwestern, and northwestern regions of the United States. These schools include public and private institutions with student populations from less than two thousand to more than thirty-five thousand. Some of these schools draw students from a predominantly upper-middle-class background while other schools have a more middle-class and working-class constituency. Some schools are essentially residential; others have a significant commuting population.

The Northern Illinois University experiment (Chapter Two) presents the first applied experiment using the approach in a college student population and lays out an extended time frame for assessing impact. The experiment used print media and cocurricular activities publicizing actual norms to change perceptions; it documented a dramatic and continuing decline in heavy drinking among students. The Hobart and William Smith Colleges experiment (Chapter Three) describes the development and results of an experimental social norms intervention implementing multiple interlinked strategies to achieve a synergistic effect in reducing misperceived drinking norms. Electronic media and curricular innovations were designed to enhance and extend print media communicating actual student norms. Results drawn from multiple survey techniques and an extensive set of survey measures over five years demonstrate both immediate and long-term reduction in high-risk drinking and negative consequences. The University of Arizona (Chapter Four) replicated the NIU print media strategy with further development of media intervention methods and coordinated the strategy with coalition building initiatives within the university, again witnessing a significant reduction in heavy drinking.

At Western Washington University (Chapter Five), another print media campaign was conducted, this time adding social norms delivery through a large peer educator program and, for students already manifesting an alcohol problem, delivery through an alcohol screening and intervention program. A significant reduction in high-risk drinking was achieved in this project as it simultaneously reinforced abstinence and the choice of substance-free housing. The Rowan University Social Norms Project (Chapter Six) reports replication of the social norms intervention approach at an East Coast university using print media as well as orientation program presentations and radio programming. Assessment results demonstrate that as exposure to campaign materials increased each year, a corresponding reduction in high-risk drinking was the result. The Small Group Norms-Challenging Model at Washington State University (Chapter Seven) introduces strategies and results of multiple efforts to reduce misperceived peer norms and related high-risk drinking through class presentations, workshop formats, and small-group interaction especially targeting high-risk groups with control group comparisons demonstrating the impact of the strategy.

The next group of studies (Part Three) consider expansion of social norms intervention to other campus applications. Chapter Eight is an evaluation of a social norms marketing intervention to reduce the onset of smoking among new college students at one university; it compares the outcome with data from another school acting as a control site. The experiment demonstrated a significant reduction in onset of smoking among students exposed to messages about accurate student norms as compared to students at the control site. Chapter Nine discusses the potential importance of using a social norms approach to build campus support for policy change, an important first step in applying policy-oriented environmental strategies. Policy controls are likely to be more effective if there is known to be significant student support, yet students often underestimate the level of support for regulations that actually exists among peers. Survey data are presented to support this claim, and the implications are discussed for building comprehensive prevention strategies.

Part Four looks beyond the college campus to research and models applying the social norms approach to young adults in general. Chapter Ten reports the results of a statewide survey of eighteen-to-twenty-four-year-old residents in Montana that examines actual and perceived norms for frequency and quantity of alcohol consumption and prevalence of drinking and driving. Results again reveal a dramatic discrepancy between actual and perceived norms for both men and women. The next chapter (Chapter Eleven) follows up this statewide research with discussion of the strategic steps taken by one social norms program to take the social norms approach for promoting health to a statewide level of implementation. It reviews important issues, from data gathering to message development to building coalitions and stakeholder support.

In Part Five, contributing authors turn their attention to middle school and high school students. Chapter Twelve reveals the pervasive pattern of misperception regarding peer tobacco, alcohol, and illicit drug norms found among middle school and high school students across the nation. The data were collected in a Web-based survey conducted in twenty-eight schools in five states across the country. The dramatic potential for introducing the social norms model in secondary education is made apparent by the prevalence of misperceived norms at these earlier age levels. The next study (Chapter Thirteen) describes a social norms experiment conducted among twelve-to-seventeen-year-olds living in seven Montana counties, with results compared to youths in the rest of the state. At the end of the experimental time period, the social norms media intervention was associated with a significantly lower rate of first-time use of tobacco compared to the rate of first-time use in the rest of the state, where other types of prevention strategies were employed. Chapter Fourteen describes the intervention conducted at two Midwestern high schools using social norms media to significantly reduce cigarette smoking and drinking among tenth grade students during a two-year period. This project was unique among social norms interventions in that it used media to change the parents' and teachers' perceptions of students as well as the students' perceptions of their peers.

In the final portion of this book (Part Six), we present further applications of the social norms model. Chapter Fifteen reports on a statewide study of parents of teenage children that examines parenting behaviors and parents' perceptions of parent norms. Parents typically misperceived parent norms, believing most parents to be less involved and more permissive in parenting as related to curfews, talking with teens about substance use, and other serious concerns than is actually the case. This study demonstrates a circumstance in which the social norms approach can be extended to family life by correcting parent misperceptions and reinforcing effective parenting. If parents can be strengthened in their resolve to pay conscientious attention to their children's social lives, it is likely to reduce substance abuse among youth. This chapter also presents examples of media intervention resulting from these findings.

The phenomenon of misperceived norms goes well beyond alcohol and other drug use and can be observed in such areas of prevention work as hate speech, sexual aggression among men, and eating disorders among women. Many educators, counselors, and clinicians working on problems of substance abuse may also be working on other such problems of health and well-being in their practice and professional work with adolescents and young adults. Thus one does not have to limit the use of a social norms approach strictly to a focus on substance use. Much of what has been learned in applying the model to substance abuse prevention can be translated to other areas as well, although care must be taken in translating this approach to other topics. Chapter Sixteen extends the horizon for using a social norms approach to these areas and presents a review of the limited work of relevance. It speculates about the utility as well as limitations of a social norms approach for these other areas.

In Chapter Seventeen, I conclude the book with a look at the promise of the social norms approach on the basis of available research. I also address common questions and criticism about this method of promoting health, and I point out what future studies are needed to address remaining questions and lead to further advances in substance abuse prevention work.

References

Agostinelli, G., and Brown, J. M. "Effects of Normative Feedback on Consumption Among Heavy Drinking College Students." *Journal of Drug Education*, 1995, *25*, 31–40.

Baer, J. S., and Carney, M. M. "Biases in the Perceptions of the Consequences of Alcohol Use Among College Student." *Journal of Studies on Alcohol*, 1993, *54*, 54–60.

Baer, J. S., Stacy, A., and Larimer, M. "Biases in the Perception of Drinking Norms Among College Students." *Journal of Studies on Alcohol*, 1991, *52*, 580–586.

Beck, K., and Treiman, K. A. "The Relationship of Social Context of Drinking, Perceived Social Norms, and Parental Influence to Various Drinking Patterns of Adolescents." *Addictive Behaviors,* 1996, *21,* 633–644.

Berkowitz, A. D., and Perkins, H. W. "Current Issues in Effective Alcohol Education Programming." in J. Sherwood (ed.), *Alcohol Policies and Practices on College and University Campuses.* (Monograph series.) Columbus, Ohio: National Association of Student Personnel Administrators, 1987.

Borsari, B. E., and Carey, K. B. "Understanding Fraternity Drinking: Five Recurring Themes in the Literature." *Journal of American College Health,* 1999, *48,* 30–37.

Borsari, B. E., and Carey, K. B. "Effects of a Brief Motivation Intervention with College Student Drinkers." *Journal of Counseling and Clinical Psychology,* 2000, *68*(4), 728–733.

Clapp, J., and McDonnell, A. L. "The Relationship of Perceptions of Alcohol Promotion and Peer Drinking Norms to Alcohol Problems Reported by College Students." *Journal of College Student Development,* 2000, *41,* 19–26.

Haines, M., and Spear, S. "Changing the Perception of the Norm: A Strategy to Decrease Binge Drinking Among College Students." *Journal of American College Health,* 1996, *45,* 134–140.

Hansen, W. B. "School-Based Alcohol Prevention Programs." *Alcohol Health and Research World,* 1993, *17,* 54–60.

Hansen, W. B., and Graham, J. H. "Preventing Alcohol, Marijuana, and Cigarette Use Among Adolescents: Peer Pressure Resistance Training Versus Establishing Conservative Norms." *Preventive Medicine,* 1991, *20,* 414–430.

Jeffrey, L. R. *The New Jersey Higher Education Consortium Social Norms Project: Decreasing Binge Drinking in New Jersey Colleges and Universities by Correcting Student Misperceptions of College Drinking Norms.* Glasboro, N.J.: Center for Addiction Studies, Rowan University, 2000.

Johannessen, K., Collins, C., Mills-Novoa, B., and Glider, P. *A Practical Guide to Alcohol Abuse Prevention: A Campus Case Study in Implementing Social Norms and Environmental Management Approaches.* Tucson: University of Arizona Campus Health Service, 1999.

Johnston, L. D., O'Malley, P. M., and Bachman, J. G. *Monitoring the Future: National Survey Results on Drug Use, 1975–2000.* Vol. 2: *College Students and Adults Ages 19–40.* Rockville Md.: National Institute on Drug Abuse, U.S. Department of Health and Human Services, 2001.

Linkenbach, J. "Imaginary Peers and the Reign of Error." *Prevention Connection,* 1999, *3,* 1–5.

Merton, R. K. "The Self-Fulfilling Prophecy." In *Social Theory and Social Structure.* New York: Free Press, 1957.

Nagoshi, C. T. "Perceived Control of Drinking and Other Predictors of Alcohol Use and Problems in a College Student Sample." *Addiction Research,* 1999, *7*(4), 291–306.

Page, R. M., Scanlan, A., and Gilbert, L. "Relationship of the Estimation of Binge Drinking Among College Students and Personal Participation in Binge Drinking: Implications for Health Education and Promotion." *Journal of Health Education,* 1999, *30,* 98–103.

Perkins, H. W. "Confronting Misperceptions of Peer Drug Use Norms Among College Students: An Alternative Approach for Alcohol and Other Drug Education Programs." In *Peer Prevention Program Resource Manual.* Fort Worth: Higher Education Leaders/Peers Network, Texas Christian University, 1991.

Perkins, H. W. "The Contextual Effect of Secular Norms on Religiosity as Moderator of Student Alcohol and Other Drug Use." In M. L. Lynn and D. O. Moberg (eds.), *Research in the Social Scientific Study of Religion.* Greenwich, Conn.: JAI Press, 1994.

Perkins, H. W. "College Student Misperceptions of Alcohol and Other Drug Norms Among Peers: Exploring Causes, Consequences, and Implications for Prevention Programs." In *Designing Alcohol and Other Drug Prevention Programs in Higher Education: Bringing Theory into Practice.* Newton, Mass.: Higher Education Center for Alcohol and Other Drug Prevention, U.S. Department of Education, 1997.

Perkins, H. W. "Social Norms and the Prevention of Alcohol Misuse in Collegiate Contexts." *Journal of Studies on Alcohol,* 2002a, supplement no. 14, 164–172.

Perkins, H. W. "Surveying the Damage: A Review of Research on Consequences of Alcohol Misuse in College Populations." *Journal of Studies on Alcohol,* 2002b, supplement no. 14, 91–100.

Perkins, H. W., and Berkowitz, A. D. "Perceiving the Community Norms of Alcohol Use Among Students: Some Research Implications for Campus Alcohol Education Programming." *International Journal of the Addictions,* 1986, *21,* 961–976.

Perkins, H. W., and Craig, D. W. *A Multifaceted Social Norms Approach to Reduce High-Risk Drinking: Lessons from Hobart and William Smith Colleges.* Newton, Mass.: Higher Education Center for Alcohol and Other Drug Prevention, U.S. Department of Education, 2002.

Perkins, H. W., and Wechsler, H. "Variation in Perceived College Drinking Norms and Its Impact on Alcohol Abuse: A Nationwide Study." *Journal of Drug Issues,* 1996, *26,* 961–974.

Perkins, H. W., and others. "Misperceptions of the Norms for the Frequency of Alcohol and Other Drug Use on College Campuses." *Journal of American College Health,* 1999, *47*(6), 253–258.

Prentice, D. A., and Miller, D. T. "Pluralistic Ignorance and Alcohol Use on Campus: Some Consequences of Misperceiving the Social Norm." *Journal of Personality and Social Psychology,* 1993, *64,* 243–256.

Schroeder, C. M., and Prentice, D. A. "Exposing Pluralistic Ignorance to Reduce Alcohol Use Among College Students." *Journal of Applied Social Psychology,* 1998, *28,* 2150–2180.

Steffian, G. "Correction of Normative Misperceptions: An Alcohol Abuse Prevention Program." *Journal of Drug Education,* 1999, *29*(2), 115–138.

Wechsler, H., Lee, J. E., and Kuo, M. "Trends in College Binge Drinking During a Period of Increased Prevention Efforts: Findings from Four Harvard School of Public Health College Alcohol Study Surveys: 1993–2001." *Journal of American College Health,* 2002, *50*(5), 203–217.

Wood, M. D., Nagoshi, C. T., and Dennis, D. A. "Alcohol Norms and Expectations as Predictors of Alcohol Use and Problems in a College Student Sample." *American Journal of Drug and Alcohol Abuse,* 1992, *18,* 461–476.

PART TWO

CASE STUDIES OF COLLEGE EXPERIMENTS TO REDUCE ALCOHOL ABUSE

CHAPTER TWO

THE NORTHERN ILLINOIS UNIVERSITY EXPERIMENT

A Longitudinal Case Study of the Social Norms Approach

Michael P. Haines, M.S.; Gregory P. Barker, Ph.D.

Traditional attempts to change student drinking behavior and alcohol-related negative consequences have been relatively ineffective. The purpose of the long-term study reported in this chapter was to assess a new method for reducing alcohol use and alcohol-related negative consequences: the social norms approach.

The effect of social norms on personal and social behavior in general is well documented in the research literature. Theory about social norms maintains that people are influenced by their perception of norms, even if the perception is not accurate (Hechter and Opp, 2001). When a whole population holds an inaccurate perception of the prevailing norms, it is referred to as *pluralistic ignorance* (Miller and McFarland, 1991; Prentice and Miller, 1993; Cialdini, 1993). In the context of college alcohol consumption, if the population mistakenly believes that most college students drink heavily, this misperception leads to a higher drinking rate. Essentially, there is a tendency to do as the Romans do; in the context of social norms theory and college alcohol consumption, it is a tendency to do as they *believe* the Romans do (Berkowitz, 1997; Perkins, 1997).

Social norms research has demonstrated the prevalence of widely held but false norms about drinking among college students (that is, pluralistic ignorance of peer drinking behavior). Students believe that heavier drinking is normative (that the majority of college students are heavier drinkers), when in fact the majority of college students drink moderately or not at all (Perkins and Berkowitz, 1986; Baer, Stacy, and Larimer, 1991; Perkins and others, 1999).

Additional research describes a strong, positive correlation between student drinking norms (whether true or false) and actual student drinking behavior (Marks, Graham, and Hansen, 1992; Wood, Nagoshi, and Dennis, 1992; Perkins and Wechsler, 1996). That is, if students believe it is typical for college students to drink heavily, then there is a greater likelihood that they too will drink more heavily while at the same time believing that safety and moderation are uncommon.

Further research has demonstrated that student perceptions about the drinking behaviors and attitudes of other students are a stronger predictor of heavier drinking than gender or membership in a fraternity or sorority (Perkins and Wechsler, 1996) or alcohol availability (Graham, Marks, and Hansen, 1991). These relationships suggest that if the number of students who overestimate heavier drinking as normative behavior (false norm) is reduced, there will be a corresponding reduction in actual heavier drinking. This strategy has been used successfully in micro applications with small groups of high school youths (Hansen and Graham, 1991), with groups of college students who were heavier drinkers (Baer and others, 1992; Agostinelli, Brown, and Miller, 1995; Barnett, Far, Maus, and Miller, 1996), and in direct mail feedback to collegiate heavier drinkers (Walters, 2000). The NIU experiment was the first attempt to test the social norms hypothesis as a campuswide longitudinal case study among college students.

Project Overview

Located in DeKalb, Northern Illinois University (NIU) is a comprehensive teaching and research institution with a student enrollment of more than twenty-three thousand. It is a residential campus with approximately seventeen thousand students living on campus or in the immediate area. In 1988, NIU began an intervention, initially funded by the U.S. Department of Education (DOE), to reduce alcohol-related injuries by reducing student drinking (quantity per occasion). The project began in the 1987–88 school year and continued through the 1997–98 school year. During 1987–88, baseline data were collected to establish the students' perceptions of peer drinking behavior, their own drinking behavior, and the frequency of alcohol-related physical injuries.

During the 1988–89 school year, a traditional approach to reducing alcohol use and alcohol-related student injuries was employed. After trying the traditional strategy without success, NIU initiated a social norms intervention in the 1989–90 school year to change student perceptions of peer drinking (reduce misperceptions of heavier episodic drinking as the norm), thereby reducing the actual level of drinks per occasion and, ultimately, reducing alcohol-related student injuries. The NIU effort was unique in that it was the first attempt to use the social norms approach on a macro level to achieve a positive impact with a large population. Essentially, it was an experiment in changing mass behavior.

The Traditional Approach at NIU

The DOE funding supported an expansion of NIU's alcohol abuse prevention efforts during the 1988–89 school year. This traditional approach to reducing alcohol-related injuries and heavier drinking at NIU included a combination of fear appeals (scare tactics), abstinence support, and examples of responsible use skills delivered through small group educational programming. For example, trained peer educators carried out alcohol education programs in residence halls and Greek houses. These programs described the risks and negative consequences associated with heavier drinking, tips for responsible drinking, and nonalcohol social strategies to maintain abstinence. Additionally, the university participated in National Collegiate Alcohol Awareness Week, wherein peer educators and local public safety professionals conducted a simulated car crash to dramatize the risks of drunk driving; informational materials with content similar to the programs were distributed.

Introducing the Social Norms Approach at NIU

The NIU social norms strategy was designed to have an impact on *all* students rather than focusing on a small subset of the population. Two assumptions were fundamental to this mass intervention. First, though drinking in college is widespread and heavier drinking not uncommon, there was no simple way to identify and reach heavier drinkers as a discrete target population. Because heavier drinking was found across a variety of social and demographic factors (Johnston, O'Malley, and Bachman, 2001; Wechsler and others, 2002; Presley, Leichliter, and Meilman, 1998), it was difficult to select a student *type* or *site* that was likely to represent most of the heavier drinkers. It was easier to reach those at greatest risk of harm (heavier drinkers) with an indiscriminate, environmental approach.

Second, like most adults in society, college students have multiple social affiliations and identities. The diversity of even ordinary social interaction means that there may be many (sometimes competing) social norms that could potentially influence a student's behavior. For example, a male Latino student drinker is simultaneously gender affiliated (male), culturally affiliated (Latino), occupationally affiliated (student), and recreationally affiliated (drinker). Each of these groups has norms, and determining which of those norms are most influential was not easy. Again, an indiscriminate, environmental approach was believed to be the most effective means of reaching the entire population of students.

Social marketing was chosen as the least expensive, most effective, most credible, and most wide-reaching strategy to reach the large and diverse student population at NIU. Social marketing "is the application of commercial marketing technologies to the analysis, planning, execution, and evaluation of programs designed to influence the voluntary behavior of target audiences in order to improve their personal welfare and that of their society" (Andreasen, 1995, p. 7). Social marketing is data-driven and uses market research to design and refine strategies to effectively change the behavior of a large social group.

The social marketing approach used on NIU's campus relied heavily on print media: posters, flyers, and advertisements and articles in the student newspaper. Print media seemed an effective method to reach a large portion of the NIU campus population regardless of residence or year in school. Survey research in 1994 indicated that the messages appearing on posters and in advertisements in the campus paper were read by 78 percent of NIU students. Interestingly, the data also indicated that the heavier drinkers were more likely to read the media (84 percent readership) than were light drinkers (70 percent readership) and abstainers (60 percent readership; Haines, 1996). Furthermore, students indicated that these media are a more believable source of alcohol information than peer educators, resident advisors, friends, or faculty (Haines, 1996; American College Health Association, 2001). Population behavior change research also suggests media methods are more effective than interpersonal methods for large-scale public health initiatives (McAlister, 1991).

The media chosen for NIU's social marketing strategy used a simple *wellness* formula to (1) describe the desired behavior of moderate and safer alcohol use as the campus norm, (2) model behavioral strategies for safer use and moderate consumption, and (3) reinforce the desired behavior in three ways. First, the media focused on the desired behavior of moderate drinking and protective or safer actions instead of admonishing students about heavier drinking and the dangers associated with that behavior. Second, the desired behavior was normalized by informing the student audience that *moderate drinking at a party* is the most common drinking behavior among college students. Therefore, the media used ego protection and social acceptance as reward mechanisms. Finally, the media transferred positive value to the desired behavior by promoting positive images (photographs of good looking, typical college students having fun in a variety of settings) to link the safer behavior with the positive feelings evoked by the graphic elements. Positive transference is a common promotional strategy used in commercial marketing.

It is important to stress that the social marketing media chosen for the campaign attempted to defeat the false norm ("most students are heavy drinkers") by identifying and promoting the true norm ("most students drink moderately"). This shift to emphasizing and reinforcing the true norm of safety, moderation, and protection was important because it allowed the intervention to address the campus environment with an optimistic, positive strategy. (Samples of media and articles describing the methods in greater detail can be found at www.socialnorm.org.)

In addition to displaying the message through numerous media channels, three promotional tactics were used to increase student reading and recall of the media content:

1. Early in the campaign, students were given dollar bills by costumed "Blues Brothers" look-alikes if they could repeat the true student drinking norm.
2. In an attempt to influence members of fraternities and sororities, "MOST of Us" buttons were distributed to all Greek students. Any student found wearing the button who could recite "Most of us drink five or fewer when we party" got a five dollar bill on the spot.
3. Every year since 1994, residence hall students were randomly rewarded with five dollars for displaying a poster in their rooms containing the true drinking norm and other health messages. It was entitled "Name This Poster" to further encourage students to read and discuss the norm message.

These promotional efforts were specifically designed to increase the "public conversation" about the true norm message while reinforcing the media impact. Even with the addition of these paid incentives, the media campaign was a low-cost way (less than $8,000 annually) to reach thousands of students.

Data Collection Methods

As was noted earlier, at Northern Illinois University approximately seventeen thousand of the state school's twenty-three thousand students live on campus or in the immediate area.

All the data were drawn from a self-report survey sampling of undergraduates. The survey has been conducted every April at NIU since 1988. (A copy of the instrument may be downloaded from the National Social Norms Resource Center, www.socialnorm.org.) The surveys were administered by a health educator in large classes. The classes were chosen to ensure a diverse and representative student sample that approximated the university population. This "cluster sampling" method yielded annual cross-sectional data sets with a high proportional response (89 percent of those attending class) that were quite representative of the demographics of NIU undergraduates. The administration methods remained the same throughout the eleven-year sampling period.

Two questions were used to measure the students' drinking behavior and their perception of their peers' drinking behavior. To measure the former, students were asked, "When you 'party,' how many drinks do you have on average? (One drink is defined as a beer, a glass of wine, a shot of liquor, or a mixed drink.) State your best estimate." To assess the latter, students were asked, "How many drinks, on average, do you think most students have when they party?"

The data were dichotomized so students who responded that they consumed six or more drinks per party were classified as heavier drinkers and students who consumed zero to five drinks were classified as moderate drinkers. The same classification scheme was used to dichotomize student perception of their peers' drinking behavior. In this way, a direct comparison could be made between the students' own drinking behavior and the perceived drinking behavior of their peers.

Two additional questions included in the 1988–1991 surveys and again in the 1995–1998 surveys were used to measure the number of alcohol-related injuries on campus. Specifically, students were asked, "If you drink alcohol, within the last school year, have you physically injured yourself as a consequence of your drinking?" and "If you drink alcohol, within the last school year, have you physically injured another person as a consequence of your drinking?" Response data to these two questions were combined so that students were classified either as having physically injured themselves or another person or as not having injured themselves or another person as a consequence of their drinking.

Results

Figure 2.1 displays the findings across school years for the three primary dependent variables. Specifically, these were (1) student misperception of their peers heavier drinking behavior as the norm, (2) the students' self-reported heavier drinking behavior, and (3) the students' self-reported incidence of alcohol-related injury to themselves or others. Chi-square significance tests were used to compare student responses from the 1989 survey year (following implementation of the traditional intervention strategy) to the baseline 1988 survey year and subsequent survey years (1990 through 1998, following implementation of the social marketing intervention) to the 1989 survey year. The results of these analyses are in Table 2.1 and in the trend lines of Figure 2.1.

As Figure 2.1 and Table 2.1 indicate, there was no significant change in the three primary dependent variables between the 1988 and the 1989 surveys. That is, implementation of the traditional alcohol intervention strategy during the 1988–89 academic year failed to reduce student perceived and heavier drinking behavior or alcohol-related injuries.

In contrast, following implementation of the social marketing strategy in the 1989–90 academic year, there was a significant decline in both student misperception of the peer norm as heavier drinking and the students' self-reported

FIGURE 2.1. HEAVIER DRINKING, NORM MISPERCEPTIONS, AND INJURIES AMONG NIU STUDENTS, 1988–1998.

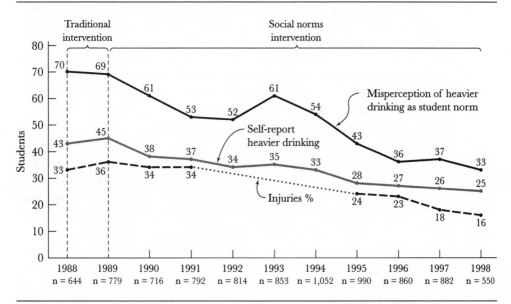

Note: During survey years 1992–1994, comparable injury questions were not included.

TABLE 2.1. SELF-REPORTED HEAVIER DRINKING, MISPERCEPTION OF PEER NORM, AND INJURY TO SELF OR OTHERS AT NIU, 1988–1998.

Survey Year	Self-Reported Heavier Drinking			Misperception of Peer Norm			Injury to Self or Others		
	Percentage	n		Percentage	n		Percentage	n	
1988	43	639		70	637		33	637	
1989	45	779	n.s.	69	779	n.s.	36	778	n.s.
1990	38	713	*	61	672	*	34	673	
1991	37	782	*	53	771	*	34	697	
1992	34	810	*	52	808	*	n/a		
1993	35	849	*	61	846	*	n/a		
1994	33	1049	*	54	1043	*	n/a		
1995	28	987	*	43	982	*	24	989	*
1996	27	858	*	36	856	*	23	856	*
1997	26	880	*	37	878	*	18	880	*
1998	25	549	*	33	541	*	16	549	*

Notes: An asterisk denotes a significant decrease (*p* < .05) from the 1989 survey year.

There was no significant (n.s.) reduction from the 1988 to the 1989 survey year.

During survey years 1992–1994, comparable injury questions were not available.

heavier drinking behavior. Indeed, chi-square tests comparing the 1990 through 1998 survey years to the 1989 survey year all yielded significant differences. These data strongly suggest the social marketing strategy implemented during 1990 and continued through the 1998 survey year reduced the students' misperceptions of the peer heavier drinking norm and, in turn, the students' own heavier drinking behavior.

As with perceived and actual drinking behavior, there was no significant difference in the students' self-reported incidence of alcohol-related injury to themselves or others between the 1988 and 1989 survey years. Although there were declines in the proportion of students reporting alcohol-related injuries in the 1990 and 1991 survey years (the years following implementation of social marketing strategy), these declines were not significant. However, in the 1995 survey year and every following survey year, when the same survey questions were again asked, a significant decline was found in the proportion of students reporting alcohol-related injuries compared to the 1989 survey year. These data suggest that although the effect was not immediate, reducing student misperception of the peer norm as heavier drinking and the students' own heavier drinking behavior eventually led to a corresponding decline in alcohol-related injuries.

To assess changes overall in drinking patterns that considered abstaining as well as moderate and heavier drinking at NIU, students' actual drinking responses were recoded into three categories: (1) abstainers (zero drinks when partying), (2) moderate drinkers (one to five drinks when partying), and (3) heavier drinkers (six or more drinks when partying). The proportions for each category for the 1989 and 1998 survey years are presented in Table 2.2. This analysis was important in addressing the question of what was happening to abstainers when the message was that moderation is the norm.

As Table 2.2 indicates, there was a significant increase in both the proportion of students who abstained from drinking from the 1989 to 1998 survey years as well as the proportion of students who drank moderately (one to five drinks when

TABLE 2.2. SELF-REPORTED DRINKING AT NIU, 1989 AND 1998.

When Partying	Number of Drinks	
	1989	1998
	(n = 779)	(n = 549)
0 drinks	9%	19%
1–5 drinks	46%	56%
6+ drinks	45%	25%

Note: All comparisons between the 1989 and 1998 survey years were significant ($p < .05$).

partying). The significant decrease in the proportion of students who reported drinking heavily (six or more drinks when partying) noted previously corresponds to the increase in both abstinence and moderation. Thus reducing misperception of heavy drinking by communicating the actual norm of moderation was not detrimental to the abstaining group of students. Rather, revealing the accurate norm reduced heavier drinking and permitted the growth of abstaining and moderation, presumably by moving heavier drinkers toward moderation or abstinence and allowing some moderate drinkers to choose abstinence as well.

Although changes to the survey response options after 1994 prevented subgroup analysis of drinking at an extremely high level of consumption (ten or more drinks per occasion) after that year, it is also worth noting the pattern found for these data between 1989 and 1994 when data on this highest consumption level could be analyzed separately. Specifically, comparison of the 1989 and 1994 survey years indicated a significant decrease in the proportion of students who drank ten or more drinks per occasion, as well as a significant decrease in the group who drank six to nine drinks per occasion. Thus, even the heaviest and most problematic of drinkers reduced their alcohol consumption.

Table 2.3 compares the 1989 and 1998 response data for the three primary dependent variables for (1) all students, (2) students under twenty-one years of age, (3) students over twenty-one, (4) student athletes, (5) fraternity and sorority members, (6) Latino students, (7) male students, and (8) female students. The intent of these analyses was to assess the impact of the social marketing strategy on a variety of social and demographic subgroups within the population.

As Table 2.3 indicates, every subgroup, with the exception of the sample of Latino students, showed significant declines in the perception of peer heavier drinking behavior, the self-reported heavier drinking behavior, and self-reported alcohol-related injuries. Although the Latino sample showed a similar decline for all three dependent variables, this decline was significant only for student perception of their peers' heavier drinking behavior. The lack of statistically significant findings for Latino students was thought to have resulted from the relatively small sample size. (Latino students were chosen for analysis as a minority subgroup because their actual drinking rate from the outset was higher than those of African American and Asian populations at NIU.)

Interpreting the Positive Results

This project represents the first longitudinal effort to produce mass behavior change in a collegiate context using the social norms approach. Not only did this approach significantly reduce the overestimation of heavier drinking perceived by students (which in turn led to a reduction in heavier drinking and alcohol-related

TABLE 2.3. SELF-REPORTED DRINKING, MISPERCEPTIONS, AND INJURY AT NIU BY DEMOGRAPHIC CATEGORY, 1989 AND 1998.

All Students

	1989		1998		
	Percentage	n	Percentage	n	
Self-reported heavier drinking	45	767	25	549	*
Misperception of peer norm	69	767	33	541	*
Injury to self or others	36	767	16	549	*

Under 21

	1989		1998		
	Percentage	n	Percentage	n	
Self-reported heavier drinking	45	664	28	374	*
Misperception of peer norm	70	664	33	372	*
Injury to self or others	37	664	18	375	*

Over 21

	1989		1998		
	Percentage	n	Percentage	n	
Self-reported heavier drinking	44	103	19	175	*
Misperception of peer norm	66	103	34	169	*
Injury to self or others	29	103	11	174	*

Athletes

	1989		1998		
	Percentage	n	Percentage	n	
Self-reported heavier drinking	52	50	29	42	*
Misperception of peer norm	70	50	44	41	*
Injury to self or others	42	50	21	42	*

Greeks

	1989		1998		
	Percentage	n	Percentage	n	
Self-reported heavier drinking	66	119	40	62	*
Misperception of peer norm	70	119	43	61	*
Injury to self or others	49	119	21	62	*

TABLE 2.3. SELF-REPORTED DRINKING, MISPERCEPTIONS, AND INJURY AT NIU BY DEMOGRAPHIC CATEGORY, 1989 AND 1998, Cont'd.

Latino

	1989		1998		
	Percentage	n	Percentage	n	
Self-reported heavier drinking	55	29	29	24	
Misperception of peer norm	66	29	33	24	*
Injury to self or others	31	29	21	24	

Male

	1989		1998		
	Percentage	n	Percentage	n	
Self-reported heavier drinking	64	355	42	225	*
Misperception of peer norm	70	355	41	221	*
Injury to self or others	41	355	20	225	*

Female

	1989		1998		
	Percentage	n	Percentage	n	
Self-reported heavier drinking	28	413	13	321	*
Misperception of peer norm	69	413	27	317	*
Injury to self or others	31	413	13	321	*

Note: An asterisk denotes a significant decrease ($p < .05$) from the baseline survey year.

injuries), it did so without significant changes in alcohol-use policy. It is also noteworthy that the approach was effective in a variety of subgroups in the population (student athletes, Greeks, under twenty-one, and so forth). Specifically, there was a significant increase in the proportion of NIU students who drank moderately or abstained and in the perception of moderation as the peer norm, *and* there was a significant *decrease* in the proportion of NIU students who drank more heavily (more than five drinks per occasion) and in the perception of peers who drank heavily being the norm.

Together, these findings suggest a trend toward greater moderation in drinking at NIU. A broader analysis of national trends in college drinking behavior during the same ten-year interval adds support to the assumption that the social norms intervention at NIU was the likely cause of the reported effect, instead of some "background" demographic change in youth drinking behavior. *Monitoring the Future: National Survey Results on Drug Use, 1980–2000* (Johnston, O'Malley, and Bachman, 2001), a highly respected government-funded study, showed virtually no change in heavier drinking by American college students. In addition, Harvard's College Alcohol Study (Wechsler and others, 2002) reported similar findings.

The traditional approach appeared to have no apparent effect on student drinking behavior, perceptions, or alcohol-related injuries. One possible explanation for the apparent failure of the traditional method is that fear appeals did not affect the students who drank most heavily. Previous researchers have shown a negative correlation between student drinking level and perceived risk of alcohol-related harm. That is, the more heavily a student drinks, the less harm the student perceives (Agostinelli and Miller, 1994). Therefore, exposing heavier drinking students to traditional scare tactics may not have any effect on their drinking behavior because they believe they are not at any risk for alcohol-related harm.

Another explanation may be that the traditional approach did not reach enough students to have an impact. Interpersonal methods are expensive (two or three hours of time to reach twelve to fifteen students), they require students to take time from their schedule to attend (active participation), and they eliminate participant anonymity. Also, previous unpublished research at NIU showed a direct negative correlation between drinks per week and likelihood of attending an alcohol education program. That is, the more a student drank, the less interest he or she had in attending an alcohol education program. Interestingly, the abstainers showed the greatest likelihood of attendance.

It is essential to stress that NIU's social marketing strategy used an environmental approach to have an impact on *all* students. In contrast, a *targeted* social norms approach may succeed *and* fail because it is *so precisely focused.* A social norms intervention aimed at a segment of the college community could successfully change the perception of the subgroup momentarily, only to have the gains fade when the group again confronts the pervasive false norm held by other students, faculty, and staff. Thus use of a campuswide environmental strategy, because it is not specifically targeted, may have a greater chance of hitting its target (student drinking norms) simply because of the widespread impact of the intervention. It hits the target(s) and the social setting simultaneously because it is so pervasive in scope. It may be that a social norms effort *must* be campuswide for sustained impact. In other words, the entire campus environment must undergo a change of drinking norm perception if the heavier drinkers are to maintain the perception of the true norm of moderation.

The alcohol wellness approach used by NIU is fairly uncommon in the literature. Prevention efforts have focused primarily on eliminating alcohol deviance and pathology or supporting alcohol abstinence and temperance initiatives. Both of these strategies ignore the fact that most college students fall somewhere between these two extremes. Both abstinence and alcohol abuse are not normative. The overwhelming majority of college students drink alcohol and *do not* have serious health consequences, run into trouble with authorities, or commit harm to others. A national survey of college students, conducted annually by the American College Health Association, reports that 95 percent of college students routinely take precautions (use a designated driver, set a limit, avoid drinking games, and so on) when drinking (American College Health Association, 2001). The NIU model identifies safer, protective, and salutary practices already used by students, and it then augments them with reinforcing media. This intervention combines elements of normative influence, behavior modification, and social marketing to promote more protection and safety—characteristics that are already prevalent, but often hidden, within the college social environment.

References

Agostinelli, G., Brown, J. M., and Miller, W. R. "Effects of Normative Feedback on Consumption Among Heavy Drinking College Students." *Journal of Drug Education,* 1995, *25*(1), 31–40.

Agostinelli, G., and Miller, W. R. "Drinking and Thinking: How Does Personal Drinking Affect Judgments of Prevalence and Risk?" *Journal of Studies on Alcohol,* 1994, *55,* 327–337.

American College Health Association. *National College Health Assessment: Reference Group Executive Summary, Spring 2000.* Baltimore: American College Health Association, 2001.

Andreasen, A. R. *Marketing Social Change: Changing Behavior to Promote Health, Social Development, and the Environment.* San Francisco: Jossey-Bass, 1995.

Baer, J. S., Stacy, A., and Larimer, M. "Biases in the Perception of Drinking Norms Among College Students." *Journal of Studies on Alcohol,* 1991, *52,* 580–586.

Baer, J. S., and others. "An Experimental Test of Three Methods of Alcohol Risk Reduction with Young Adults." *Journal of Consulting and Clinical Psychology,* 1992, *60,* 974–979.

Barnett, L. A., Far, J. M., Maus, A. L., and Miller, J. A. "Changing Perceptions of Peer Norms as a Drinking Reduction Program for College Students." *Journal of Alcohol and Drug Education,* Winter 1996, *96,* 39–61.

Berkowitz, A. D. "From Reactive to Proactive Prevention: Promoting an Ecology of Health on Campus." In P. C. Rivers and E. Shore (eds.), *A Handbook on Substance Abuse for College and University Personnel.* Westport, Conn.: Greenwood Press, 1997.

Cialdini, R. B. *Influence: The Psychology of Persuasion.* New York: Morrow, 1993.

Graham, J. W., Marks, G., and Hansen, W. B. "Social Influence Processes Affecting Adolescent Substance Use." *Journal of Applied Psychology,* 1991, *76*(2), 291–298.

Haines, M. P. *A Social Norms Approach to Preventing Binge Drinking at Colleges and Universities.* Newton, Mass.: Higher Education Center for Alcohol and Other Drug Prevention, 1996.

Hansen, W. B., and Graham, J. W. "Preventing Alcohol, Marijuana, and Cigarette Use Among Adolescents: Peer Pressure Resistance Training Versus Establishing Conservative Norms." *Preventive Medicine,* 1991, 20, 414–430.

Hechter, M., and Opp, K. *Social Norms.* New York: Russell Sage Foundation, 2001.

Johnston, L., O'Malley, P., and Bachman, J. *Monitoring the Future: National Survey Results on Drug Use, 1975–2000.* Vol. II: *College Students and Adults Ages 19–40.* (NIH publication 00–4802.) Rockville, Md.: National Institute on Drug Abuse, 2001.

Marks, G., Graham, J. W., and Hansen, W. B. "Social Projection and Social Conformity in Adolescent Alcohol Use: A Longitudinal Analysis." *Personality and Social Psychology Bulletin,* 1992, *18,* 96–101.

McAlister, A. L. "Population Behavior Change: A Theory-Based Approach." *Journal of Public Health Policy,* Autumn 1991, 345–361.

Miller, D. T. and McFarland, C. "When Social Comparison Goes Awry: The Case of Pluralistic Ignorance." In J. Suls and T. Wills (eds.), *Social Comparison: Contemporary Theory and Research.* Hillsdale, N.J.: Erlbaum, 1991.

Perkins, H. W. "College Student Misperceptions of Alcohol and Other Drug Norms Among Peers: Exploring Causes, Consequences and Implications for Prevention Programs." In *Designing Alcohol and Other Drug Prevention Programs in Higher Education: Bringing Theory Into Practice.* Newton, Mass.: Higher Education Center for Alcohol and Other Drug Prevention, U.S. Department of Education, 1997.

Perkins, H. W., and Berkowitz, A. D. "Perceiving the Community Norms of Alcohol Use Among Students: Some Research Implications for Campus Alcohol Education Programming." *International Journal of the Addictions,* 1986, *21,* 961–976.

Perkins, H. W., and Wechsler, H. "Variation in Perceived College Drinking Norms and Its Impact on Alcohol Abuse: A Nationwide Study." *Journal of Drug Issues,* 1996, *26,* 961–974.

Perkins, H. W., and others. "Misperceptions of the Norms for the Frequency of Alcohol and Other Drug Use on College Campuses." *Journal of American College Health,* 1999, *47,* 253–258.

Prentice, D. A., and Miller, D. T. "Pluralistic Ignorance and Alcohol Use on Campus: Some Consequences of Misperceiving the Social Norm." *Journal of Personality and Social Psychology,* 1993, *64,* 243–256.

Presley, C., Leichliter, J., and Meilman, P. *Alcohol and Drugs on American College Campuses: A Report to College Presidents.* Carbondale: CORE Institute, Southern Illinois University, 1998.

Walters, S. A. "In Praise of Feedback: An Effective Intervention for College Students Who Are Heavy Drinkers." *Journal of American College Health,* 2000, *45,* 235–238.

Wechsler, H., Lee, J. E., and Kuo, M. "Trends in College Binge Drinking During a Period of Increased Prevention Efforts: Findings from Four Harvard School of Public Health College Alcohol Study Surveys: 1993–2001." *Journal of American College Health,* 2002, *50*(5), 203–217.

Wood, M. D., Nagoshi, C. T., and Dennis, D. A. "Alcohol Norms and Expectations as Predictors of Alcohol Use and Problems in a College Student Sample." *American Journal of Drug and Alcohol Abuse,* 1992, *18,* 461–476.

CHAPTER THREE

THE HOBART AND WILLIAM SMITH COLLEGES EXPERIMENT

A Synergistic Social Norms Approach Using Print, Electronic Media, and Curriculum Infusion to Reduce Collegiate Problem Drinking

H. Wesley Perkins, Ph.D.; David W. Craig, Ph.D.

Pervasive misperceptions of peer norms regarding alcohol use exist on most college campuses (Perkins and others, 1999). Students typically believe that campus drinking norms are more permissive than is really the case among peers, even when the actual level of use and risk-taking is quite high. Exaggerated perceptions contribute significantly to the problem of substance abuse on campus, so prevention strategies that reduce misperception to a more accurate level of actual peer norms have demonstrated significant positive effects (Perkins, 2002).

Initial research on this topic began at Hobart and William Smith Colleges (HWS) several years ago (Perkins and Berkowitz, 1986). Studies of this student population demonstrated a pervasive and continuing pattern of misperception about alcohol norms among student peers. Even though actual patterns of use were quite high because of the social and demographic characteristics of the student population, the misperceptions still far outpaced the actual norms and reinforced the heavy drinking that did occur.

The authors gratefully acknowledge the financial support of U.S. Department of Education Drug and Violence Prevention in Higher Education grants to implement this campus intervention (grant no. S184H980041) and to analyze and disseminate results (grant no. P183A960126). The authors are also grateful to William Badger, Ethan Healy, and Michael Ruiz for their technical and creative assistance in producing project materials, and to Deborah Herry for her administrative and research assistance in all aspects of this project.

Even though research and theory about the social norms strategy emerged from the HWS Alcohol Education Project in the 1980s, and we continued conducting research on student drinking and the effects of perceived social norms through the early 1990s, no intensive and ongoing application of the model was introduced during that period. Indeed, the broad-based prevention strategy remained largely untested on our campus until Northern Illinois applied our theory in a practical application using a creative print media intervention (Haines and Spear, 1996; Haines, 1996).

Bolstered by these promising results as well as continuing research and theory development concerning misperceived norms (Perkins and Wechsler, 1996; Perkins, 1997), we decided to launch the HWS experiment as an intensive and sustained test of the model. We intended this experiment to expand applied intervention research on the social norms approach in several ways. First, a broad-based social norms strategy had not been tested in a small college setting. Other intensive experiments with this strategy were being conducted in larger university contexts (Johannessen, Collins, Mills-Novoa, and Glider, 1999). Second, selective liberal arts colleges in the Northeast typically experience relatively heavy alcohol consumption among their students compared to larger universities with a more diverse population and compared to students in other regions of the country (Presley, Meilman, and Cashin, 1996). Therefore it seemed particularly appropriate to see how effective this strategy could be in reducing alcohol abuse in an environment of traditionally heavy alcohol consumption. Third, the design of this experiment was not only to use print media strategies as employed elsewhere but also to combine them with new electronic media strategies and curriculum infusion. Our idea was that the various strategies could be combined to act synergistically in reducing misperception, actual use, and harm caused by use even in an environment of this kind. What follows is an accounting of this work as an applied experiment and the remarkable results that were achieved in a short period of time.

Campus Setting for This Experiment

HWS is a selective undergraduate liberal arts institution of higher education with approximately 135 faculty and eighteen hundred students. Hobart, for men, and William Smith, for women, exist in a coordinate structure sharing a single faculty, campus grounds, academic classes and facilities, provost, and president of the institution. Male and female students maintain separate student governments and athletic programs and are supervised by separate dean's offices. More than 95 percent of students who attend this institution are single, are of traditional college age (between seventeen and twenty-four), and have moved away from family to attend college. More than 85 percent of the student population live in campus housing, which includes small and large single-sex and coeducational residence halls, small cooperatives and special theme houses, and fraternities (no sororities exist on this campus). Although students come from all over the United States as well as from other countries, the large majority come from states in the Northeast. More than two-thirds of each entering cohort played a varsity sport during their senior year in high school, and more than one-third arrive at HWS expecting to play an intercollegiate sport.

The sociodemographic profile of HWS and its entering student population each year are important factors explaining the pervasiveness and persistence of a heavier drinking pattern among students in comparison with institutions of higher education in general. Research nationally (Presley, Meilman, and Cashin, 1996; Wechsler, Dowdall, Davenport, and Castillo, 1995) has established that heavy alcohol use among college students is more predominant (1) in the Northeastern region of the United States, where the abstinence rate among students is far below the national norm; (2) at undergraduate colleges and smaller schools (with fewer graduate students to moderate the social atmosphere on campus), and especially if these undergraduate students are predominantly single and mostly of a traditional, young age; (3) at a residential college (where family or outside employment are less of a constraining factor); (4) in a student population with low religious interest and participation; (5) at a school where Greek social organizations exist; (6) at a school where athletic participation is prevalent among students; and (7) at a school with a mostly Caucasian student body. HWS and its students, like many selective liberal arts colleges in the Northeast, match all of these high-risk factors. Thus, regardless of their high academic selectivity and low faculty-student ratios in educational programs, such schools will continue to find themselves on the front line of student alcohol abuse with each new high-risk cohort of students that enters the campus community.

Despite the formidable sociodemographic circumstances facing HWS, we believed that a dramatic reduction in high-risk drinking in the student population could be achieved with the social norms approach. One challenge or question often posed to this approach involves skepticism about its ability to work in a context where the norm is actually quite high, because presumably one could not demonstrate a majority with moderate drinking norms. But as we shall see, even in a context where heavy drinking is prevalent, the majority typically exhibit moderate patterns, the perceived norms are still higher than the actual norms, and misperception still works perniciously to spawn or exacerbate problem behavior. Thus, demographic characteristics that predispose an institution such as HWS to greater drinking problems, according to social norms theory, should still not prevent the possibility of substantial reduction in the problem by reducing misperceptions.

The HWS Project formally began intervention activities in the late fall of 1996. It is important to note that during the 1995–96 academic year and following introduction of the social norms experiment in subsequent years, no new alcohol education or prevention initiatives were undertaken by any other campus constituency. Moreover, at the end of spring term 1995 the coordinator of alcohol prevention, whose formal administrative role was to coordinate ongoing alcohol prevention initiatives and develop new programs, left HWS to relocate in another area of the country. This position was not filled at the time, given a reorientation of program initiatives and also new strategies that were being planned, including what ultimately began in late 1996 as the HWS Project's experiment. The departure of the coordinator left the ongoing counseling and disciplinary programs intact, but no other new college prevention initiatives or personnel were introduced during the first three-year period of this experiment (through spring 1999). Thus the historical circumstance was the perfect time to test and evaluate a new strategy with minimal confounding effects from any other new program activity related to alcohol on campus. Any significant improvement with regard to campus alcohol use in subsequent years after the project's experiment was initiated could be strongly linked to project interventions. Moreover, the lack of change in high-risk drinking that was observed nationally throughout the 1990s (Wechsler and others, 2002) makes any change observed locally more strongly attributable to local interventions.

Planning Intervention Initiatives as a Synergistic Strategy

In the late fall of 1996, the Hobart and William Smith Colleges Alcohol Education Project (the HWS Project) launched a major new initiative, with support of an institutionwide U.S. Department of Education Drug and Violence Prevention Programs in Higher Education grant. This project initiated a comprehensive campaign to reduce harmful misperceptions about student drinking norms and reduce actual alcohol abuse by developing innovative social marketing strategies as well as new strategies for teaching about alcohol in the academic curriculum. Major initiatives included creation and delivery of a mass-media campaign using multiple media channels and development of academic venues involving both faculty and students to communicate data-based messages about actual social norms.

Significantly, the mass communications campaign combined traditional print media with unique electronic media approaches to expand the exposure of normative information to the campus community. The campus computer network was used to produce and rapidly deliver multimedia sound and video content all over campus. By combining traditional print media with electronic media and curriculum infusion, we planned to simultaneously deliver social norms communications to the college community through multiple methods, to produce a *synergistic* effect. We hypothesized that if we could foster intense social norms exposure through mutually reinforcing mechanisms, on a foundation of credible data showing more moderate norms than typically perceived, then heavy consumption could be reduced even in this high-risk collegiate context; furthermore, we might be able to produce a notable reduction in the problem rate in a shorter time frame.

In the next sections of this chapter, we describe how the HWS Project initiatives were each designed to work together in our comprehensive campuswide project to reduce harmful misperception about alcohol use and thereby reduce actual problem use.

Data Collection

Any social norms prevention campaign must begin with collecting information about the norms of the community. The HWS Alcohol Education Project had been collecting data on alcohol use and perceived norms for many years prior to the social norms intervention, which afforded us an extended baseline assessment. Data collection continued along with introduction of some new survey measures as the experiment began. The data collected in these surveys served several purposes. They shaped the content of the social norms messages that we delivered to the campus community. It was very important that the data be collected systematically and representatively, and that as many students as possible participate in providing data to enhance the credibility of the data in the eyes of students. We believed that information obtained consistently over time and from multiple survey instruments could have a powerful impact on the campus. Almost every student on our campus, at one time or another, participates in at least two of our surveys during his or her time here. Finally, the survey results allow us to assess our progress in reducing harmful misperception, actual high-risk use, and resulting consequences.

Surveys were conducted of all entering students during fall orientation and of all graduating seniors at the end of each academic year. In addition, periodic campuswide surveys, and surveys of students enrolled in large introductory courses, were conducted throughout the project and combined with periodic campus life surveys conducted by the deans' offices. Selected results from these surveys appear in examples of social norms messages and in the impact evaluation presented in the next sections of this chapter.

Print Media Campaigns

Over the course of the four intervention years described in this report (fall 1996 through spring 2000), more than twenty print media posters were created containing messages about actual norms for alcohol use. These messages presented norms that were much more moderate than students typically perceived. (Many examples can be found in Perkins and Craig, 2002; a complete catalogue is available at http://alcohol.hws.edu.)

Posters were regularly rotated among display cases distributed across campus in both academic and residential buildings, and new posters were introduced into the rotation with each new survey administration. These same posters were reproduced in black-and-white formats for the campus newspaper, and at least one was printed in most weekly editions of the paper during the intervention period. We were careful to follow any reports in the campus newspaper of alcohol-related incidents. Whenever there was a report of an incident, we immediately followed in the next issue with a poster advertisement that showed how the majority of students did not, in fact, drink in ways that led to such consequences.

We produced and distributed three poster sequences of particular note. The first was our silent numbers campaign. Our goal in this campaign was to communicate to the campus that a large majority of students consume alcohol moderately or not at all while a minority consumes heavily. We wanted to impress upon students that, in fact, the distribution of consumption levels is quite skewed, so students would have less of a sense that they were all in one camp as drinkers in opposition to administrators or health educators. We wanted to create a sense of a political divide between the heaviest drinkers, who cause most of the damage, and other students so that the latter would be able to resist heavy drinking and speak out more often in opposition to it. Our slogan for this campaign was "2/3 = 1/4," signifying that two-thirds of the students drink only one-fourth of the alcohol consumed among students, a message based on representative local survey data. During a one-week period, we blanketed the campus with the first poster only, showing the slogan with no explanation. The mystery generated a great deal of attention and conversation as to the meaning of the contradictory equation. The next week, we sent out the second poster with only vague hints. More theories were generated by students and staff. Then four days later, we distributed the answer (see Figure 3.1). This was followed by a visual poster graphically representing the skewed distribution and other follow-up posters communicating the same point.

A second campaign was our "Reality Check" poster and ad series. These posters were specifically designed to dispel myths. Each poster begins with a myth

FIGURE 3.1. HWS CAMPAIGN POSTER:
SILENT NUMBERS—"HERE IS THE ANSWER!"

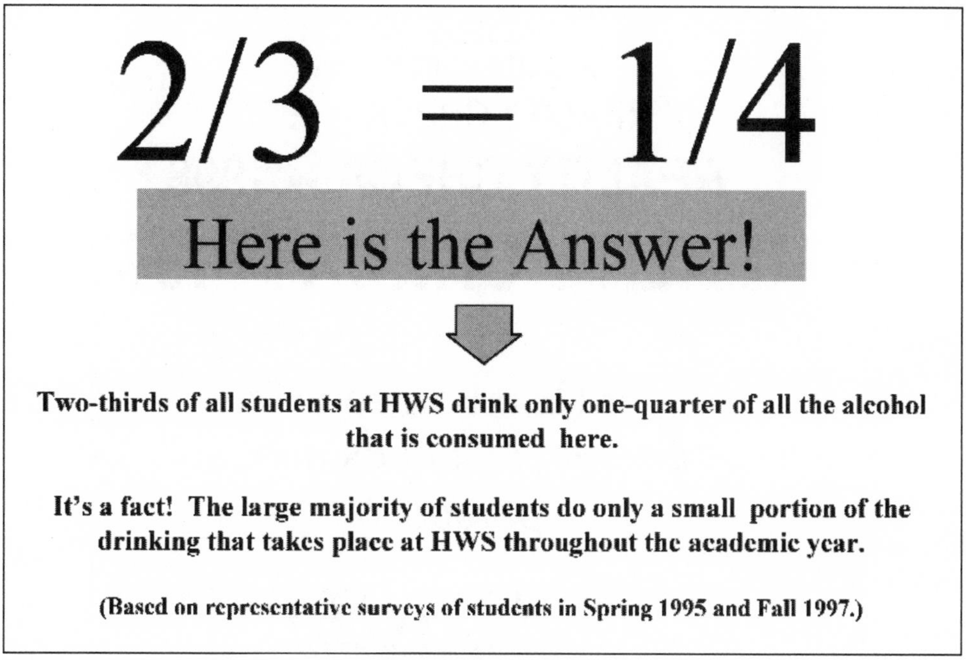

2/3 = 1/4

Here is the Answer!

Two-thirds of all students at HWS drink only one-quarter of all the alcohol that is consumed here.

It's a fact! The large majority of students do only a small portion of the drinking that takes place at HWS throughout the academic year.

(Based on representative surveys of students in Spring 1995 and Fall 1997.)

Source: Used by permission of HWS Alcohol Education Project.

and then follows with the facts from the survey results. They were run repeatedly in the newspaper as well as prominently placed in our campus display cases. One example from this poster series is shown in Figure 3.2.

Our final campaign poster series became most important in the later years of the experiment, as we were able to show reduction in risky and harmful behaviors. We called this campaign "Healthy Choices Are on the Rise" and used an aerial balloon logo on each of these posters, as shown in the sample in Figure 3.3. An increase in the number of students who did not miss class or engage in risky sexual practice because of drinking was featured in these posters to encourage others to join with the majority and not feel the pressure created by their own misperception.

Our "Campus Factoids"™ newspaper column communicated information to the community on topics ranging from opinions on controversial social issues, to the academic success of students, to demographic information of the entering class, and of course student alcohol norms. About one fact in seven that were printed had to do with alcohol or other drugs. We wanted to create a column that

**FIGURE 3.2. HWS CAMPAIGN POSTER:
REALITY CHECK.**

REALITY CHECK -- 1996
REALITY CHECK -- 1997
REALITY CHECK -- 1998
REALITY CHECK -- 1999

Ever Hear Someone Say
*"Everybody drinks a lot at
parties"*?

IN REALITY

The majority of HWS seniors drink only 1 to 4 drinks

or do not drink at all!

Source: Higher Education Data Sharing Consortium Senior Survey conducted annually
each spring at participating U.S. Colleges. HWS data based on:
  1996 survey of 440 HWS graduating seniors
  1997 survey of 344 HWS graduating seniors
  1998 survey of 345 HWS graduating seniors
  1999 survey of 288 HWS graduating seniors
  (Data also available in Campus Factoids)

Source: Used by permission of HWS Alcohol Education Project.

FIGURE 3.3. HWS CAMPAIGN POSTER:
HEALTHY CHOICES ARE ON THE RISE.

What % NEVER have unprotected sex as a consequence of drinking?

1995
83%

1998
90%

The Majority of Students Drink Responsibly or Do not Drink at All

Data: Comparison of 1995 and 1998 representative campus surveys conducted by BD295, n=551.

Source: Used by permission of HWS Alcohol Education Project.

attracted students with a broad range of information about the community. Some of it was humorous and some troubling, but all of it was informative about campus characteristics. Any reader could find facts of interest, and as readers scanned the facts at least one on alcohol would typically be encountered in the newsprint listing.

Electronic Media Campaign

The success of any media campaign relies on broad exposure to the community. Community members must pass by and read poster displays or read newspaper advertisements. Many community members may be missed using these particular strategies alone; however, what if media advertisements could be brought to student, faculty, and staff computers wherever they are on campus? Realizing that we could accomplish this distribution task using a campus network infrastructure, we decided to introduce social norms interventions through this attractive medium.

Advantages of Electronic Media

Using electronic media channels in a social norms prevention program expands the breadth and intensity of audience exposure to messages beyond that of more traditional print media. Distinct features of electronic media in message delivery are (1) bringing messages to the desktop, (2) instantaneous targeted updates and delivery, (3) reduced costs, (4) incorporating multimedia sound and video, (5) interactive engagement with the viewer, and (6) immediate assessment of exposure through server log files.

Students, faculty, and staff spend much of their workday at a computer. Bringing social norms messages to computer desktops brings them messages where they work. We don't have to worry about individuals who might not otherwise read a campus newspaper or pass by a poster display. Messages can be delivered through electronic media such as screen savers and interactive multimedia applications. Models of these delivery mechanisms are discussed later in this chapter.

Campus computer networks join student and staff computers to servers that can instantaneously deploy messages and poster graphics to them. Data presented on social norms can be updated or new data added to a server as they become available. The server can instantaneously deploy the new or updated information to the entire campus. Furthermore, it is possible to target messages by location and by user (athlete data delivered to athletic facilities, Greek data to fraternities and sororities, data to an identified subpopulation through targeted electronic mail lists, and so on).

Electronic media delivery is inexpensive when compared to a print media campaign. Distribution of messages uses existing network infrastructure. There are no printing costs; nor are there reprinting costs when new data become available. Inexpensive and readily available database and graphics editing software allow staff to quickly and inexpensively edit and deploy new messages with a minimum of training. Staff time is not required to travel from location to location around campus changing displays. On our campus, we automatically change electronic displays every twenty seconds all over campus.

Print media are static, but electronic media can incorporate animation, video, and sound. These additional modes of communication offer a mechanism to more powerfully communicate social norms messages. Students can talk to other students, music can attract attention and expand the intensity of engagement in the message.

Electronic media can also be interactive. Students and staff can select and search out specific messages or data of interest. Students and staff can engage in interactive debate with others in the community. Quiz competitions or survey questions asked, as well as responses, can be recorded automatically to central servers.

It is also possible to assess message exposure through computer server log files. This information yields important formative assessment measures of the intervention and can guide prevention specialists in where and how to most effectively direct their efforts.

Models for Electronic Media Delivery

In this section, we present the primary electronic media models we devised and used on the HWS campus for delivering social norms messages. Using data and messages already created as well as new material, these strategies incorporated each of the advantages noted earlier.

Campus Factoids™ Screen Saver: Automated Message Display. A screen saver program that randomly displayed facts and posters from our Campus Factoids™ database was installed on student-accessed college-owned computers in libraries and laboratories throughout the campus, and on many faculty and administrative office computers as well. All facts printed in the newspaper and the entire set of posters as well as other pictures of campus life were included in this database. Normative messages start appearing randomly on the screen whenever a computer remains idle for ten minutes. The main advantage of this program was that it was not necessary to rely on an individual to actively seek a particular Website or launch a particular application. The computer operating system starts its screen saver application automatically. The data are updated from a network server whenever a user logs on or the computer is rebooted.

Multimedia Campus Factoids™: Interactive Access to Campus Data. As successful as the screen saver was in bringing normative messages across campus, it was not able to employ the interactive and multimedia capabilities of modern computer networks. Interactive multimedia access to Campus Factoids™ was created to incorporate these capabilities into our electronic media campaign. Students and staff were able to browse and search the database by subject and see graphical displays of our posters and video clips containing information relevant to the factoid being displayed. Many of the video clips used information put together and presented by student peers. A sample screen shot of the program display is shown in Figure 3.4.

In addition, we decided to expand the program to allow users to react to facts and engage in online discussion about any factoid that compelled them to react. Students were required to identify themselves when submitting comments because we did not want students to make careless graffiti entries; we wanted them to feel responsible for the conversation and thus be less prone to contribute to exaggerated perceptions. They could not make personal attacks or use language in poor taste, but otherwise all entries were posted along with the facts. Thus students could react to facts as they read them, react to other student comments, or simply read the discussion that had taken place on any particular factoid.

How the inclusion of reactions ("reactoids") served our agenda of communicating social norms about alcohol is evident in an example. Among the factoids in the online database was a fact about first-year students entering in fall 1998 (class of 2002). The fact, which was based on a September 1998 survey of the entering class with 446 respondents, stated that "91 percent of the entering class expressed the opinion that students should not drink to an intoxicating level that affects academic work or other responsibilities." The first reaction submitted by a sophomore student as a response to reading this fact was: "This really surprises me. I agree with the statement, but don't feel that this attitude is prominent here. It would be interesting to compare this statistic with the opinion of the graduating class." The student's reaction to the fact is a classic example of the misperception phenomenon where most students hold a moderate attitude but think they are rare among their peers.

This student's reaction then motivated the next reply, from a student who affirmed the fact and responded to the other student's skepticism about seniors by remarking: "As a graduating senior, I would agree with this factoid. Because we are such a small school, it often appears that we are surrounded by those people who fall into the 9 percent, however, it is often the 9 percent who are being vocal about their social life, while the 91 percent remain silent. Perhaps we need to encourage good role models for the younger classes. Leading by example is always the best way."

FIGURE 3.4. MULTIMEDIA CAMPUS FACTOIDS™ WITH GRAPHICAL ENHANCEMENTS (SCREEN IMAGES).

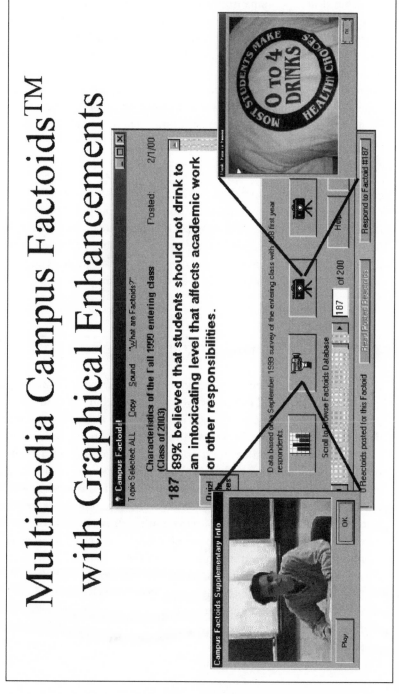

Multimedia Campus Factoids™
with Graphical Enhancements

Source: Used by permission of HWS Alcohol Education Project.

This ideal reply came from a peer voluntarily and unsolicited. Certainly not all student reaction is so positive, but for every student who voices a potential misperception another student armed with the actual data from the fact and a larger campus conversation about norms usually voices support. The senior student who made the preceding comment may or may not have ever made that expression verbally in conversation. But even if spoken, the comment would have been heard by only a few people on a single occasion. In this form, her thoughts are "recycled" each time another student reads the chain of discussion. It can be read and considered by hundreds of students even after the student has graduated.

Posters promoting the interactive program were displayed throughout the campus; mouse pads promoting it were placed with every college-owned computer in a public area or computer laboratory. A quiz game on knowledge of the facts about alcohol and other drug (AOD) social norms as well as other campus facts was subsequently built into the online program. Following introduction of the quiz online, there were announcements of weekly winners and prizes, all designed to attract more students to read the database.

Curriculum Infusion and Curriculum Development

Although print and electronic media campaigns permeate space and time occupied by students and faculty between classes and in the evenings, they do not penetrate many classroom discussions; nor do they always reach commuting students who live off campus. Developing strategies to expand the conversation about alcohol use and campus norms into the classroom can increase the breadth and intensity of social norms message exposure, further enhancing the effectiveness of a social norms prevention program. It is not necessary to design a new course, nor is it necessary to choreograph a major curriculum reform to infuse conversation about alcohol and other drugs into the curriculum. Numerous activities in curriculum development were conducted at HWS to expand conversation about alcohol norms in classrooms. Most notable among these activities at HWS were (1) workshops for faculty to explore ways of introducing AOD content into their courses, (2) development of a model interdisciplinary course on alcohol use and abuse, and (3) teacher education workshops to train student teachers and their teacher partners in the schools about the social norms approach (more documentation of each of these activities can be found at http://alcohol.hws.edu).

Laying the Ground Work: Assessing and Building Faculty Interest

At the beginning of the project, a comprehensive survey of all faculty was conducted to identify the current state of AOD issues presented in the curriculum and to assess interest in expanding that content. We discovered that a number of faculty were already introducing it into their courses and that there was significant interest among the faculty on our campus to expand this content. Luncheon addresses by the project directors were presented about the faculty's role in increasing the health and safety of students while enhancing learning in their courses at the same time. Workshops were offered for interested faculty to develop AOD content. Course resources such as library holdings and World Wide Web resources were made available to faculty, and extensive discussion took place about the wide-ranging possibilities for bringing AOD material into the classroom in a variety of academic disciplines.

The key here for our social norms initiative in both the luncheon addresses and the faculty workshops was the opportunity to introduce faculty to the theory and empirical data about misperceived student norms and the role they could play in challenging those misperceptions. Faculty can easily initiate conversation about actual and misperceived social norms in many courses in sociology, psychology, gender studies, first-year general education, philosophy and ethics, creative writing, and health education. For example, a course on Theories of Masculinity at HWS examines the social forces that shape the lives of men and the nature of men's experience, especially in relation to the question of manhood; prevailing models of what it means to be a man are examined. Connections between alcohol use and masculinity, both real and perceived, are examined through popular literature and history. This is a fruitful forum for a discussion of campus alcohol norms. In sociology research methods courses, students learn how to collect, analyze, and report survey data, which frequently involves studies of student drinking patterns. Students are learning the research craft while also learning about actual HWS alcohol norms. Sociology courses have also made use of the Campus Factoids™ online program and the reactoid discussion function of this program to amplify conversation about actual cultural norms; again, discussion of perceived and actual drinking patterns is encountered in this process.

In the natural sciences, there are many opportunities to study substance abuse, and even in the process of teaching the science of AOD phenomena—be it an examination of metabolism, the risk of fetal alcohol syndrome, addictive processes, and the like—faculty can be prepared to challenge the misperception revealed in the classroom comments of students about patterns of peer use. The chemistry department, for example, introduced a seminar, "The Science of

Feeling Good and Bad with Ethanol," as part of its weekly evening seminar; it was attended by all students in intermediate and advanced chemistry courses. The lecture incorporates a drinking demonstration with breath alcohol determination to illustrate the speed of absorption and onset of pharmacological effects. Importantly, the lecture concludes with facts about the healthy norms for the majority of HWS students with regard to alcohol.

At the most basic level, it was important to address the misperceptions of faculty who, as "carriers," sometimes help spread misperception in their causal comments and practices, exacerbating the problem. For example, the professor who says to a class "I know you are all going to go out drinking this weekend, but you still have to be in class or at least turn in your paper on Monday" helps perpetuate the myth that all students will be drinking and drinking heavily; he or she unintentionally encourages a few more students to actually do so than would otherwise be the case. Even worse is the occasional circumstance where a faculty member may cancel a class or permit late paper submissions because he or she assumes that most students will be recovering from a big drinking night or weekend party. Here the minority of students who do drink heavily in ways that affect their academic participation are actually "enabled" in their behavior by the faculty member's misperception of the student norm.

An Interdisciplinary Course Promoting Social Norms Research and Education About Alcohol

A model interdisciplinary course on alcohol use and abuse, team-taught by the project directors, was developed. It serves as one of the capstone research courses for the public policy program at HWS, bringing together students from the social and natural sciences and from the humanities to look comprehensively at the phenomenon of alcohol abuse in our society and in college life specifically. Any question raised about alcohol use in this course requires both natural scientific and sociocultural perspectives. Students come together from several disciplines to contribute essential perspectives in the struggle to understand the complexities and consequences of substance abuse and in finding solutions to reduce its harm. Discussions of social norms permeate this course, and students learn even more about the social norms approach as they study various prevention strategies in practice.

Several activities came out of this course that contributed directly to other components of the campus intervention. Students helped to design and administer a campuswide survey on alcohol norms on alternating years. They produced video clips used in the multimedia Campus Factoids™ program and poster displays of their projects to communicate key concepts to the broader community. In many ways, this core group of students became participants in delivering the social norms prevention strategy at these colleges. The residential campus became a laboratory for them to apply principles learned in class in designing, delivering, and assessing a comprehensive prevention program based on sound academic research methods.

Student-Teacher Workshops

Secondary teacher certification programs require education in substance abuse. The HWS intervention contributed workshops for the teacher certification program. HWS students involved in student-teacher training experiences in middle and high school settings attended these workshops, along with several teacher partners and administrators from various local schools. These workshops were an opportunity to introduce students to the phenomenon of misperceived AOD norms and the social norms prevention strategy as well as problem behaviors and risks associated with AOD use among middle and high school students. In addition to catalyzing dissemination in secondary schools, these student-teacher workshops contributed directly to our social norms intervention on the HWS campus as well. Research on college student social norms was presented here to help explain the approach; thus student-teachers were hearing about their own norms and misperceptions once again. This strategy was also important for increasing social norms exposure because a large number of HWS students are involved in the teacher education program.

Assessing the Intervention Impact

Although no one evaluation strategy for a prevention program in a college population can furnish absolute definitive proof of specific program impact, the strongest evidence is likely to include (1) use of multiple evaluation techniques, (2) inclusion of longitudinal assessment strategies with preintervention and postintervention data, (3) consistency in method of data collection over time (measurement items and sampling techniques), (4) selection of demographically representative samples reflecting the target population, (5) a reliable response rate in addition to sufficient sample size when surveying a target population, and (6) rigorous statistical analyses that incorporate significance tests of sample differences and controls for demographic variation in comparison groups. All of these criteria were crucial components in evaluating program effectiveness for the HWS Project's social norms experiment.

Three types of data are presented here to indicate the project's positive impact on HWS students. First, data are drawn from senior exit surveys and from electronic login records to monitor student exposure to project media campaigns. Second, data are provided by a fall-term survey administered to students in introductory courses before the introduction of project initiatives and repeated each subsequent year to assess short-term impact. Third, data are drawn from a cross-sectional mail survey of a sample representing the entire student body conducted in the spring academic term before, and at two subsequent points after, the intervention was introduced that allow a longer-term assessment of impact.

Program Exposure Data

We collected data on student exposure to various project initiatives throughout the experiment. If efforts to reduce misperception were going to produce more accurately perceived norms and consequently reduce high-risk drinking and related problems, then it was important to know if communications about social norms were being noticed. A reduction in drinking problems at the end of the experiment might be satisfactory evidence of impact since no other new interventions were introduced simultaneously, but demonstrating significant exposure to intervention material certainly strengthens any positive findings on outcome. Monitoring of these data has also served to help shape the ongoing work of the project by informing project staff about whether students were receiving certain forms of information and indicating when new initiatives might be valuable in promoting student attention to the social norms campaign.

Following the launch of the Campus Factoids™ initiative on campus, graduating seniors each year were asked, as part of an exit survey administered to all seniors just before graduation, how often during their senior year they had read the newspaper column or logged into the interactive electronic program. About three-quarters of the seniors had read Campus factoids™ at least once during the immediate year in each graduating class from 1997 through 1999, and about half had read it more than once. For the class of 1997, 34 percent had logged into the online program during the last nine months. The figure grew to 44 percent for the next year's class of 1998 and to 61 percent for the class of 1999. About 25 percent of seniors in 1998 and 1999 had used the online program multiple times within the year. The use of both print and electronic media served to broaden and intensify exposure. For example, 80 percent of seniors in those years had read the column or logged online during their final year at least once, and 23 percent had done both multiple times during their final year. On the basis of electronic log records, one can estimate that more than seven thousand online reader sessions in this multimedia program were initiated by students and staff during the intervention period of this study. During the 1999–2000 academic year, there were 1,903 campus logons to this interactive program, in which a combined total of

12,612 factoid and 5,109 reactoid items were read. In the latter part of spring term, when the online quiz was introduced, it was taken 951 times on this campus of about eighteen hundred students.

Fall-Term Introductory Class Surveys

A survey devised to assess actual and perceived norms about student alcohol use was administered in introductory courses to quickly achieve a high response rate from students with diverse academic interests. Specifically, all introductory sociology and chemistry courses were selected because (1) they embraced a broad spectrum of humanities, social science, and natural science students; (2) each fall there were multiple sections of relatively large classes (large, that is, by the standards of a small college where the student-faculty ratio is about 13:1); and (3) faculty cooperation was assured for access to every class in subsequent years. Although enrollment in these introductory courses predominantly represented first-year and second-year students, this profile was of particular interest given that the first two years of college are a critical juncture for developing collegiate alcohol abuse, and these initial years were heavily targeted in the programming implemented by the project.

Surveys were administered during a one-month time span in the middle of the fall academic term. The first administration occurred in 1996, just before new project initiatives at HWS were introduced. All of the students attending each selected class responded to this voluntary and anonymous survey. Comparing the response (156 students) to enrollment lists indicated that in the five classes constituting the baseline data (89 percent of students officially enrolled in the classes had been surveyed). In fall 1997 and 1998, students in all sections of the same courses were surveyed using the same instrument and procedures. Again, all students in attendance participated (90 percent of the official enrollment), producing a total postintervention sample of 274 respondents from nine classes over the two fall terms.

This fall-term evaluation was an important component of the initial postintervention analysis because it provided an early assessment of program effect by demonstrating how quickly the misperception reduction campaign, when intensively delivered, could begin to produce effects. None of the students in the 1997 fall survey had been exposed to more than one year of social norms programming, and first-year students obviously could have been exposed to no more than two months of intervention. Again in the survey of introductory classes in fall 1998, first-year students had only about two months of exposure, second-year students had less than one year, and even the relatively few juniors and seniors in the sample had received less than two years' exposure to social norms messages.

Comparing the survey results in fall 1996 (preintervention sample) with combined survey results of fall 1997 and 1998 (postintervention samples) revealed differences with lowered perception of peer norm use of alcohol, less perception of permissive peer attitudes, and less personal drinking behavior as predicted on virtually every survey item. Table 3.1 has examples of differences with statistical significance. These data indeed indicate a substantial and consistent reduction in average perceptions of peer drinking norms in a fairly short time of program intervention for most students. Furthermore, declines in actual drinking behavior were associated with declines in perception. Even though (as theory predicts) perceived norms continued to be exaggerated relative to actual behavior, both were moving in a more moderate direction as perceptions of drinking were scaled back.

It is also important to note that these lowered perceptions and behaviors in the postintervention sample cannot be explained by any change in entering cohorts of students between 1996 and 1998. First, the sociodemographic background characteristics of students were quite similar across admission cohorts, as revealed in analysis of HWS entering class survey data. These data were collected using the nationally administered CIRP Freshman Survey (Sax, Astin, Korn, and Mahoney, 2001). All entering HWS students were surveyed at arrival during orientation. Furthermore, in this CIRP survey of incoming students each year, we found virtually no change throughout the 1990s in drinking patterns in high school the year prior to attendance at HWS.

Moreover, the response distribution on a survey item about personal attitudes in the fall introductory course surveys (where students were asked to indicate what level of drinking was appropriate, from no consumption to frequent intoxication) were virtually identical in preintervention and postintervention cohorts. That these groups held the same attitudes about drinking, thus suggesting the groups did not differ in basic character, is not counter to program impact. Recall that changing personal attitudes was not the fundamental goal of the approach, because most students were already relatively moderate in their attitudes. What was most problematic were the exaggerated perceptions of peer norms and the concomitant behavior frequently associated with them. (In theory, misperception pushes some students to drink in excess of their attitude and allows other students with the most liberal attitude to act out in accordance with the attitude.)

Student perception of other students' attitudes regarding the same response categories did reflect a dramatic difference between the preintervention and postintervention samples of our fall introductory class survey. In 1996, 45 percent of the sample erroneously believed the most common attitudinal response of their peers in the survey would be that frequent intoxication and drinking affecting responsibilities was OK. (In reality, only 7 percent actually held this attitude personally in

TABLE 3.1. PERCEIVED AND ACTUAL DRINKING ATTITUDES AND BEHAVIORS AMONG STUDENTS BEFORE AND AFTER SOCIAL NORMS INTERVENTION (FALL TERM CLASS SURVEYS).

	1996 Before Intervention (n = 156)	1997–98 After Intervention (n = 274)	Rate of Change (Percentage)	(*p* <)
Perceptions of others' attitudes and behaviors				
Thinks moderate or conservative attitude is typical of most students (%)	55	79	+44	(.001)
Estimated percentage heavy drinkers (5+ in a row; mean)	70	55	−21	(.001)
Friends' average drinks at party or bar (mean)	6.5	5.8	−11	(.05)
Males' average drinks at party or bar (mean)	8.5	7.7	−8	(.01)
Females' average drinks at party or bar (mean)	5.6	5.1	−9	(.01)
Athletes' average drinks at party or bar (mean)	6.6	5.8	−12	(.01)
Average drinks by all at party or bar (mean)	6.7	5.8	−13	(.001)
Average student drinks at residence hall "get-together" (mean)	5.3	4.7	−11	(.10)
Actual (personal) attitudes and behaviors				
Moderate attitudes (%)	93	93	0	n.s.
Abstaining (%)	15	18	+20	n.s.
Drinking 5+ in a row weekly (%)	47	39	−17	(.10)
Average drinks at party or bar (mean)	5.1	4.4	−14	(.05)
Average drinks at residence hall "get-together" (mean)	3.9	3.2	−18	(.05)

the pretest or posttest assessment.) In the 1997 and 1998 sample years, however, only 21 percent believed that other students would typically choose the most permissive attitude, thus representing a reduction in the misperceived norm by more than half.

Again these rather dramatic postintervention effects were observed among students who in most cases had one year or less of program exposure. We were also interested in seeing if a significant impact was achieved specifically for first-year students who had been on campus for about two months. Counselors and health educators commonly point to the crucial adaptation period of the first few months at college, noting this as a particularly vulnerable time for an increase in high-risk drinking. One objective of the social norms approach was indeed an attempt to dispel myths and highly exaggerated stereotypes held by new students about the normality of heavy drinking in college life. A crucial part of the HWS experiment was the effort to get the message to new students as a preemptive strike against such misperception leading to new student drinking problems.

To assess the immediate impact of the program on new students, we selected out the first-year students who participated in each of the fall surveys and examined their rate of high-school-to-college increase in high-risk drinking (having five or more drinks when at a party or bar). For this analysis, we also added the entering first-year students from our fall 1999 survey, which was again administered to students in all introductory sociology and introductory chemistry courses using the same procedures as before. (Again, comparing the response of 133 students to enrollment lists indicated that in the four classes 89 percent of students in the class had been surveyed.)

We compared the rate of high-risk drinking at parties prior to entering college as reported by each entering cohort in our CIRP survey to the first-year student rate of current high-risk drinking at parties, as reported in the introductory course surveys after two months in college. Thus, a comparison could be made between the high-risk drinking rate in the student population at matriculation with that of the sample of first-year students in the middle of fall term. The entering cohort rate was statistically adjusted in this comparison to account for limited variation in the gender distribution of fall introductory survey samples and for small differences among entering class characteristics. In the 1996 sample (before social norms project intervention) of first-year students (n = 86), the increase in high-risk drinking from high school to college was clearly evident, with a statistically significant 11 percent increase ($p < .05$). In contrast, the 1997 to 1999 first-year students (n = 183) in the introductory class samples who had all received orientation exposure and four to eight weeks of social norms messages during the first term demonstrated only a statistically insignificant 2.5 percent increase in the high-risk behavior after entering college.

Spring-Term Cross-Sectional Mail Survey

In the middle of spring term 1995, we devised and conducted an extensive survey of alcohol use in collaboration with students in our interdisciplinary course on alcohol use and abuse. The survey contained items we constructed, items from national research that had been used in previous campus surveys at HWS and elsewhere, along with questions developed by students in the course. A random sample of 150 students, stratified for gender and class year, was computer generated from the list of all students enrolled at HWS. Surveys were sent out and returned anonymously through campus mail. In addition, to cost-effectively enlarge the sample size and engender greater interest in the survey among students in the course, these students distributed the survey to an additional quota sample. Each student distributed eight surveys—selecting one male and one female representing each class year—to students who had not received the survey in the random mail sample. The surveys distributed to this quota sample were returned anonymously through the mail with the same return format as used for the random sample that received the survey in the mail. A total of 232 surveys were returned (64.8 percent response); they were highly representative of the student body as a whole in terms of academic and demographic characteristics.

In the middle of spring term 1998 (eighteen months after programming strategies began), another survey of alcohol use was devised and administered using all the same procedures as the 1995 survey. The content of the 1998 survey was again formulated with assistance of students in the Alcohol Use and Abuse course and retained all of the crucial items for comparison with 1995 data. A stratified random sample of 400 students was selected to receive the anonymous survey and return it through campus mail. Again, an additional quota sample was collected by students in the academic course to match the procedures used in 1995. The 1998 survey produced 319 respondents from the random and quota samples (50.5 percent response). Respondents were academically and demographically representative of HWS students overall. A second postintervention survey using all of the same procedures employed in 1995 and 1998 was conducted in spring 2000 with a stratified random sample of 422 students and the additional quota sample solicited by students enrolled in the Alcohol Use and Abuse course. The 2000 survey produced 327 respondents (50.6 percent response) that were, likewise, academically and demographically representative of HWS students overall.

In each of the survey years, the random sample and quota sample returns produced similar distributions by gender and class year (differences were statistically insignificant at $p > .05$). We conducted an additional test for biases in method of survey administration by comparing survey results in the random sample with those of the quota sample on fourteen alcohol attitudes, perceptions, and use measures of interest for this project for each survey year. Among the forty-two random and quota sample comparisons for the three survey years, only two comparisons produced differing results using a $p < .05$ significance level—the exact number of significant differences that should occur simply by chance if there were no systematic differences in the subsets of respondents. Thus, we pooled the random and quota sample data in the spring surveys for analyses of program impact.

Finally, there were no significant differences across survey years in gender and class year distribution. Thus we were confident that demographic differences and sampling bias would not be a significant influence on any difference that we might observe in these data among survey years.

In Table 3.2, we compare the results of the 1995 baseline spring survey with results from the first postintervention spring survey in 1998 (eighteen months after the social norms campaign began) and the second follow-up survey in spring 2000 (after continuing the social norms campaign for an additional two years). These results give us further strong support for program impact. Students' perceptions of the norms for alcohol use moved closer to the actual norms, and problem drinking was significantly reduced over the time period.

In 1995, 84 percent of this cross-section of the student body expressed a conservative personal attitude (opposing any intoxication) or relatively moderate attitude (opposing frequent intoxication or any intoxication that interfered with any responsibilities). Yet that moderate or conservative normative attitude in opposition to drunkenness was correctly identified by only 48 percent of students at that time. That is, 52 percent believed that support for frequent and problematic intoxication was the most typical attitude among other students in general at HWS. Thus over half of the sample perceived that a highly permissive attitude was the norm among peers. In 1998, even though the distribution of personal attitude had not changed (recall most attitudes were not problematic to begin with and personal attitude change was not the focal target of the project), the percentage of students misperceiving a permissive attitude as the norm among peers dropped from 52 percent to 44 percent and dropped further to 32 percent in 2000. Consequently, the percentage of students holding an accurate perception of the norm as being moderate or conservative increased from 48 percent to 56 percent and then to 68 percent across this time period.

As perceptions of peer norms were becoming more moderate and more accurate, we observed changes in actual drinking behavior that demonstrated improvement. As seen in Table 3.2, abstaining (though quite uncommon) increased from 1995 to 2000. More important, there was a statistically significant decline in the number of drinking days and the number of drinks consumed in a two-week period and in the average number of drinks students consumed at a party or bar.

TABLE 3.2. PERCEIVED AND ACTUAL DRINKING ATTITUDES AND BEHAVIORS AMONG STUDENTS BEFORE AND AFTER SOCIAL NORMS INTERVENTION (SPRING TERM RETURN MAIL SURVEYS).

	1995 Before Campus Campaign (n = 232)	1998 After Eighteen-Month Campaign (n = 319)	2000 After 3.5 Years of Campaign (n = 326)	1995–2000 Rate of Change (Percentage)
Perceptions of others' attitudes and behaviors				
Thinks moderate or conservative attitude is typical of most students (%)	48	56	68	+42***
Friends' average drinks at party or bar (mean)	7.1	6.4	6.3	–11*
Males' average drinks at party or bar (mean)	8.6	8.0	7.4	–14**
Females' average drinks at party or bar (mean)	5.4	5.0	4.7	–13***
Average drinks by all at party or bar (mean)	6.8	5.9	5.5	–19***
Actual (personal) attitudes and behaviors				
Moderate or conservative attitudes (%)	84	85	87	+4
Abstaining (%)	5	6	10	+100
Days drinking in last two weeks (mean)	4.4	4.0	3.6	–18*
Drinks consumed in last two weeks (mean)	23.5	18.1	17.8	–24**
Average drinks at party or bar (mean)	6.0	5.3	5.2	–13*
Drinking 5+ in a row three or more times in last two weeks:	41	34	28	–32**
Rarely or never experience any negative consequence (no more than one during an entire academic year, %)	30	42	45	+50***

Note: * Change is significant at $p < .05$ level; ** $p < .01$; *** $p < .001$.

Even more important, we observed a consistent decline in the percentage of students in the highest-risk or frequent heavy drinking category (drinking five or more drinks in a row on three or more occasions in the last two weeks). With the observed reduction from 41 percent to 34 percent and then 28 percent, this heaviest drinking group was cut by almost one-third (32 percent reduction).

Thus, the heaviest drinking group was scaled back considerably, and drinking overall declined as we communicated (and students began to more accurately perceive) that moderation was the peer norm. More students started behaving in accordance with their already moderate attitude, and more of the highly permissive students started constraining their behavior in accordance with a more accurately perceived norm (that is, a peer norm perceived as less permissive). Also noteworthy is the fact that abstaining did not decline as students were told that other students most typically drink a moderate amount of alcohol. We actually observed a relatively large (albeit statistically insignificant) increase in the number who abstained.

Finally, in the survey we also examined the overall incidence of a range of possible negative consequences of one's drinking during the academic year as revealed in students' self-reported experiences. Respondents were asked to indicate which of fifteen consequences had occurred once or multiple times during the entire academic year as a result of their own drinking:

1. Physical injury to oneself
2. Physical injury to others
3. Fighting
4. Behavior that resulted in negative reaction from others
5. Damage to property
6. Missing class
7. Inefficiency in a homework, classroom, or lab assignment
8. A late paper or missed exam, or failure to study for an exam
9. Damaged friendships or relationships
10. Impaired driving
11. Attempting intimate physical or sexual contact not desired by another person
12. Being sexually active when the person otherwise might not have chosen to be active
13. Engaging in unprotected intercourse when the person otherwise would not have
14. Inability to remember events that occurred while drinking
15. Missing or performing poorly in an athletic event

Considering all of these possible effects of drinking, it was not uncommon for students to have noted at least some effect of their drinking on an aspect of their lives, especially given that this question covered the entire academic year. Nevertheless, we observed a significant increase in the percentage of students who rarely or never experienced such a consequence of their drinking, from 30 to 45 percent, thus producing a 50 percent growth rate in the size of this low-incidence category.

Local Arrests for Liquor Law Violations

In addition to the self-report data provided in anonymous surveys, other archival data available on negative consequences dramatically reinforce the picture of a decline in alcohol problems over the course of the intervention period. As part of the crime reporting regulations required of all colleges in recent years, academic institutions were required to standardize the process of assembling and publicly reporting crime violations among students. The Office of Campus Safety, which is responsible for recording these statistics, reported the number of arrests for liquor law violation—a particular interest for this experiment—as part of its systematic reporting for calendar years from the beginning of 1997 through the end of 2000. The total number of students arrested both on campus and in the local community declined substantially, from eighty-four arrests in 1997 to seventy-two in 1998, and forty-five in 1999. Thus, the number arrested dropped by 46 percent. In the middle of the 2000 calendar year, the academic calendar was converted from a trimester to semester system, uniquely extending the number of weeks students were in residence during spring and fall of that calendar year compared to previous calendar years. So arrest rates had to be adjusted for the difference in student residence time for 2000. Adjusting for this difference produced an estimate of forty-four arrests, a figure similar to the low rate of the previous year.

Reflecting on Accomplishments

We launched this social norms experiment during the 1996–97 academic year with optimism about what the positive effect of reducing misperceptions in our campus context might be. We knew that students grossly misperceived the peer drinking norm in an exaggerated direction even in our local context, where overall consumption was actually high compared to national patterns. Our theory proposed that challenging these misperceptions by publicizing accurate data about student norms could lead already heavy drinkers and potentially problematic students to reduce or avoid a risky level of consumption. Therefore our goal was to see if we could produce a substantial positive effect through communicating accurate norms and see if it could be brought about quickly through the synergistic impact of multiple strategies communicating accurate peer norms simultaneously. We wanted to produce a new and more integrated academic and social climate, one where students had a more realistic awareness of peer disapproval of alcohol use and abuse and where a more responsible level of conversation about drinking could take place. The expectation was that, as perceptions of drinking norms became more realistic and responsible discussion of alcohol was increasingly integrated into the curriculum, a significant reduction in student alcohol abuse would be the result.

In conducting this experiment, we were pleased to learn that developing print media, electronic media, and curricular and cocurricular presentations about actual peer norms was made much easier by this synergistic approach. Almost all of the material created for one venue could be recycled or amplified through its reintroduction in one of the other modes of communication. In the end, the most gratifying result, of course, was the marked reduction we observed immediately (and also in the long run) in misperceived norms, in personal high-risk drinking, and in associated consequences among our students.

One must always be cautious about concluding that one's program was influential if the claim is based on limited data collection, which is always imperfect. Our confidence in the existence and strength of this positive result, however, was significantly bolstered by several factors. First, the results were subjected to standard significance tests that repeatedly demonstrated a reduction not likely due to sampling error. Second, we observed a decline in heavy drinking that continued over multiple time points as the social norms campaign went on. Third, these observations were based on surveys regularly conducted in both fall and spring that included multiple assessment measures of perceived norms and problem drinking, all demonstrating the same basic pattern of change overall. Fourth, it is important to add that the findings of this extensive database of anonymous survey results have been reinforced both by informal anecdotal comments of administrative colleagues at our institution, who believe they have seen fewer problems in years following the introduction of the social norms strategy, and by the reality of declining alcohol-related arrests among students.

Finally, it is important to note again that the primary objective of the social norms intervention was not to change attitudes overall, because the attitudinal norm was already relatively moderate. Rather, the intention was to help make student perception of the attitudinal norm more accurate, so they could behave in accordance with that moderate attitude, whether or not it was personally held. This point is especially important for schools such as HWS, where the behavior norms of the average consumption level are relatively high to start with. When students were apprised of the actual norm of moderate drinking attitudes, the accuracy of their perception increased; simultaneously, the heavy drinking rate declined precipitously.

In this chapter, we have shown how the HWS Project's strategy of integrating a comprehensive set of initiatives to reduce harmful misperception about student norms was successful for this undergraduate residential campus. As a final note, it is also important to stress that strategies developed in this experiment are by no means restricted to small schools or residential institutions. Indeed, the media campaigns—electronic as well as print—and curricular infusion strategies we introduced at HWS are highly transportable to quite different settings. Electronic media can be potentially even more useful as an efficient cost-saving medium of message delivery in a larger institution. Curriculum-based social norms efforts may be even more important for a school with a large commuting population in which classroom contacts are the primary or only intervention context for reaching most students. If media and classroom social norms efforts can be constructed as linked strategies in any of these higher education settings, then the work of substance abuse prevention will be greatly strengthened.

References

Haines, M. *A Social Norms Approach to Preventing Binge Drinking at Colleges and Universities.* Newton, Mass.: Higher Education Center for Alcohol and Other Drug Prevention, 1996.

Haines, M., and Spear, S. F. "Changing the Perception of the Norm: A Strategy to Decrease Binge Drinking Among College Students." *Journal of American College Health,* 1996, *45,* 134–140.

Johannessen, K., Collins, C., Mills-Novoa, B., and Glider, P. *A Campus Case Study in Implementing Social Norms and Environmental Management Approaches.* Tucson: University of Arizona Campus Health Service, 1999.

Perkins, H. W. "College Student Misperceptions of Alcohol and Other Drug Norms Among Peers: Exploring Causes, Consequences and Implications for Prevention Programs." In *Designing Alcohol and Other Drug Prevention Programs in Higher Education: Bringing Theory Into Practice.* Newton, Mass.: Higher Education Center for Alcohol and Other Drug Prevention, and U.S. Department of Education, 1997.

Perkins, H. W. "Social Norms and the Prevention of Alcohol Misuse in Collegiate Contexts." *Journal of Studies on Alcohol,* 2002 (Supplement no. 14), pp. 164–172.

Perkins, H. W., and Berkowitz, A. D. "Perceiving the Community Norms of Alcohol Use Among Students: Some Research Implications for Campus Alcohol Education Programming." *International Journal of the Addictions,* 1986, *21,* 961–976.

Perkins, H. W., and Craig, D. W., *A Multifaceted Social Norms Approach to Reduce High-Risk Drinking: Lessons from Hobart and William Smith Colleges.* Newton, Mass.: Higher Education Center for Alcohol and Other Drug Prevention, and U.S. Department of Education, 2002.

Perkins, H. W., and Wechsler, H. "Variation in Perceived College Drinking Norms and Its Impact on Alcohol Abuse: A Nationwide Study." *Journal of Drug Issues,* 1996, *26,* 961–974.

Perkins, H. W., and others. "Misperceptions of the Norms for the Frequency of Alcohol and Other Drug Use on College Campuses." *Journal of American College Health,* 1999, *47,* 253–258.

Presley, C. A., Meilman, P. W., and Cashin, J. R. *Alcohol and Drugs on American College Campuses: Use, Consequences, and Perceptions of the Campus Environment.* Vol. 4: *1992–1994.* Carbondale, Ill.: Core Institute, 1996.

Sax, L. J., Astin, A. W., Korn, W. S., and Mahoney, K. M. *The American Freshman: National Norms for Fall 1999.* Los Angeles: Cooperative Institutional Research Program, American Council on Education, UCLA, 2001.

Wechsler, H., Dowdall, G., Davenport, A., and Castillo, S. "Correlates of College Student Binge Drinking." *American Journal of Public Health,* 1995, *85,* 921–926.

Wechsler, H., and others. "Trends in College Binge Drinking During a Period of Increased Prevention Efforts: Findings from Four Harvard School of Public Health College Alcohol Study Surveys: 1993–2001." *Journal of American College Health,* 2002, *50*(5), 203–217.

CHAPTER FOUR

THE UNIVERSITY OF ARIZONA'S CAMPUS HEALTH SOCIAL NORMS MEDIA CAMPAIGN

Koreen Johannessen, M.S.W.; Peggy Glider, Ph.D.

The social norms campaign at the University of Arizona (UA) is part of a two-pronged approach to alcohol and other drug abuse prevention that also targets campus alcohol use policies and enforcement practices for change. The overall outcome objectives for the UA program were to:

- Decrease the rate of heavy drinking among undergraduates
- Reduce the consumption of alcohol by heavy drinkers to a more moderate level
- Correct the campus misperception that most college students are heavy drinkers who typically harm others or themselves when they drink
- Identify, implement, and consistently enforce campus alcohol and other drug policies that could increase campus safety
- Prevent entering freshmen and freshwomen from misperceiving campus alcohol norms

Portions of this chapter were adapted from *A Practical Guide to Alcohol Abuse Prevention: A Campus Case Study in Implementing Social Norms and Environmental Management Approaches* (Johannessen, Collins, Mills-Novoa, and Glider, 1999), an in-house publication of the University of Arizona's Campus Health Service. Funding for the UA Campus Health Alcohol and Other Drug Prevention Program was provided by the U.S. Department of Health and Human Services, the U.S. Department of Education, and the Campus Health Service of the University of Arizona.

- Correct key campus community misperceptions so that faculty, staff, advisors, and others are not carriers of misperception about student alcohol use
- Target campus and community events, associated in the past with unsafe drinking practices, for policy and enforcement change through partnership with key community groups

The UA social norms media has three goal-related objectives: (1) to publicize student alcohol use norms and change existing misperceptions; (2) to support those norms with educational information; and (3) to change the public conversation about alcohol use among UA students, staff, administration, and the community. When the project began in 1994, normative (majority) messages were advertised primarily through print media: the *Arizona Daily Wildcat*, the campus newspaper, featured one or two ads per week. Feature articles and inserts supplemented the ad campaign. Posters and flyers were developed and distributed (predominantly in residence halls and other high-traffic areas) to reinforce the newspaper campaign. The student alcohol misperceptions and alcohol use data for the media campaign were collected from Campus Health random mail-out surveys, residence halls, and fraternity and sorority housing mail-out surveys.

Steps for Developing a Social Norms Print Media Campaign

A successful social norms media campaign requires a commitment to data gathering and analysis. Several surveys and other data collection instruments were used throughout the study period to address questions about behavior, perceptions, and information gathering regarding alcohol and other drug (or AOD) use among UA students (see the section on quantitative measures for more detailed information).

Accurate majority (normative) data that address campus drinking misperceptions are at the center of the social norms strategy. This derives from the finding that college students greatly overestimate the amount of alcohol their peers are consuming (Perkins, 1997; Perkins and others, 1999). To correct this misperception at UA, a media campaign was developed to broadcast actual student drinking norms.

The UA campaign broadcast information about campus drinking that survey data revealed as having a high incidence of misperception by students: amount consumed per occasion (how much), frequency of occasion (how often), level of intoxication (from not intoxicated to extremely intoxicated), and endorsement of protective factors that slow intoxication (for example, eating, or tracking drinks) or increase safety (such as selecting a designated driver, or watching out for a friend at a party).

Determining Survey Measures

Shifting from a problem-focused perspective ("How often do you drink heavily?") to a more specific behavioral focus was the key to uncovering norms. Commonly asked questions included "If you drink, . . .":

- ". . . when you party, how many drinks do you usually have?"
- ". . . how many nights a week do you usually party?"
- ". . . how many drinks did you have the last time you drank?"
- ". . . over the course of how many hours did you drink?"
- ". . . please estimate the amount of drinks you have during the first hour, second hour, third hour. . . ."

Surveys also included questions about gender and weight so that staff could calculate average blood alcohol concentration (BAC) levels. In addition, questions about protective behavior—what the respondents do to drink safely—were also included. For example, "When I drink I always, usually, rarely, or never . . .":

- ". . . eat before and during the time I'm drinking"
- ". . . choose beverages with alcohol content I know"
- ". . . have one or fewer per hour when I drink" [for women]
- ". . . have two or fewer per hour when I drink" [for men]

Traditionally, practitioners have solicited information that would identify behaviors they hoped to correct; but in this model the goal is to uncover majority information that supports the drinking behaviors the practitioner wants to increase.

Determining the Method of Communication

There are a variety of ways that normative information can be broadcast to students in print. Campaigns have used campus newspaper display and classified ads as well as feature articles and editorials. Flyers and posters on classroom bulletin boards, kiosks, and bus advertising space, as well as table tents, door hangers, and promotional giveaway items are popular. At UA the choice to use print media as the primary source of broadcasting campus drinking norms was highly influenced by data gathered by Campus Health staff regarding how students prefer to get their information. Surveys included questions about how often students read the *Wildcat*, how often they listened to KAMP radio (the campus radio station), and whether they would hang a health-related poster in their living space. Students' responses guided Campus Health staff in their decisions about where to invest their marketing dollars.

The format selected for the UA ad campaign was a three-by-eight-inch black-and-white ad published weekly in the *Wildcat*. Norms information was also imbedded in health-related feature articles, inserts, and supplements to the paper. A majority of students read the *Wildcat* three or four times per week during the first three years of the study period. (We have seen this trend decline over the years and as a result now publish ads at least twice per week.) Students highly endorsed posters and flyers as other messaging formats; but at a large school, multiple distribution of such items could create a logistical problem.

Design selection was also influenced by gathering information about the target population from a variety of sources (magazines, design books, stock photography). Color and style trends in commercial advertising campaigns aimed at young adults were an important resource in making design choices.

The design for our alcohol social norms newspaper campaign used attractive photos of students set in a familiar campus location to capitalize on the norm of moderate drinking and good health, and to emphasize the campus context of the peer group. A photo shoot was conducted and images were selected for the campaign.

Next, images were paired with messages in three or four pilot print designs. Research at NIU (Haines, 1996) and market research at the UA revealed that effective print designs should consist of these elements: a normative message, an engaging photo of students in a familiar campus location (or eye-catching graphic for text-only ads), a credible data source, drink equivalency information, and a recognizable logo (in this case, the UA Campus Health logo). The overall goal was to engage students on an optimistic, emotional level with material that is intelligent, accurate, familiar, and not "preachy" (see Figures 4.1 and 4.2).

We make these suggestions to help ensure a successful pilot piece:

- Hire a photographer and graphic designer, or enlist the help of a talented amateur, and shoot campus-specific photographs.
- Select student models who drink moderately or not at all and who are perceived as drinking moderately.
- Obtain campaign-specific consent forms from students used in the photo shoot.
- Strive for realism. Use groups of students who know each other well and place them in settings where they are naturally engaged with one another.
- Select photos that are conceptually consistent with or connected to the message. If your message is moderate drinking, images of students who appear to be intoxicated or hung over are not appropriate.

FIGURE 4.1. UA CAMPAIGN POSTER:
STUDENTS HAVE 4 OR FEWER DRINKS (WITH BULL'S-EYE TARGET).

Source: Martin Valencia, graphic designer. Used by permission of Health Promotion and Preventive Services, University of Arizona.

FIGURE 4.2. UA CAMPAIGN POSTER: MOST OF US ARE SAFE.

Source: Martin Valencia, graphic designer. Used by permission of Health Promotion and Preventive Services, University of Arizona.

- Use white space effectively in the design to help the ad stand out among other ads competing for reader attention. Limit the amount of information and strive for clarity and simplicity in the ad layout. Ads with multiple messages and multiple elements were not seen as often.
- Repeat some visual design elements across all campaign ads. For example, lead with the most important information, and adjust font size to emphasize key information.
- If resources prevent the inclusion of a photograph with the main message, develop a text-only media campaign. Experiment with graphics, font sizes, and font styles to create an appealing and effective ad.
- Negotiate good placement for display ads and other print media.

Test Marketing Campaign Materials

Market testing was a mandatory step for the UA campaign, ensuring that the information was easy to understand and packaged in a way that appealed to the target population (UA students).

There are several ways to collect information for modifying the ads. At UA we used *subject intercepts* during the design phase of the media campaign. These are brief interviews that ask subjects to compare design elements or messages. Questions gave insight into which designs were most appealing and potentially effective for the target population:

- "Which of these pictures caught your eye?"
- "Can you tell me a story about the people in the picture?"
- "Do you think you could be friends with these people?"
- "What does the message say?"
- "What do you think these people do on a weekend to have fun?"
- "What feelings do you get when you look at this picture?"
- "Can you repeat the information you just saw in this ad?"

Sampling of the target population for media design and wording preferences was conducted until consistent patterns emerged within the data. Sample sizes varied (from twenty to one hundred) depending upon the element being tested.

Paper-and-pencil market tests were used when piloting new campaign ads and served as a final test before final production and distribution. During this process, samples of four or five completed ads or posters were shown to target groups of students who completed a one-to-two-page questionnaire comparing the ads and posters. Students were asked which they liked best and least, which provided the most and least information, and which caught their eye first. Paper-and-pencil surveys were typically conducted in the residence halls or in classrooms; subjects received a small reward or prize for participating.

Market-testing questions were also included on the annual Campus Health Wellness Survey to gather student opinions about the social norms media campaign—how visible and credible they perceived the ads and posters to be. Often *key informant interviews* (one-on-one interviews with students in the target group) and *small focus group interviews* were used to help develop new survey questions.

Regular and frequent exposure to the normative message was critical to the success of the UA campaign. The information targeting misperceptions was conveyed through:

- Campus newspaper advertisements in the *Daily Wildcat*, placed fifteen times throughout the semester
- Campus newspaper inserts, centerfolds, and special supplemental issues
- A poster campaign designed for residence hall rooms and common areas (students who hung the poster in their room received a small cash award)
- Bulletin board displays placed in strategic locations such as residence hall bathrooms, game rooms, laundry rooms, elevators, and front desks
- Inclusion of normative information in a variety of student newsletters (this included feature articles, news briefs, and display ads)
- Semiannual memoranda about alcohol, and other health-related student norms to faculty, staff, and administrators

Cost Analysis of UA's Social Norms Newsprint Campaign

In general, the cost of implementing a social norms media campaign in a college or university setting depends on the vehicle for the campaign, production and placement costs, and staff training time. The analysis given here is from the UA experience with a student body of thirty-four thousand, and with costs specific to the Tucson area in 2002. This information may give an idea of campaign cost, but actual costs of course vary from campus to campus.

Student Newspaper Ad Campaign: Costs for 2001–02 School Year

Ad placement in the campus paper (*Arizona Daily Wildcat*) (3 × 8-inch ad cost is $170, placed twice a week for 30 weeks)	$10,200
Student workers for market research and testing ($7/hour for 5 hours/week during development phase, which lasts 6 weeks)	$210

Models for photographs	$500
(Compensated with gift certificates to the bookstore)	
Media team time	$11,800
(Director of health promotion @ 4 hrs/month, AOD coordinator	
@ 16 hrs/month, 2 prevention specialists @ 4 hrs/month,	
graphic designer @ 44 hrs/month)	
Photography (for 25 usable images per year)	$2,000
Total	$24,710

The total cost per ad of the *Wildcat* campaign is $24,710 divided by sixty ads, or $412. The cost per reader per ad is $412 divided by fifteen thousand (the approximate daily readership of the paper), or three cents.

Evaluating UA's Social Norms Media Campaign

A solid evaluation plan was a critical component of the UA's social norms media campaign. Evaluation procedures not only provided needed information for the campaign and for key stakeholders but more important offered evidence of the program's success in changing the heavy drinking rate and resulting negative consequences at UA. What follows is a description of the quantitative and qualitative evaluation strategies used for UA's social norms media campaign and environmental strategies.

Quantitative Measures

The Campus Health staff worked with a team of quantitative evaluators to determine the best strategies and instruments for collecting data. The Core Alcohol and Drug Survey (Presley and Meilman, 1989) was selected because it is a national instrument. Use of a nationally recognized instrument had several benefits, notably that it incorporated sound psychometric properties and allowed comparison on AOD-related behaviors, perceptions, and trends between local and national data sets over time. The Core Survey mailed to a random sample of 1,500 undergraduates (February and March) in 1995 and 1998 provided data for this case study. The list of students was generated through the Office of the Registrar using a computer program. The return rates were fairly consistent, with 30 percent in 1995 (322 surveys returned of the 1,097 deliverable surveys—those with accurate addresses) and 25 percent in 1998 (317 of the 1,268 deliverable surveys). A demographic breakdown of survey respondents each year is in Table 4.1.

TABLE 4.1. DEMOGRAPHIC CHARACTERISTICS OF SURVEY RESPONDENTS BY YEAR FOR CORE ALCOHOL AND DRUG SURVEY AND HEALTH ENHANCEMENT SURVEY.

Core Survey	1995 (Percentage)	1998 (Percentage)
Freshmen	34.2	15.2
Sophomores	33.5	17.4
Juniors	10.2	30.0
Seniors	11.5	34.1
Graduate or professional	9.0	1.3
Nondegree seeking	1.5	1.3
Aged 18–22	79.6	68.8
Males	38.2	38.1
Females	61.8	61.9

Health Enhancement Survey	1996 (Percentage)	1998 (Percentage)
Freshmen	42.2	32.1
Sophomores	27.5	37.6
Juniors	19.9	22.6
Seniors	10.2	7.3
Graduate or professional	0.2	0.4
Aged 18–22	97.6	97.8
Males	30.3	22.9
Females	69.7	77.1

Some flexibility is lost when using a national instrument. The Core Survey did not contain information specific to several program interests (one example being protective factors used when drinking). Also, there are no questions that allow us to measure the relationship between program exposure and other responses (attitudes, perception, and behaviors). It was decided that an additional, program-specific instrument would be necessary to capture this information.

The Health Enhancement Survey (HES) was developed from a set of items that tapped the knowledge, attitudes, perceptions, and behaviors targeted by each component of the AOD prevention approach. In addition, this instrument featured a checklist of program activities to which the respondent could have been exposed, and it asked how often he or she read the *Wildcat*. Frequency of program exposure gave insight into the relationship between exposure to the program and desired outcomes. The HES was distributed via campus mail to all students living in residence halls or a Greek house (approximately four to five thousand each year). Baseline data were collected in September 1995, and subsequent collections were done in April and May. Data in spring of 1996 and 1998 are given for this case study. Response rates were 17 percent in 1996 (842 returned) and 15 percent in 1998 (746 returned). The demographic data of respondents in 1996 and 1998 are also presented in Table 4.1.

Given that drinking patterns vary throughout the school year (generally peaking in the first semester), it was determined that all surveys would be best collected early in the spring semester (prior to spring break) each year.

Qualitative Measures

Campus Health staff used qualitative evaluation measures to garner insight as to how the media campaign affected the campus environment and key stakeholder networks. Using qualitative measures preserved the context in which AOD behaviors occurred and permitted a more holistic examination of processes and outcomes related to the social norms media campaign. Information gathered from qualitative methods was combined with quantitative data for a clearer picture than either data set might offer in isolation. The primary qualitative evaluation methods used were:

- Key informant (stakeholder) interviews using a standardized interview protocol
- Focus group interviews with students, conducted to obtain feedback on the media campaign and to produce contextual data regarding their AOD experiences on campus
- Observation of key AOD-related events and interventions (Homecoming, Bid Night, sporting events) using a standardized observation protocol
- Informal surveys and interviews with staff and the target audience regarding implementation of the project
- Analysis of secondary data sources containing information related to campus AOD issues (newspaper articles, newsletters, memos, television stories related to the intervention or having potential impact on the students and stakeholders, student records and reports, critical incidents and anecdotes collected regularly by staff)

These methods allowed staff to make changes to the social norms media campaign and permitted them to monitor the public conversation about heavy drinking among students, faculty, staff, and administrators, from "everyone drinks heavily" to "most drink moderately."

HES 1998 survey results revealed that 81 percent of UA students living on campus in a residence hall or a Greek residence had seen the social norms media campaign ads, and usually multiple times. Table 4.2 presents data comparing results from the UA 1995 and 1998 Core Surveys broken down by gender. Table 4.3 likewise presents data comparing results of the 1996 and 1998 HES surveys

TABLE 4.2. COMPARISON OF 1995 AND 1998 UNIVERSITY OF ARIZONA UNDERGRADUATE CORE ALCOHOL AND DRUG SURVEY RESULTS BY GENDER.

Undergraduates Reporting That They:	*Males*			*Females*		
	1995 Percentage (n = 94)	1998 Percentage (n = 98)	*p*	1995 Percentage (n = 180)	1998 Percentage (n = 177)	*p*
Had five or more drinks in one sitting in the past two weeks	52.1	41.7	n.s.	37.4	24.9	.010
Used alcohol in the past thirty days	75.3	70.5	n.s.	71.9	60.6	.024
Increased use of alcohol in the past year	27.7	15.2	.032	27.5	18.8	.050
Increased use of drugs other than alcohol in the past year	10.8	6.9	n.s.	11.9	6.3	n.s.
Got into a fight or argument due to AOD use in past year	30.9	21.3	n.s.	32.0	18.9	.005
Got in trouble with police, residence hall, or other college authorities due to AOD use in the past year	20.2	9.3	.029	16.3	4.0	.000
Had a memory loss due to AOD use in the past year	32.3	28.0	n.s.	31.5	21.1	.027
Were taken advantage of sexually due to AOD use in the past year	8.6	8.3	n.s.	17.4	7.0	.003
Performed poorly on a test or important project due to AOD use in the past year	21.3	17.6	n.s.	21.8	13.8	.050
Missed class due to AOD use in the past year	31.2	29.0	n.s.	33.3	20.9	.009

TABLE 4.3. COMPARISON OF 1996 AND 1998 UNIVERSITY OF ARIZONA UNDERGRADUATE HEALTH ENHANCEMENT SURVEY RESULTS BY GENDER.

Undergraduates Reporting That They:	Males			Females		
	1996 Percentage (n = 252)	1998 Percentage (n = 168)	p	1996 Percentage (n = 586)	1998 Percentage (n = 573)	p
Used alcohol in the past thirty days	75.7	65.9	.029	73.5	66.9	.014
Believe alcohol-free events are not as much fun as events with alcohol	46.0	33.3	.012	33.5	27.4	.029
Say they would rather go to a party that served alcohol than one that did not	40.8	36.0	n.s.	57.5	45.8	<.001
Believe most UA students have four or fewer drinks when they party	44.1	59.9	.002	46.7	64.2	<.001

broken down by gender. The pattern of data shows positive changes on all items in Tables 4.2 and 4.3 for both males and females, though statistical significance was found more often among the females than among males. This difference in significance reflects the larger sample size for females and in some instances a larger difference over time as well. Although overall response rates for the Core Survey and Health Enhancement Survey were lower than desired, consistency across survey sets supports the credibility of each data set.

Comparison was also made between the UA Core Survey data and national data for the Core Survey furnished by the Core Institute for this study. Table 4.4 demonstrates that decreases between 1995 and 1998 in UA student overall alcohol use, heavy drinking, and consequences due to AOD use (trouble with the police, residence hall or other college authorities, and arguing or fighting) cannot be explained as a nationwide trend. Indeed, national results on these items revealed an opposite trend. In addition, there was a decrease of 22.5 percent in UA students who believed the social atmosphere promotes alcohol use, compared to only a 4 percent decrease in the national time comparison.

TABLE 4.4. COMPARISON OF NATIONAL CORE AND UA CORE SURVEY, 1995–1998.

1. Frequency of Alcohol Use in the Past Year (Percentage)

	Males		Females		All UA		National	
	1995 (n = 107)	1998 (n = 112)	1995 (n = 199)	1998 (n = 182)	1995 (n = 322)	1998 (n = 317)	1995 (n = 14,012)	1998 (n = 32,283)
Nonuser (no use in past year)	12.5	17.1	15.2	17.8	14.5	17.2	22.8	14.9
Infrequent (1 to 6 times/year)	14.4	17.1	25.3	28.3	20.4	24.5	22.1	17.6
Moderate (once/month to once/week)	44.3	39.6	42.9	43.3	43.1	41.7	37.5	43.1
Frequent (3 times/week or more)	28.8	26.2	16.6	10.6	22.0	16.6	17.5	24.4

2. Frequency of Having Five or More Drinks in One Sitting in the Last Two Weeks (Percentage)

	Males		Females		All UA		National	
	1995	1998	1995	1998	1995	1998	1995	1998
None	49.5	58.0	66.2	75.3	59.8	69.4	66.0	55.1
Once	14.0	15.2	13.1	12.1	12.8	13.2	11.6	14.0
Twice	12.1	10.7	7.1	6.0	9.0	7.6	8.7	10.7
Three or more times	24.3	16.1	13.6	6.5	18.4	9.8	13.8	20.2

3. Frequency of Being in Trouble with Police, Residence Hall, or Other College Authorities Due to AOD Use in the Past Year (Percentage)

	Males		Females		All UA		National	
	1995	1998	1995	1998	1995	1998	1995	1998
Never	82.2	90.9	85.3	96.1	84.4	93.9	90.4	86.7
One or two times	14.9	6.3	13.7	3.9	14.1	5.1	7.4	11.7
Three or more times	2.8	2.7	1.0	0	1.5	1.0	2.1	2.1

4. Frequency of Getting into an Argument or Fight Due to AOD Use in the Past Year (Percentage)

	Males		Females		All UA		National	
	1995	1998	1995	1998	1995	1998	1995	1998
Never	71.7	79.3	70.6	81.6	70.5	80.2	74.6	70.8
One or two times	18.9	9.0	22.8	13.8	21.6	12.3	16.7	19.7
Three or more times	9.3	11.7	6.6	4.6	7.9	7.5	8.7	9.5

5. Agree with the Statement (Percentage)

	Males		Females		All UA		National	
	1995	1998	1995	1998	1995	1998	1995	1998
Social atmosphere on campus promotes alcohol use	78.8	57.9	75.8	58.3	76.8	59.5	64.7	61.5

Here are highlights of the project findings:

- The rate of heavy drinking (defined as five or more drinks at a sitting in the last two weeks) decreased by 29 percent at the UA, from 43 percent of undergraduates in 1995 to 31 percent in 1998 on the Core Survey.
- The alcohol use rate (used in past thirty days) decreased from 74 percent in 1995 to 65 percent in 1998.
- Eighteen percent of undergraduates reported increasing their alcohol use (in the past year) in 1998, compared to 28 percent in 1995.

Qualitative methods also revealed a positive impact of the social norms media campaign. Data indicated that over the first four years of the study the sentence "Sixty-four percent of UA students have four or fewer drinks when they party" became a campus tag line readily recognized and repeated by students and staff alike. Even incoming freshmen and freshwomen were documented as accurately repeating the "four or fewer" phrase. This fueled speculation that the message was filtering down from UA students to incoming students.

Qualitative findings also demonstrated that public conversation regarding heavy drinking became less tolerant. Increasingly over the last five years, there has been greater effort at all levels of UA administration to take the emphasis off alcohol at campus and community events. This activity began more than ten years ago with the tragic death of a UA police officer at an off-campus fraternity party. Interviews, memos, and documented anecdotal conversations with and from key stakeholders in administration indicated that they no longer viewed heavy drinking as a rite of passage for college students. Rather, it was increasingly referred to as a public health risk to students and the community.

Furthermore, Campus Health evaluation staff monitored selected campus events as minicase studies for viewing the effect of policy change and enforcement on alcohol-related behavior at these events. Homecoming, traditionally a heavy drinking event at the UA, was one such key campus and community event. Observations and police reports of alcohol-related incidents conducted and gathered during Homecoming over the past several years indicated a decline in alcohol-related negative behaviors. Qualitative data revealed that the social norms media campaign, coupled with consistent enforcement of more uniform alcohol-related policies (for example, more uniform restrictions on alcohol availability, monitoring of alcohol distribution and consumption, increased attention to student and faculty academic and community achievements, an earlier game time so that party time before the game is shortened), were deemed responsible for this reduction in alcohol-related incidents during UA's Homecoming (Johannessen and others, 2001).

Sustaining Social Norms Efforts over Time

Social norms and environmental change efforts require a college or university's commitment to a public health approach as well as long-term commitment of time and resources. The UA saw an impressive 29 percent drop in the heavy drinking rate over three years of implementation. Our program success was based on our commitment to adherence to data gathering and social marketing practice techniques; majority data interpretation and broadcast; redirecting the conversation among student affairs professionals, faculty, staff, and others away from the negative impact of problem drinkers and instead toward the actual use norms and protective behaviors of the moderate drinking majority; a proactive (instead of reactive) stance on alcohol issues by administrators and policy makers; and communitywide environmental change (DeJong and others, 1998).

The social norms media campaign continues to be a cost-effective method for reducing heavy drinking and related negative behavioral consequences for college students at this large residential campus in an urban setting. Broadcasting existing alcohol use norms through print media permits consistent and controlled exposure to well-researched messages.

The social norms media campaign at the UA is part of a larger public health agenda encouraged by the Campus Health Service. The goal is to increase the health and safety and decrease the harm and risk associated with heavy drinking for every student and all members of the campus community. This public health frame has allowed us to influence campus alcohol policy regarding a safer level of use for students and other members of the campus community.

More traditional strategies that stress general alcohol knowledge and awareness, or that attempt to scare or intimidate heavier drinking students into drinking more responsibly or not drinking, have not proven effective in preventing or reducing heavy or high-risk drinking. These strategies—which traditionally have targeted the individual through campus presentations—are not cost-effective, and they may undermine the credibility of a social norms campaign. Other strategies that might do the same are selective enforcement of campus policies (for example, allowing bar promotion on a campus bulletin board, or alcohol in the stadium for a private party) or media advocacy and peer-based campaigns that emphasize the rights of the nondrinking minority.

By turning up the volume on the moderate drinking norms at UA, protective factors and attitudes held by the majority gives the larger community a different standard by which to judge student civility. Problem drinkers can more easily be identified and referred for treatment. Problem environmental issues—alcohol availability, sponsorship, promotion, enforcement, and policy—become more visible. These issues are in the community domain and can be addressed through campus community coalitions—neighbors, administrators, health educators, and public officials working together.

References

DeJong, W., and others. *Environmental Management: A Comprehensive Strategy for Reducing Alcohol and Other Drug Use on College Campuses.* Newton, Mass.: Higher Education Center for Alcohol and Other Drug Prevention, 1998.

Haines, M. *A Social Norms Approach to Preventing Binge Drinking at Colleges and Universities.* Newton, MA: Higher Education Center for Alcohol and Other Drug Prevention, 1996.

Johannessen, K., Collins, C., Mills-Novoa, B., and Glider, P. *A Practical Guide to Alcohol Abuse Prevention: A Campus Case Study in Implementing Social Norms and Environmental Management Approaches.* Tucson: Campus Health Service, University of Arizona, 1999.

Johannessen, K., and others. "Preventing Alcohol Related Harm at Homecoming." *American Journal of Drug and Alcohol Abuse,* 2001, *27*(3), 587–597.

Perkins, H. W. "College Student Misperceptions of Alcohol and Other Drug Norms Among Peers: Exploring Causes, Consequences, and Implications for Prevention Programs." In *Designing Alcohol and Other Drug Prevention Programs in Higher Education: Bringing Theory into Practice.* Newton, Mass.: Higher Education Center for Alcohol and Other Drug Prevention, U.S. Department of Education, 1997.

Perkins, H. W., and others. "Misperceptions of the Norms for the Frequency of Alcohol and Other Drug Use on College Campuses." *Journal of American College Health,* 1999, *47*(6), 253–258.

Presley, C. H., and Meilman, P. W. *The Core Alcohol and Drug Survey.* Carbondale: Core Institute, Southern Illinois University, 1989.

CHAPTER FIVE

APPLYING THE SOCIAL NORMS MODEL TO UNIVERSAL AND INDICATED ALCOHOL INTERVENTIONS AT WESTERN WASHINGTON UNIVERSITY

Patricia M. Fabiano, Ph.D.

Empirical evidence suggests that it is possible to reduce the proportion of college students engaging in heavy frequent drinking (defined as five or more drinks once a week or more often) by changing their perception of drinking norms through interventions collectively known as the "social norms approach." Encouraging results from our research at Western Washington University (WWU) on both universal (primary prevention) efforts and indicated (secondary prevention) efforts support the strong correlation between (1) introduction of social norms interventions and (2) reduction in high-risk consumption and alcohol-related problems.

WWU, located in the far northwestern corner of Washington, is one of the state's six public four-year institutions of higher education. Although WWU enrolls twelve thousand students from all fifty states and forty other nations, 93 percent of students come from Washington state; about 13.2 percent are ethnic minority students.

Prior to introducing alcohol interventions using the social norms approach in fall 1997, WWU could be characterized as a campus where most students drank

The research for this article was funded by an FY1997 validation grant (#S184H70021) and an FY2000 model program grant (#S184N000007) from the U.S. Department of Education to Western Washington University. The author would like to thank Christopher Stark, Elva Giddings, and Maggie Feeney for their careful assistance in preparing this manuscript.

moderately or not at all, with some students engaging in episodic heavy drinking. The one characteristic all students shared—regardless of their actual reported frequency or quantity of consumption—was overestimation of how frequently their peers drank. When WWU received a validation grant from the U.S. Department of Education in fall 1997, researchers decided to develop and test social norms delivery strategies with students who drank moderately, frequently and heavily, or not at all. Because the social norms approach has often been equated with mass-media delivery strategies, researchers at WWU developed alternative norms-delivery strategies tailored to address students who differed in level of involvement with alcohol, consequences experienced, and decision-making strategies in their use or nonuse of alcohol.

This chapter describes three alcohol interventions at WWU that use the social norms model: (1) a large-scale universal prevention application for *all* WWU students before the onset of alcohol-related problems, (2) a smaller scale universal prevention application of social norms focused on nondrinking students living in substance-free residences, and (3) an indicated prevention infusion of the model into WWU's risk reduction intervention for students who have already developed signs and symptoms of alcohol-related problems.

The Moderate Alcohol Culture at WWU

Data from both quantitative and qualitative studies suggested that WWU already had a moderate drinking culture prior to initiation of the social norms model in our universal and indicated alcohol interventions.

Quantitative Data on Alcohol Use

A partnership established in 1992 between WWU's Prevention and Wellness Services and the Office of Institutional Assessment and Testing allowed researchers to establish alcohol-use baseline data prior to initiation of the social norms interventions in the fall of 1997. Data on student alcohol use and consequences collected in spring 1992 and spring 1997 showed that the WWU drinking culture was not monolithic; it was several "cultures." The data revealed student groups ranging from complete abstainers to those who typically drank a low-to-moderate amount of alcohol (one to four drinks on a typical occasion) with no drinking-related problems, and those who were at increased risk for episodic heavy drinking (five or more drinks on a typical occasion) and drinking-related problems.

A cross-sectional comparison of the data for the 1992 and 1997 cohorts indicated that the percentage of students in these three groups remained remarkably the same. For example, the percentage of students who reported they did not drink at all in the last month remained statistically the same in 1992 (23.4 percent) and 1997 (21.5 percent). Approximately one-fifth of the sample that consistently reported not drinking at all was removed from the analyses of both survey administrations, so that trends among *drinkers*—the population with potential risk of alcohol related problems—could be assessed.

The campus drinking culture saw little change from 1992 to 1997 (see Table 5.1). Among students who drank, those who reported low-to-moderate use and those who reported high use remained statistically the same. These data make clear that a moderate alcohol-use culture already existed at WWU—a culture similar to that in other institutions of higher education in the Western United States that consistently report less frequent heavy drinking than schools in the Eastern, Central, or Southern regions of the country (Presley, Meilman, and Cashin, 1996). The fact that WWU has never had affiliation with Greek organizations, which historically have been linked to heavier drinking than non-Greeks, also contributed to the cultural norm of moderate alcohol use (Meilman, Leichliter, and Presley, 1999; Wechsler, Kuh, and Davenport, 1996).

Qualitative Data on Alcohol Use

In addition to the biennial administration of the WWU Lifestyles Survey, the alcohol prevention assessment plan included regular collection of qualitative data on student alcohol use. Data were collected in focus groups to clarify the complexity of decision-making strategies within student-use groups.

Focus group participants were recruited from large classes with majority first-year student enrollment where extra credit could be earned through participation in social science research outside of class. After completing a basic demographic and alcohol-screening questionnaire, students were placed in groups according to

TABLE 5.1. TYPICAL WEEKEND ALCOHOL CONSUMPTION: DRINKERS ONLY, 1992–1997.

"On a Given Weekend Night, How Much Alcohol Do You Typically Consume?"

Quantity	1992	1997
1–2 drinks	38.2%	33.8%
3–4 drinks	28.0%	32.0%
5 or more drinks	33.8%	34.2%

gender, age, and typical alcohol consumption level. Content analysis of focus groups composed of either all men or all women who were nondrinkers, moderate drinkers, or heavy drinkers yielded qualitative data that helped the research team understand (1) changes in student drinking between high school and college, (2) alcohol-related decision-making strategies, (3) attitudes toward alcohol-free activities, (4) students' choices for substance-free housing, and (5) perception of use among students in the several alcohol use or nonuse groups (Hyun, Snyder, Harwick, and Fabiano, 1998).

Perceptions of the Frequency of Peer Alcohol Use

WWU researchers began collecting data on student perception of other students' drinking in the spring 1997 administration of the WWU Lifestyles Survey. Using students' perception of frequency of peer alcohol use, researchers were able to document a significant gap between the actual and perceived frequency of drinking reported by students in 1997. When all students—both nondrinkers and drinkers—were asked "How often in the last month did you drink alcohol?" only 32 percent of respondents reported drinking alcohol once a week or more, with the majority drinking far less often. When asked "How often in the last month do you think the typical student at WWU drank alcohol?" 89 percent of students thought the typical student drank alcohol once a week or more, indicating a large gap between actual and perceived drinking frequency.

Applying Social Norms to Universal Alcohol Interventions

Universal or primary prevention programs target the "general student body." From a public health perspective, the goal of universal prevention is to reduce the risk for and deter the onset of disease or a problem in a population *before* it occurs (Modeste, 1996). WWU researchers focused universal prevention efforts on the two subpopulations who fit the criterion of "preproblem onset": low-to-moderate consumers and nondrinkers.

Universal Prevention Strategies Targeted at Low to Moderate Drinkers

Researchers at WWU initiated a mass-media intervention using the social norms model after five years of survey research had shown no decrease in the percentage of students reporting frequent drinking. We hypothesized that low-to-moderate consumers would show the greatest potential to be influenced by a mass media effort to market accurate campus drinking norms. Previous focus group research revealed that, although both nondrinkers and heavy drinkers identified no situa-tion-specific moderating effect on their alcohol use or nonuse, low-to-moderate drinkers modified their drinking according to specific social settings. When so-cializing with nondrinkers or low-consumers, the low-to-moderate drinkers often reduced their personal consumption. Conversely, when socializing with a higher-consuming individual or group (especially if the person or group was significant), the low-to-moderate consumers often increased their personal consumption.

Although researchers hoped that the social norms marketing project would have an impact on *all* students, they hypothesized that students in the low-to-moderate con-sumption group, whose drinking norms seemed more context-dependent, would ben-efit most. Researchers hoped that the social norms marketing campaign would contribute to and strengthen a normative campus context that would support low-to-moderate drinkers, as well as acknowledge nondrinkers.

Mass Media Campaign

The social norms mass media campaign that began at WWU in the fall 1997 as the initial intervention was modeled on templates developed at Northern Illinois University (see Chapter Two, by Haines and Barker, in this volume) and at the University of Arizona (Johannessen and Glider, Chapter Four in this volume) and profited from the many lessons learned in these other projects (Haines, 1996; Johannessen, Collins, Mills-Novoa, and Glider, 1999).

Between September 1997 and May 1998, one six-by-eight-inch ad per week ran in the student newspaper—a newspaper whose readership crossed the lines between WWU's on-campus (n = 3,500) and off-campus students (n = 8,000). The ads repeated the message that "Most (66%) Western students drink 4 or fewer drinks when they party" (see Figure 5.1).

Each ad was composed of these elements:

- Pictures of students who gave informed consent to appear in an alcohol pre-vention advertisement
- Information about the exact amount of alcohol in "one drink"
- Statement disclosing the number of WWU students who responded to the sur-vey upon which the ad was based
- Information about the origin of the ad (Prevention and Wellness Services) and the funding source (U.S. Department of Education)

Each social norms marketing ad was duplicated in an eleven-by-seventeen-inch poster distributed widely on campus, thereby multiplying the "dosage" of the weekly message. Researchers concurrently placed classified ads in the same student

FIGURE 5.1. CAMPAIGN POSTER: MOST WESTERN STUDENTS HAVE 4 OR FEWER DRINKS (THREE STUDENTS).

Source: WWU Social Norms Marketing Ad, 1997. Used by permission of Prevention and Wellness Services, Western Washington University.

newspaper to present supportive normative information about the effect of alcohol on studying, concentration, sexuality, and nutrition.

Lifestyle Advisors

Two hundred health opinion leaders, called "lifestyle advisors," increased the effect of the normative message by using typical social interactions to educate their peers about actual alcohol use norms on campus (Kelly and others, 1991). In a four-credit course taught by Prevention and Wellness Services staff, these students learned about social norms theory and the power of perception to influence individual behavior. Further, they studied how the social norms approach can (1) correct student misperception about campus alcohol use and (2) acknowledge and reinforce student perception of the actual protective behaviors that they and their peers practice.

During the academic course, these students kept field notes to document the content and social context of their social norms interventions and to reflect on their successes and challenges. After completion of the course, students made a commitment to correct misinformation about campus alcohol use in settings ranging from parties to casual conversation with their peers. Researchers considered each health opinion leader to be a carrier of accurate social norms data to fellow students in a natural social venue that other mass media channels might not reach.

Outcomes Survey

To measure the effect of the social norms mass media approach, the third WWU Lifestyles Project Survey on alcohol and drug usage among WWU students was administered in May 1998 to a randomly selected sample of 25 percent of WWU's student population (n = 2,500). Forty-five percent (n = 1,127 of 2,500) returned the survey in 1998, compared to a 48 percent response rate in 1992 (n = 1,217 of 2,500) and a 49 percent response rate in 1997 (n = 489 of 1,000). Researchers were particularly pleased with this response rate because, for the first time in the history of administering the WWU Lifestyles Survey, a confidential coding system approved by WWU's Institutional Review Board was used with the 1998 cohort so that the 1999 survey administration could be used to assess the impact of additional exposure to the social norms marketing intervention on the same individuals. On the one hand, the 45 percent response rate dispelled researchers' fear that using a coding system might adversely affect the overall response rate. On the other hand, the research team acknowledged the potential liability of the coding system in influencing students to respond more conservatively regarding the frequency and quantity of their consumption.

Results from the 1998 survey were compared to the 1992 and 1997 administrations of the survey. Table 5.2 compares sample size, return rate, and demographic make-up of students in all three administrations of the WWU Lifestyles Project Survey (1992, 1997, and 1998). Table 5.2 also illustrates that men were 51.2 percent of the sample in the spring 1998 administration while women made up only 48.9 percent of the sample. Males were thus overrepresented in the 1998 sample because, during this same period, the WWU student body consisted of 44 percent men and 56 percent women. However, this discrepancy did not concern the research team because past surveys indicated that males drink more than females at WWU. Therefore, researchers felt that the nearly equal gender balance would make any positive trends indicated by the findings even more impressive.

TABLE 5.2. WWU LIFESTYLES PROJECT SURVEY DEMOGRAPHICS: 1992, 1997, AND 1998 COMPARED.

Item	1992 Survey	1997 Survey	1998 Survey
Number surveys returned, of number in random sample	n = 1,217 of 2,500	n = 489 of 1,000	n = 1,127 of 2,500
Percent response rate	49.0	48.0	45.0
Sample stratified to match institution for sex and ethnicity	n = 1,217	n = 489	n = 638
Gender (Percentage)			
Female	64.4	57.2	48.9
Male	35.6	42.8	51.2
Ethnicity (Percentage)			
African American	1.5	1.0	1.4
Asian American	9.2	7.4	6.9
Euro-American	84.1	86.2	87.3
Hispanic American	2.1	2.5	2.7
American Indian	1.6	1.8	2.2
Age (Percentage)			
20 or less	44.2	43.1	40.8
21 or over	56.6	56.6	59.2

These were the three most important findings from the 1998 administration of the WWU Lifestyles Project Survey as compared with previous administrations:

1. In 1997, 89 percent of students estimated that other students drank once a week or more; in 1998, only 49.6 held a similar view, a significant 44.4 percent reduction in student misperception of what they thought was typical ($p < .001$). Students' perceptual accuracy increased in 1998 because fewer of them thought that other students drank once a week or more. The data on student perceptions was gathered from *all* student respondents. However, changes in the reported rate of drinking that follow apply to only those students who reported drinking alcohol.

2. The percentage of drinking students who reported consuming five drinks or more on a typical weekend occasion dropped from 34.15 percent in 1997 to 27.3 percent in 1998, a significant 20.6 percent reduction ($p < .024$). Given that (1) men were overrepresented in the sample and (2) male college students tend to drink more than females, researchers compared the rate of reduction in heavy drinking between men and women. Table 5.3 shows the changes that occurred between 1997 and 1998 in the typical consumption rate reported by men and women students. There was a 25 percent reduction in men who reported heavy drinking, from 48.5 percent in 1997 to 36.3 percent in 1998. There was a 23 percent reduction in women who reported heavy drinking, from 23.5 percent in 1997 to 17.9 percent in 1998. The overrepresentation of men who may tend to more heavy drinking might be thought of as working against the effect of the social norms marketing intervention, but in fact an equal effect was found in both men and women.

3. The percentage of drinking students who reported at least one negative effect of alcohol use on the Rutgers Alcohol Problems Inventory (RAPI) scale

TABLE 5.3. TYPICAL WEEKEND CONSUMPTION BY GENDER: DRINKERS ONLY, 1997 AND 1998.

"On a Given Weekend Night, How Much Alcohol Do You Typically Consume?" (Percentage)

Quantity	Male		Female		Overall	
	1997	1998	1997	1998	1997	1998
1–2 drinks	26.2	44.5	39.7	54.2	33.8	49.2
3–4 drinks	25.4	19.2	36.9	27.8	32.1	23.5
5+ drinks	48.5	36.3	23.5	17.9	34.15	27.3

decreased from 60.9 percent in 1997 to 51.3 percent in 1998—a 15.7 percent reduction in self-reported alcohol-related negative consequences. The RAPI measures common problems students experience as a direct result of drinking: concern about drinking, irresponsibility and neglect, symptoms of alcohol dependence, interpersonal conflict, and family conflict.

A Panel Study Follow-up

In May 1999, a follow-up survey was sent to all registered WWU students who responded to the spring 1998 WWU Lifestyles Survey. Researchers examined the data to determine first how one additional year of the social norms marketing campaign might affect the same students' actual and perceived alcohol use patterns, and second the possible differential effects of social norms mass media interventions on drinkers and nondrinkers.

Of the 800 follow-up surveys mailed out, 347 surveys were returned, a response rate of 43 percent. Demographic comparison of the 1998 and 1999 samples showed that frequent heavy drinkers were less likely to fill out the follow-up survey than those who drank nothing or who drank moderately. Given the limitations of (1) the demographic differences between the 1998 and 1999 respondents, (2) the modest response rate, (3) the fact that one year of maturation might temper the alcohol use of the 1999 respondents, and (4) the possible conservative effect of the coding system on students' responses, we could not draw strong conclusions from the follow-up data as compared to the previous year's data overall.

Nevertheless, though many local and national surveys have highlighted the initial effect of social norms marketing interventions on cross-sectional cohorts, no previous surveys had looked at whether this approach could continue to affect behaviors, beliefs, attitudes, and perceptions of the *same students*. Therefore, because of the novelty of the panel design in the 1999 WWU Lifestyles Follow-Up Survey, the research team used paired sample t-tests to assess changes in the same students who responded to both the 1998 and 1999 surveys. We were able to draw several tentative conclusions regarding the effects of an additional year of exposure to a social norms marketing campaign among the same individuals. Students reported drinking slightly more often in 1999 than in 1998, but a significant decrease was noted in their typical quantity per weekend occasion, their peak quantity during the last month, and their misperception of other students who drank five or more drinks in the past two weeks. Further, there were more students who reported no alcohol-related consequences in 1999 than there were in 1998. Specifically, we observed:

- A significant decrease in the typical number of drinks the same students reported from 1998 to 1999 ($p < .001$). Student participants reported consuming fewer drinks on a typical weekend evening in 1999 ($M = 2.12$, SD 2.81) than they did in 1998 ($M = 2.64$, SD 2.76).

- A significant decrease in the peak number of drinks (that is, the most they drank in the past month) reported from 1998 to 1999 ($p < .01$). Student participants reported consuming fewer drinks on a peak occasion in 1999 ($M = 3.65$, SD 3.94) than they did in 1998 ($M = 4.08$, SD 3.94).

- A significant decrease in the perception of other students who drank five or more drinks in the past two weeks reported from 1998 to 1999 ($p < .01$). Student participants estimated that a lower percentage of other students consumed five or more drinks in the past two weeks in 1999 ($M = 36.29$, SD 23.96) than their estimates reflected in 1998 ($M = 41.58$, SD 22.52).

- A significant increase in the proportion of students who reported no negative alcohol-related RAPI consequences from 1998 to 1999 ($p < .05$). There was a significantly higher proportion of students reporting zero negative consequences in 1999 (38.3 percent) than in 1998 (31.3 percent).

Targeting Specific Groups

Theoretically coherent, empirically validated, and cost-effective interventions such as WWU's social norms marketing approach to student alcohol abuse prevention are urgently needed on college campuses. Yet as promising as this model may be as a universal prevention strategy targeting *all* students, the Prevention and Wellness Services team at WWU continued to ask questions about the applicability of the social norms approach to specific student groups: nondrinkers living in WWU's substance-free residences, and frequent heavy drinkers sanctioned into WWU's alcohol screening and intervention program. The remainder of this chapter reports on further research conducted at WWU to answer questions regarding how to tailor the social norms model to meet the needs of various student audiences who engage in higher-risk drinking or who do not drink at all.

Universal Prevention Strategies Targeting Nondrinkers

Researchers at WWU used the social norms approach to design two labor- and cost-effective interventions targeting nondrinking students who live by choice in substance-free residence halls: (1) marketing information for prospective students and their parents that promoted accurate campus norms about student life in substance-free residences, and (2) a focused social norms marketing campaign that targeted only the substance-free residence halls. WWU's substance-free residence halls give students an opportunity to live in an alcohol-free, drug-free, and to-bacco-free living space. Although students who live in these halls are not neces-sarily abstinent all the time, they sign a "community agreement" not to use alcohol, drugs, or tobacco in the substance-free halls. Enforcement of the com-munity agreement is conducted by resident advisors, who require that violating students attend WWU's alcohol risk reduction program.

The decision to choose a substance-free residence was normalized in WWU's residence hall admissions literature using specific language suggested by non-drinking students in focus groups. The literature on housing options simply said that substance-free halls were a "choice that many WWU students find comfort-able." Once students made the choice to live in a substance-free residence, the re-search team made available a series of posters and dining hall table tents that promoted and reinforced nondrinking campus data: "Nearly a quarter of WWU students make the choice not to drink, and those who do drink, drink moderately."

The research team chose three outcome measures to assess the impact of this low-key normative approach to marketing substance-free housing. First, the num-ber of requests to live in substance-free housing during the subsequent academic year was analyzed. Further, researchers evaluated data on alcohol use among stu-dents living in substance-free halls compared to others and on the perception of use among students living in substance-free halls compared to other halls:

• Demand for substance-free housing. Since substance-free housing became available at WWU in 1993, the demand has increased each year. Between 1997 and 1998—the period corresponding to application of our social norms market-ing strategies—there was a 42.8 percent increase in students who requested place-ment in a substance-free residence.

• Actual alcohol use. As might be expected, students living in a substance-free residence reported far less alcohol use than their peers. In every administra-tion of the WWU Lifestyles Survey, students living in a substance-free hall reported less drinking on typical occasions than both students who lived on cam-pus in a residence that was not substance-free and students who lived off campus. However, qualitative data from focus groups with nondrinkers helped the research team understand that students also chose to live in a substance-free hall for sec-ondary benefits, such as less noise and fewer distractions when studying, not sim-ply because they do not drink or have a moral aversion to drinking.

• Perceived alcohol use. Repeated administration of the WWU Lifestyles Survey has shown that students who live in a substance-free residence are the sub-group most likely to estimate accurately the percentage of other students who do not drink alcohol. However, their perception of students who drink heavily (five or more on a typical occasion) suffers from the same overestimation as other students on campus.

To address the concern that a social norms mass media campaign might influence nondrinkers to initiate alcohol consumption, the research team conducted two analyses. First, we compared the overall incidence of nondrinkers in 1998 and 1999. In 1998, 22.3 percent of students reported they had not consumed alcohol in the past thirty days; in 1999, 21.9 reported no drinking in the past thirty days. For all intents and purposes, the overall proportion of nondrinkers remained the same between 1998 and 1999.

Second, we used the coded data set and analyzed how many of *the same students* who reported that they did not drink in 1998 remained nondrinkers in 1999. The analysis included only those participants who completed both surveys. Of the 110 participants who reported consuming no alcohol in the 1998 survey, 75 remained nondrinkers in 1999. However, of the 232 participants who reported that they did drink alcohol in 1998, 24 reported not drinking in 1999. Although the 35 students who shifted from nondrinking to drinking status between 1998 and 1999 may present a concern, it is not possible to unequivocally attribute their initiation of drinking to continued exposure to the social norms marketing campaign. One possible alternative explanation is that the recall time period (thirty days) is short and therefore yields only a snapshot of the nondrinkers, not a long-term picture of abstinence. Therefore, those who reported not drinking in the past thirty days in 1998 might, in fact, have consumed some alcohol in 1998; those who reported drinking in the past thirty days in 1999 might, in fact, have not consumed alcohol for the rest of 1999. A second possible explanation of the net loss of 35 nondrinkers between 1998 and 1999 is that college drinking patterns are neither fixed nor static but change considerably over time (Grant, Harford, and Grigson, 1988). The variations existing in the stability of college student drinking might also explain the net gain of 24 nondrinkers in 1999.

Applying Social Norms to Indicated Alcohol Interventions

Indicated prevention programs focus on students who are already manifesting at least some alcohol-related problems (Modeste, 1996; Institute of Medicine, 1990). The research team chose to integrate social norms feedback into WWU's alcohol screening and intervention program, which was modeled on the alcohol skills training intervention developed at the University of Washington (Dimeff, Baer, Kivlahan, and Marlatt, 1999). The WWU alcohol screening and intervention program is designed for students who are sanctioned for infringement of alcohol policy in the residence halls and for students who are found eligible for diversion by the local municipal court following charges of being a minor in possession.

Students who enter the alcohol screening and intervention program complete an intake assessment that measures their (1) frequency and quantity of drinking, (2) negative consequences resulting from alcohol use over the past six months, (3) use of other psychoactive substances in the past six months, (4) sexual behavior, including risky sex behavior involving alcohol and other drug use, (5) alcohol outcome expectancies, (6) interest in changing and degree of readiness to change drinking, (7) symptoms of psychological distress, and (8) indices of alcohol dependence (Dimeff, Baer, Kivlahan, and Marlatt, 1999). These data are used to develop a three-page Personalized Feedback Profile, which offers nonjudgmental information on personal drinking patterns and consequences as well as moderation tips on reducing risks for alcohol-related harm.

The intake assessment also measures the sanctioned student's perception of other students' (1) frequency and quantity of drinking, (2) average blood alcohol, (3) range of alcohol-related negative consequences, (4) amount of money spent on alcohol, and (5) amount of calories consumed from alcohol. These data constituted a focused and individualized strategy for confidentially assisting students to compare their own drinking and alcohol-related consequences to WWU norms.

From a motivational interviewing perspective, the primary objective in working with students who have no desire to change their behavior (that is, precontemplators) is to assist them through a change process that decreases defensiveness and increases motivation to begin thinking about the connections between alcohol use and unwanted consequences (Prochaska and DiClemente, 1984). WWU's risk reduction specialists used comparison of individual use patterns with WWU norms to introduce ambivalence into the student's thinking. Once ambivalence was adequately addressed, the primary task shifted from comparing drinking profiles to assisting students to determine the best route for change.

Heavy-drinking students typically reacted with more surprise and concern to the normative feedback than to any other part of the data presented in the Personalized Feedback Profile. Some challenged the accuracy of the norms used in the graphic comparisons, reasoning that most college students would intentionally underestimate the amount of alcohol they drank when completing a questionnaire for university researchers. In these circumstances, risk reduction specialists typically responded in the nondefensive manner recommended by Dimeff and her associates (1999), that is, by telling students that although some "may attempt to falsify their report, the data from our studies are consistent with national figures" (p. 105).

When students challenged the veracity of the normative data, the risk reduction specialists were able to use the opportunity to introduce specific information about how college students typically associate with persons with similar lifestyle habits, thereby making it difficult for a student to get a good sense of how their drinking may be far out of the "normal" range of all college students.

The comparison between a student's Personalized Feedback Profile and actual campus drinking norms provided the introduction to the next stage of motivational interviewing: training in moderation skills and general lifestyle behaviors that may increase health-protective behaviors and reduce alcohol-related negative consequences in the student's life. In some cases, the gap evidenced by the difference between the campus norms and a student's Personalized Feedback Profile created an opportunity to talk with the student about possible need for medical consultation or other outside treatment services.

The 446 mandated students who completed risk reduction services in 1998–99 were assessed at the completion of the intervention and at a three-month follow-up. Of these 446 students, 196 (or 44 percent) completed and returned the voluntary follow-up assessment. To measure the impact of the intervention on alcohol use and consequences, researchers used paired sample t-tests to analyze the responses of participants who had completed both the baseline intake assessment and the follow-up surveys. From the results of these analyses, researchers observed these changes in alcohol-related behaviors from baseline to follow-up:

- Significant decrease ($p < .001$) in typical number of drinks consumed from intake (M = 3.82, SD 1.26) to follow-up (M=3.45, SD 1.22)
- Significant decrease ($p < .001$) in peak number of drinks consumed from intake (M= 4.89, SD = 1.80) to follow-up (M = 4.29, SD = 1.77)
- Significant decrease in time spent drinking ($p < .012$); students spent more hours drinking per occasion at baseline (M = 3.63, SD = 1.38) than at follow-p (M= 3.37, SD = 1.42)
- Significant decrease in drinking frequency per month ($p < .001$); students reported a higher number of episodes of drinking per month at baseline (M = 3.39, SD = 1.09) than at follow-up (M = 3.13, SD = 0.98)
- A statistically nonsignificant 10 percent decrease in overall negative alcohol-related consequences reported between baseline and follow-up

Researchers at WWU tentatively concluded that the infusion of personalized social norms comparisons into the alcohol screening and intervention for sanctioned students could be a significant enhancement within an indicated prevention strategy. A limitation to this observation is the fact that the specific effects of the personalized social norms feedback cannot be differentiated from the treatment effects of other feedback categories of the Personalized Feedback Profile. However, these preliminary results at WWU are consistent with findings from studies showing the effect of brief interventions using individualized feedback (Marlatt and others, 1998; Baer, Kivlahan, and Marlatt, 1995) and studies showing the effect of modifying contextual variables such as drinking norms (Baer, Stacey, and Larimer, 1991; Perkins and Berkowitz, 1986) on reducing high-risk drinking and alcohol problems in the college student population.

The prevention field's enthusiasm for the social norms approach to reducing alcohol consumption and its related negative consequences on college campuses is well founded. Social marketing projects that are based on social norms, like the one conducted at WWU, have produced heartening results that suggest this relatively low-cost strategy has considerable promise as part of a comprehensive campus approach to prevention.

However, the central intervention of these projects—media promoting accurate drinking norms—is directed at all members of the population—in this case, all students at a particular college or university. Because college students are not a monolithic category, but rather a highly diverse group of people with vastly different levels of involvement with alcohol, universal prevention efforts may not be equally effective for everybody. Social norms marketing may remain the central intervention for a campus wishing to reach a large target audience with positive, empowering information about healthy alcohol behaviors, but other social norms delivery strategies may have increased efficacy with a specific student population.

The question of whether the social norms approach can be tailored to meet the needs of varying student populations remains unanswered. Researchers at WWU have found success in using social norms delivery strategies that range from development of a campuswide mass media campaign to focused use of health opinion leaders or infusion of normative data into screening and brief interventions. Varying the social norms delivery approach for the target audience holds promise for those seeking to broaden the base of effective outcomes-based prevention models that meet the needs of all of our students.

References

Baer, J. S., Kivlahan, D. R., and Marlatt, G. A. "High-Risk Drinking Across the Transition from High School to College." *Alcoholism: Clinical and Experimental Research*, 1995, *19*, 54–61.

Baer, J. S., Stacey, A., and Larimer, M. E. "Biases in Perception of Drinking Norms Among College Students." *Journal of Studies on Alcohol*, 1991, *52*, 580–586.

Dimeff, L. A., Baer, J. S., Kivlahan, D. R., and Marlatt, G. A. *Brief Alcohol Screening and Intervention for College Students.* New York: Guilford Press, 1999.

Grant, B. F., Harford, T. C., and Grigson, M. B. "Stability of Alcohol Consumption Among Youth: A National Longitudinal Survey." *Journal of Studies on Alcohol*, 1988, *49*, 253–260.

Haines, M. *A Social-Norms Approach to Preventing Binge Drinking at Colleges and Universities.* (No. ED/OPE/96-18.) Washington, D.C.: U.S. Department of Education, 1996.

Hyun, Y. R., Snyder, E., Harwick, E., and Fabiano, P. M. *Assessing the Role of Alcohol Among Students at Western Washington University: A Qualitative Study.* Bellingham: Prevention and Wellness Services/Project WE CAN 2000, Western Washington University, 1998.

Institute of Medicine. *Broadening the Base of Treatment for Alcohol Problems.* Washington, D.C.: National Academy Press, 1990.

Johannessen, K., Collins, C., Mills-Novoa, B., and Glider, P. *A Practical Guide to Alcohol Abuse Prevention: A Campus Case Study in Implementing Social Norms and Environmental Management Approaches.* Tucson: Campus Health Service, University of Arizona, 1999.

Kelly, J. A., and others. "HIV Risk Behavior Reduction Following Intervention with Key Opinion Leaders of Population: An Experimental Analysis." *American Journal of Public Health,* 1991, *81,* 168–171.

Marlatt, G. A., and others. "Screening and Brief Intervention for High-Risk College Student Drinkers: Results from a 2-Year Follow-up Assessment." *Journal of Consulting and Clinical Psychology,* 1998, *66,* 604–615.

Meilman, P. W., Leichliter, J. S., and Presley, C. A. "Greeks and Athletes: Who Drinks More?" *Journal of American College Health,* 1999, *47,* 187–190.

Modeste, N. N. *Dictionary of Public Health Promotion and Education: Terms and Concepts.* Thousand Oaks, Calif.: Sage, 1996.

Perkins, H. W., and Berkowitz, A. D. "Perceiving the Community Norms of Alcohol Use Among Students: Some Research Implications for Campus Alcohol Education Programming." *International Journal of Addictions,* 1986, *21,* 961–976.

Presley, C. A., Meilman, P. W., and Cashin, J. R. "Alcohol and Other Drug Use by Region." In *Alcohol and Drugs on American College Campuses: Use, Consequences and Perceptions of the Campus Environment.* Vol. 4: *1992–1994.* Carbondale, Ill.: SIUC Press, 1996.

Prochaska, C. A., and DiClemente, C. C. *The Transtheoretical Approach: Crossing Traditional Boundaries of Therapy.* Homewood, Ill.: Dow Jones/Irwin, 1984.

Wechsler, H., Kuh, G., and Davenport, A. "Fraternities, Sororities, and Binge Drinking: Results from a National Study of American Colleges." *NASPA Journal,* 1996, *33,* 260–279.

CHAPTER SIX

THE ROWAN UNIVERSITY
SOCIAL NORMS PROJECT

Linda R. Jeffrey, Ph.D.; Pamela Negro, M.S.W.;
DeMond S. Miller, Ph.D.; John D. Frisone, Ph.D.

R owan University is a comprehensive, coeducational, nonsectarian, state-supported institution of higher education. Located in suburban southern New Jersey approximately twenty miles southeast of Philadelphia, Rowan has a student body of more than six thousand full-time and three thousand part-time students taught by four hundred faculty members.

In 1988, the institution was a founding member, and has since served as the institutional host, of the New Jersey Higher Education Consortium on Alcohol and Other Drug Abuse Prevention and Education. For a decade, the Rowan Center for Addiction Studies has administered a grant funded by the New Jersey Department of Health and Senior Services to support prevention projects at colleges across the state in peer education, curriculum infusion, and most recently social marketing.

In this chapter, lessons learned from the first four years of the Rowan University Social Norms Project and plans for further project implementation are shared.

Baseline Assessment

The Campus Survey of Alcohol and Other Drug Norms (Core Institute, Southern Illinois University)—an instrument designed to assess actual versus perceived norms—was administered at Rowan University in the spring semester of 1998 in both general education and upper-level advanced classes in the communications and psychology departments (n = 483). These departments were chosen because they serve a range of students. As found on other campuses (Fabiano and others, 1999; Haines and Spear, 1996; Perkins, 1997; and Perkins and others, 1999). Rowan students surveyed overestimated the rate of student drinking at their institution. The reported use of alcohol by students was once a week, but the perceived norm for students in general was three times a week. Male students were perceived to use alcohol three times a week, while their self-reported rate was once a week. Female students were perceived to drink once a week; their self-reported rate was twice a month. Although almost 48 percent of students reported heavy drinking (five drinks in a row) in the two weeks previous to their completing the survey, they perceived 63 percent of their fellow students engaging in heavy drinking during the same time span.

At baseline, the perceived drinking rate among Rowan students was an overestimation of 15 percentage points. This discrepancy between perceived and actual rates is targeted in the social norms approach (Perkins, 1997; Perkins and others, 1999). The public information campaign at the center of our social norms project is designed to communicate the actual use profile of the students at the institution to the campus community through a variety of media and related activities.

Institutional Support and Project Preparation

The goal of the social norms approach is to create a campuswide conversation about the campus drinking norms. This conversation was initially launched in a series of training events conducted by the project coordinator for college personnel and students. It was important that the concept of the "carrier" (Perkins, 1997) of misperception be understood by staff and students who routinely address alcohol-related problems so that they do not inadvertently undercut the fundamental message that the majority of Rowan students drink moderately or not at all.

In a series of training events, the project coordinator presented information concerning reported versus perceived campus drinking norms, and the importance of campus leaders and student support staff in spreading the word about actual campus drinking norms. The audiences for the special training included sixty peer educators, the Residence Life staff and resident assistants, the Counseling Center staff, sixty help line student volunteers, and members of five Greek houses. In these sessions, the project coordinator explained survey methodology, the empirical basis of the statistics reported, and the reasons drinking norms may sometimes be misperceived. Skeptical undergraduates, especially those who engage in heavy drinking themselves, challenged the finding that most Rowan students drink moderately or not at all, and lively discussions took place about the role of alcohol use in campus life. The project coordinator modeled reliance on empirical data and respect for those who disagreed with her—key features the students were asked to employ in their own discussion with other students.

The project coordinator also integrated misperception theory and information concerning Rowan drinking norms into the six undergraduate alcohol and other drug (AOD) counselor-training courses, and the First Thursday Seminar of the Center for Addictions Studies. Because these students are pursuing alcohol and drug counseling professionally, they have a greater awareness of the problems associated with alcohol use and are familiar with traditional fear-based alcohol prevention approaches, which are likely to emphasize the negative aspects of alcohol use, and, out of awareness of problems associated with addiction, might inadvertently exaggerate the extent of problematic alcohol use on campus. They were thus vulnerable to being carriers of the misperception. They were, however, an important group of students to reach because their specialized study of alcoholism gives their opinions added credibility in discussion with other students.

Outreach about campus drinking norms to parents and members of the surrounding community also took place. The project coordinator spoke to students and parents at new-student orientation and offered training on social norms theory and the campus drinking norms to the Gloucester County Department of Human Services staff. A key message to these audiences was that the social norms approach is not an attempt to deny the negative consequences of student heavy drinking or the reality that a certain proportion of students engage in risky drinking practices. The emphasis was placed on the positive message that the majority of Rowan students drink moderately or not at all, that alcohol abuse is not necessary for an authentic college experience as the majority of our students experience it, and that fatalistic resignation in the face of alcohol abuse by a minority of students is not necessary or inevitable.

It was interesting to note that parents and students who took part in orientation all had a lot to say about the misperception of social norms. In fact, both groups initially expressed disbelief about the survey results on excessive drinking. One father stated: "I don't believe for a minute that so few students are drinking here at Rowan. When I went to school here over twenty years ago, I was a member of a fraternity and we drank every night of the week. Of course, we just drank beer for the most part and stayed in the house. We weren't out at bars or driving around drunk hurting other people. I expect my son will do the same thing. It's what you do at college." From another father: "Alcohol was never off limits to me in my home growing up, and I learned how to drink responsibly there. I raised my son the same way; he knows his limits." A number of parents agreed that they didn't think drinking in college was such a big deal. Some students seemed to share the view that drinking was the expected norm at college and were surprised to hear that the college had programs in place to address the issue of high-risk drinking.

Linkage between the social norms project and other elements of the campus' comprehensive alcohol prevention program was consistently highlighted, and the project director and coordinator offered information about the social norms approach to the all-campus alcohol prevention task force. Strategies were developed to connect the media campaign to the increased number of alcohol-free campus social events.

At the heart of the social norms project was a team of undergraduate and graduate students who developed and implemented the print and radio media products and related activities. The visibility of the students and their availability to dialogue with other students were essential features of the social norms project.

Media Campaign and Related Activities

The centerpiece of the social norms approach is a public information media campaign informing students of the actual campus drinking norms. At Rowan, students were informed of the actual drinking norms through posters, flyers, and weekly multiple half-page student newspaper advertisements, as well as brief personal advertisements and student radio spots. The drinking norms were publicized on the back of theater programs for the campus center for the arts. Promotional items such as balloons, pens, Frisbees, highlighters, and magnets conveying the campus drinking norm were distributed to students. Print media and radio contests were held in which prizes were given to those who could accurately state the campus drinking rate. Letters were written to the editor of the campus newspaper focusing on the percentage of students making healthy choices. (These media materials are described in more detail in a handbook on implementing a social norms project, available from the New Jersey Consortium.)

This excerpt is an example of one of our campus newspaper articles submitted as a letter to the editor:

Is Your Perception About Drinking on Campus Pickled?

You may have noticed posters around the Rowan campus challenging your perceptions about how many students drink excessively. One, showing a brain in a fruit jar, says, "If you think drinking is a big thing on campus, maybe your thinking is a little pickled." Contrary to what most students think, the norm on campus is not to drink excessively. Surveys conducted show 63% of Rowan students choose not to drink excessively.

"These findings reflect those on college campuses across the country," says Pam Negro, Center for Addiction Studies' Project Coordinator. "Research also shows that when students learn that drinking excessively is not the norm, excessive drinking rates decline."

The "Know It" campaign was developed as part of a project on alcohol and drug abuse prevention initiated by The New Jersey Higher Education Consortium on Alcohol and Other Drug Prevention and Education. "It's part of a total effort to help ensure a safer campus environment for our students," says Negro.

The Center for Addiction Studies is distributing free giveaways on campus throughout the school year. Keep reading *The Whit* and listen to WGLS-FM to know where we'll be next! Stop by and pick up free gifts and prizes to show that you "Know It."

Residence halls were asked to compete in creating a poster concerning the campus-drinking rate. The resulting works were hung in the student center, and the event was pictured in the campus yearbook. Student actors, "Mr. and Ms. Moneybags," performed skits in the student center and gave rewards to students who could accurately state the campus drinking norm. Many contests were held, modeled on the game show "Jeopardy" and incorporating drinking norms information at awareness events throughout the academic year. Students winning the radio drinking norms contests won tickets and a limousine ride to dinner theater in Philadelphia and tickets for a dinner cruise on the Delaware River.

The Rowan University radio station and students from the communications department have been great resources for our social norms project. Our station is popular with faculty, staff, and students; there is a large audience both on campus and in the communities surrounding us. The communications students have created a number of humorous PSAs (public service announcements) to address alcohol use and abuse, incorporating statistics about actual norms that are based on survey statistics. They have also developed arresting concepts for monthly student contests. The Center for Addiction Studies also sponsors radio coverage for football, basketball, soccer, and baseball events.

The survey statistics became the focus of discussion in student government and in the campus literary magazine. Some students who drink excessively themselves found it impossible to believe that other students do not drink excessively several times a week. They were invited to review the survey statistics for reported rather than perceived rates, and as a source of empirical rather than anecdotal evidence. In sum, the social norms project activities transformed the campus discussion of drinking norms, opened up new paths and opportunities for discussion, and suggested the possibility that students had the power of choice in determining how much they wished to drink if at all.

Assessing Outcomes

Annual surveying of student alcohol attitudes and drinking behaviors is essential to the social norms approach. The credibility of the media campaign rests in how accurate and recent the data being reported are. Moreover, the project leaders need feedback about the effectiveness of the media campaigns in decreasing misperception of college drinking norms so that the frequency or content of media materials may be modified as needed.

The Campus Survey of Alcohol and Other Drug Norms was administered again at the beginning of second semester in 1999 (n = 514), 2000 (n = 494), and 2001 (n = 453), following the same classroom sampling procedure with communications and psychology department courses that was employed in the 1998 (n = 483) baseline study, and tapping a large annual sample of students comparable in gender, ethnicity, and year in school.

The students were asked how often they had seen or heard media messages (radio spots, newspaper advertisements, posters, and so on) about excessive drinking rates on campus. Responses to this question track how effectively the message about actual drinking norms is reaching the students. The results are reported in Table 6.1. A large increase in the number of students who had seen or heard

TABLE 6.1. HOW OFTEN HAD SURVEY RESPONDENTS SEEN OR HEARD MEDIA MESSAGES CONCERNING CAMPUS DRINKING RATES?

How Often Respondent Saw or Heard Message During Year	Baseline: 1998 (Before Media Campaign; n = 483) (Percentage)	1999 (After One-Semester Campaign; n = 514) (Percentage)	2000 (After Three-Semester Campaign; n = 494) (Percentage)	2001 (After Five-Semester Campaign; n = 453) (Percentage)
Never	64	18	18	17
Once or twice	14	29	27	19
3–5 times	8	25	20	13
6–10 times	12	13	14	23
More than 10 times	2	15	20	27

media messages about campus drinking rates took place after only one semester of the media campaign. After five semesters, one in four students had come in contact with the media messages more than ten times.

It was anticipated that as the media campaign continued, the actual drinking norm—that the majority of students drink moderately or not at all—would become more commonly identified. As Figure 6.1 indicates, after five semesters of the media campaign the perception of the heavy drinking rate that is based on student estimates as reported in the survey decreased 15 percent. This translates to a 24 percent decrease in the misperception of the college drinking norm. The average student impression of other students' drinking shifted after three semesters (spring 2000) of the media campaign from a belief that a majority of students drink excessively (63 percent) to a belief that half of the students drink excessively (50 percent). This is still an overestimation, even of the baseline self-reported rate of heavy drinking (48 percent), but it was a significant decrease in a brief period of time after a relatively modest intervention.

The social norm approach is based on the hypothesis that a decrease in misperception of college drinking norms will be accompanied by a decrease in self-reported heavy drinking (Perkins, 1997). As Figure 6.2 indicates, following five

FIGURE 6.1. PERCENTAGE OF STUDENTS PERCEIVED TO BE HEAVY DRINKERS (AVERAGE ESTIMATE) AND CHANGE IN THE PERCEIVED RATE.

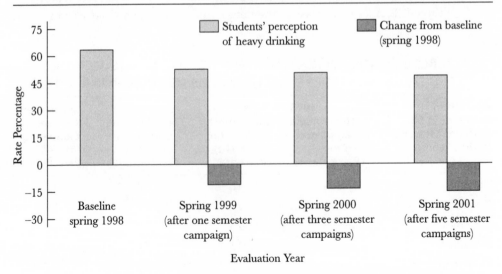

semesters of the media campaign the self-reported rate of excessive drinking declined 11 percent. This constitutes a 23 percent rate of change in reported heavy drinking. It is important to note that despite a vigorous traditional collegiate alcohol abuse prevention program in previous years, prior to the social norms campaign this institution had never before seen a decrease in the reported rate of heavy drinking.

Table 6.2 summarizes the major outcome measures of the Rowan University Social Norms Project. The degree of misperception was measured across the four years on four measures: (1) the proportion of students who erroneously believed that students most commonly thought intoxication interfering with academics or other responsibilities or frequent intoxication was acceptable; (2) students' mean estimate of the percentage of peers who drank five or more drinks in a row in the last two weeks; (3) the proportion of students who thought the typical student drank five or more drinks at a party or bar, and (4) the proportion of students who thought that other students most typically consumed five or more drinks during their last drinking occasion.

The final objective of reduced heavy drinking over time was assessed on the basis of three measures: (1) the proportion of students who personally reported typically consuming five or more drinks on average at a party or bar, (2) the

FIGURE 6.2. CHANGE IN REPORTED HEAVY DRINKING RATE.

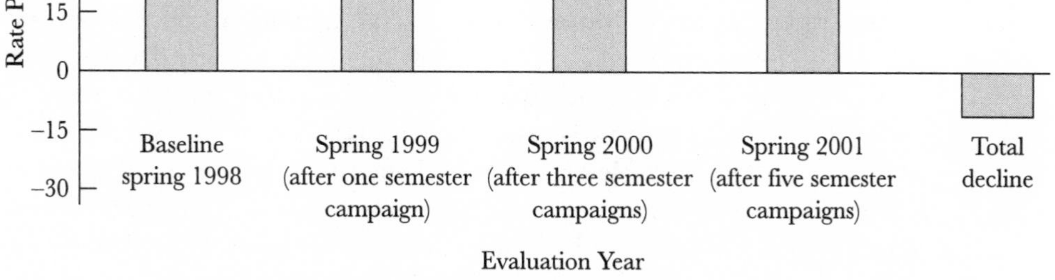

Note: Heavy drinking equals five drinks in a row in two weeks prior to survey.

TABLE 6.2. SURVEY BASELINE AND OUTCOME DATA MEASURES.

Survey Measures	1998 (n = 483; Percentage)	1999 (n = 514; Percentage)	2000 (n = 494; Percentage)	2001 (n = 453; Percentage)	p <
Media exposure:					
6+ times during year		28	34	50	.001
Misperceived norms (perceptions of other students):					
Perceive permissive attitude as typical	41	30	22	19	.001
Perceive drinking 5+ at parties and bars as typical	72	62	55	49	.001
Mean estimate drinking 5+ at once in last 2 weeks	63	52	50	48	.00l
Perceive other students drank 5+ on last occasion	73	63	67	57	.00l
Actual high-risk drinking:					
Drinks 5+ drinks on average at parties and bars	40	33	32	30	.00l
Drinks 5+ drinks in a row in last 2 weeks	48	43	41	37	.00l
Drank 5+ on last drinking occasion	44	41	39	35	n.s.

proportion of students who had five or more drinks in a row in the last two weeks, and (3) the proportion of students who reported drinking five or more drinks on their last drinking occasion. Misperception declined significantly on all four measures, and all three indications of high-risk drinking consistently declined over time, with statistically significant results on two of these three measures.

The Rowan University Social Norms Project is a work in progress, with positive results thus far. A double-digit rate of change in both the misperception of and the actual rate of student heavy drinking was obtained. The results present dramatic evidence of the impact of the social norms approach when fully implemented. By the end of three years, half of the student body was aware of frequent messages on actual drinking rates. This increase in exposure directly corresponds to a steady and significant decrease in erroneously perceived high-risk drinking as the norm among peers and a steady and significant decline in actual (nonnormative) high-risk drinking among students. Judging from all three measures of personal drinking behavior, results indicate that high-risk drinking was cut by one-quarter over the project time period. The project was quite successful in getting the message about accurate norms to the student body and producing a positive outcome.

Initially, we believed that the social norms approach would not significantly affect the behavior of students who become alcoholic prior to college or become alcohol dependent while at college. We believe that for college drinkers who are alcohol dependent, individual alcohol evaluation and treatment services are needed, and that each institution should have procedures in place for either providing such services or referring students displaying alcohol dependence to appropriate community intervention agencies as part of a comprehensive prevention program. We now realize that the social norms project may offer significant assistance in intervention with students involved in frequent heavy episodic drinking and related problems. The survey data collected as part of the social norms project offers detailed information about the heavy drinkers and may allow campus personnel to tailor more individualized interventions for students displaying frequent heavy drinking. Moreover, plans are under way at Rowan to incorporate use of social norms information in motivational interviews with students experiencing alcohol-related problems, on the basis of the Western Washington University model (Fabiano, 2000).

Finally, the survey results also facilitate development of media messages directed toward the experiences of specific groups within the campus community, including the Greeks and athletes. Indeed, the institutionalization of annual comprehensive survey evaluation of campus alcohol use as an integral part of prevention programming is transformational.

In the fall of 2001, the Rowan University Tobacco Social Norms Project was launched, applying the social norms approach to issues of campus smoking. Questions remain about the effectiveness of integrating normative messages about alcohol and tobacco use in the same media campaign or whether separate campaigns are required. These issues will be explored as we move forward at Rowan with continued implementation of the social norms approach.

References

Fabiano, P. "Beyond Mass Marketing: Developing Capacity Using Additional Norms Delivery Strategies." Paper presented at National Conference on the Social Norms Model, Denver, 2000.

Fabiano, P. M., and others. *Lifestyles, 1998: Patterns of Alcohol and Drug Consumption and Consequences Among WWU Students.* Bellingham: Office of Assessment and Testing, Western Washington University, 1999.

Haines, M., and Spear, A. F. "Changing the Perception of the Norm: A Strategy to Decrease Binge Drinking Among College Students." *Journal of American College Health*, 1996, *45*, 134-140.

Perkins, H. W. "College Student Misperceptions of Alcohol and Other Drug Norms Among Peers: Exploring Causes, Consequences, and Implications for Prevention Programs." In *Designing Alcohol and Other Drug Prevention Programs in Higher Education: Bringing Theory into Practice.* Newton, Mass.: Higher Education Center for Alcohol and Other Drug Prevention, 1997.

Perkins, H. W., and others. "Misperceptions of the Norms for the Frequency of Alcohol and Drug Use on College Campuses." *Journal of American College Health*, 1999, *47*, 253–258.

CHAPTER SEVEN

THE SMALL GROUPS NORMS-CHALLENGING MODEL

Social Norms Interventions with Targeted High-Risk Groups

Jeanne M. Far, Ph.D.; John A. Miller, M.S., M.Ed.

O ver the past thirty years, alcohol abuse and related problems have been widely documented on college and university campuses across the country. As a consequence, concerned prevention workers and researchers have been designing and implementing programs to reduce the rate of alcohol consumption among college and university students. Until recently, these efforts did not achieve significant results. In the past decade, however, promising new prevention strategies based on social norms theory (SNT) have demonstrated significant reduction in alcohol abuse. One such approach, the Small Groups Norms-Challenging Model (SGNM) intervention developed at Washington State University (WSU), is described in this chapter.

As applied to alcohol abuse prevention on college campuses, SNT states that most students significantly overestimate the attitude and behavior norms of their

The authors would like to thank several individuals who have been particularly helpful in developing, implementing, and evaluating the Small Groups Norms-Challenging Model. Alan Berkowitz and H. Wesley Perkins contributed their original ideas in 1988 and continue to provide guidance and support. Armand Mauss was instrumental in designing program evaluation as an essential and ongoing project component, and Lisa Barnett assisted with the first experimental test of the model. Colin Peeler and Thomas Brigham assisted with expansion of the model to the curriculum infusion setting.

peers with regard to alcohol use and abuse (Berkowitz, 1997; Berkowitz and Perkins, 1987; Perkins, 1997; Perkins and Berkowitz, 1986a, 1986b). They then adjust their behavior toward these inaccurate norms, and student drinking increases. The primary goal of SGNM interventions is to correct misperception of alcohol use norms among students in membership groups considered to be at high risk for alcohol abuse and related problems: fraternities and sororities; athletic teams; and small, intensive classes intended for first-year students. According to SNT, this should decrease the rate of alcohol use in these targeted groups, and in turn lead to reduction in violence and harmful consequences to health, social life, and academic work.

We were interested in developing an intervention that would target specific campus subpopulations, such as fraternities and sororities, considered to be at high risk for alcohol abuse. Alcohol abuse and related problems have been well documented in the Greek system. Members of fraternities consistently display a higher rate of problem drinking behavior than the general campus population (Baer, 1994; Borsari and Carey, 1999; Coggins and McKellar, 1994; Far, Thompson, and Miller, 1995; Goodwin, 1989; Lo and Globetti, 1993, 1995; Page, Scanlan, and Gilbert, 1999). Sorority members also drink at a higher rate than other college women. For example, a campuswide random sample survey at WSU in 1995 showed that 50 percent of Greek women have five or more drinks on the average when they "party." Only 24 percent of non-Greek women drink at that rate (Far, 1998). Perception of drinking norms in the Greek environment also plays a strong role in drinking behavior. Goodwin (1989) found a correlation of .43 between the amount a subject drinks and the belief that people at his or her house drink more than those at other houses. Lo and Globetti (1993, 1995) studied first-year college students who were nondrinkers in their senior year of high school. Forty-six percent of the survey respondents started to drink during their first year of college, and Greek affiliation was the strongest predictor of their decision to begin drinking.

At WSU, SGNM interventions have been implemented and evaluated among students living in the Greek system (Barnett, Far, Mauss, and Miller, 1996), a classroom of freshman students (Peeler, Far, Miller, and Brigham, 2000), and three athletic teams. Other studies with the Greek system, student athletes on a variety of teams, a curriculum infusion project aimed primarily at freshman students, and newly admitted students participating in the "WSU Alive!" summer orientation sessions are in progress. Significant corrections in alcohol use misperception and decrease in alcohol consumption have been demonstrated in these populations following just a single intervention. Findings from some of these studies are reported in a later section of this chapter.

Although not meant to replace prevention activities aimed at a campuswide population, SGNM interventions are proving to be a valuable tool for use with traditionally difficult-to-reach subpopulations who appear to account for a disproportionately large portion of the alcohol abuse and related problems on campus. Moreover, having an impact on these subpopulations may reduce drinking problems on campus in general, as these high-risk groups also influence on other students on campus.

The Small Groups Norms-Challenging Model Intervention

In 1988–89, we began development of the Small Groups Norms-Challenging Model (SGNM) at WSU, employing student alcohol-use norms data as suggested by the early work of Perkins and Berkowitz (1986a, 1986b). This was piloted in 1990–91 (Barnett, Far, Mauss, and Miller, 1996), with funding from the WSU Alcohol and Drug Abuse Program, and replicated in 1995–96 (Far, 1998) with funding through the Wellness Programs of the WSU Health and Wellness Services office. In 1998, Project Culture Change (PCC) was implemented with funding from the U.S. Department of Education (DOE) to further research the SGNM in the Greek system and other high-risk groups. Additional funding from the DOE was made available in 2000 through a model programs award grant to continue work with the Greek system, and a two-year grant for Project Empowerment to further research the model with student athletes, first-year students living in residence halls, and predominantly freshman classrooms.

The SGNM intervention has targeted students in classrooms (Peeler, Far, Miller, and Brigham, 2000); student athletes; and students living in fraternities, sororities, and residence halls. (Other membership or reference groups would also be appropriate, such as high school or middle school audiences—wherever people have a cohesive group identity.) The intervention consists of a one-time, forty-five-minute, intensive, interactive program facilitated by a respected group leader or peer presenter, which makes the norms correction message more credible to group members (Berkowitz and Perkins, 1986, 1987; Perkins, 1997). This model has been used with WSU Greek houses since 1991, and a significant decrease in alcohol abuse and increase in accurate perception of alcohol-use norms have been documented in this population (Far, 1998; Far, Thompson, and Miller, 1995). In the next sections, we summarize general procedures for using the model as well as several example studies.

General Procedures

Preparation for the SGNM intervention cycle begins with yearly campuswide norms data collection. The Student Life and Health Behaviors survey is mailed to a random sample of the WSU student population using an adapted form of the Dillman Total Design Survey Method (Dillman, 1978; Salant and Dillman, 1994). The data collection process consists of four waves of mailing approximately two weeks apart: (1) a letter of introduction, (2) a cover letter and copy of the survey, (3) a reminder postcard to nonrespondents, and (4) a second copy of the survey. A fifth mailing or follow-up phone call is implemented if needed. It takes approximately six to eight weeks to complete the collection process.

The random sample for each survey cycle was provided by the Office of Institutional Research. Representative samples of the approximately 17,000 WSU students have been surveyed since 1991: fall 1991, n = 585 (1,000 sampled, with 59 percent response); spring 1995, n = 596 (1,000 sampled and 60 percent response); spring 1999, n = 756 (1,000 sampled, 76 percent response); spring 2000, n = 561 (2,000 sampled, with a 28 percent response); and fall 2000, n = 506 (1,250 sampled, 41 percent response).

The campuswide surveys are used to gather baseline data about students' attitudes and behaviors regarding alcohol use, and their perception of their peers' attitudes and behaviors. Information about prosocial and protective behaviors is also gathered. Group-specific alcohol attitude and behavior data are collected prior to facilitating the SGNM intervention for a particular group (such as a fraternity, sorority, residence hall, athletic team, or classroom), using an appropriately adapted form of the campuswide survey instrument. Confidentiality is discussed with participants prior to collecting group-specific data, and their anonymity is assured. Campuswide and group-specific norms data, as well as educational information about norms and misperceptions, are presented to the target group for discussion using a prepared script. The presentation is facilitated by a respected student leader, peer educator, or peer mentor who has received specific training. The presentation is interactive and lasts approximately forty-five minutes; participant involvement is elicited throughout the presentation.

Follow-up surveys, using a shorter, adapted form of the campuswide instrument, are typically conducted about three weeks and again six to fifteen weeks following each presentation to determine the degree to which the intervention influenced (1) an increase in the accuracy of student perceptions of the alcohol-use behavior and attitude norms of their peers, and (2) a decrease in their level of alcohol use. In some studies, control groups with similar characteristics that did not take part in the intervention cycle (no-treatment control groups) received the pretest and/or posttest at the same time as the groups receiving the intervention.

Focus groups with randomly selected students from each intervention group were conducted in some studies for assistance in fine-tuning the survey instrument and the intervention process. In addition, mechanisms have been established to gather data on alcohol-related campus problems, including visits to Student Health and the emergency room, conduct incidents, alcohol policy violations, citations or arrests, academic problems, and withdrawal from school.

Development of the Survey Instrument

The survey instrument presently in use is titled Student Life and Health Behaviors. The instrument began development in 1988 and has undergone a number of adjustments and refinements since its first use in 1991 (Barnett, Far, Mauss, and Miller, 1996). The survey questions currently in use ask participants to report on their attitudes and behaviors with regard to alcohol use, including the number of drinks they have per occasion (quantity), how many times they drink per week (frequency), and how much they approve of drinking (attitude). The attitude question consists of a continuum of five position attitudes used by Perkins and Berkowitz (1986b). Participants also are asked to estimate how often and how much other significant reference groups and individuals drink and how much they approve of drinking, using identical measures with slight changes in question wording (for example, how much for "others" rather than how much for "self"). These questions, asked in both campuswide surveys and group-specific surveys, yield the quantity, frequency, and attitude data that are then delivered during the small group intervention. This current survey also contains questions measuring instances of, and student perception about, prosocial and protective behaviors, such as using a designated driver, eating before drinking, and having fun without alcohol (Haines and Spear, 1996; Johannessen, Collins, Mills-Novoa, and Glider, 1999). Other questions address interesting and untested theoretical issues related to social norms theory: students' bragging about alcohol use, perception about and instances of altruistic behaviors, and beliefs and feelings about WSU's public image with regard to alcohol.

Case Study One: Greek System Intervention, 1990–91

A brief description of this study is included here. Further details are available in Barnett, Far, Mauss, and Miller (1996).

Participants and Procedures

The first experimental test of the SGNM intervention began with a sample of 1,426 university students; of them, 639 lived in Greek houses and the rest in mixed-gender residence halls. The sample included four fraternities and four sororities; slightly more than half the sample was female. A total of 317 participants, distributed approximately equally across treatment conditions, were available after the three-month follow-up. Attrition was high in the residence halls, but sufficient participation was obtained from the Greek houses to produce analyzable data.

Group-specific preintervention data were collected at time 1 (T1), approximately one month prior to delivery of the intervention. The survey form used at T1 collected demographic data that were not included in a shortened form used for time 2 (T2), immediately following the intervention, and time 3 (T3), approximately three months after intervention.

Trained peer facilitators (nongroup members) in mixed-gender pairs conducted presentations of approximately forty-five minutes during regularly scheduled meetings of the groups participating in each of the three treatment conditions. Participants in the social norms treatment condition (Tx 1) were presented with a series of five posters showing the results of the data collected in the campuswide and group-specific surveys. The five posters contained, respectively, this information: (1) actual and perceived attitude norms about drinking; (2) actual and perceived drinking behavior; (3) annoyances experienced from the drinking behavior of others; (4) occasions when participants felt pressured to drink more than they wanted; and (5) common academic or other problems experienced while drinking, including unwanted sexual activity. The second treatment condition (Tx 2) used a values continuum exercise. Participants were read a series of alcohol-related statements and questions. Some of the questions were those on the survey instrument asking about attitudes, behaviors, and perceptions. Participants were instructed to place themselves at one of five locations around the room that corresponded to the Likert-type scale used for these survey questions (ranging from "strongly agree" to "strongly disagree"). The third treatment condition (Tx 3) combined shortened versions of the social norms presentation and values continuum exercise. No-treatment control groups completed the surveys at the same time as the treatment groups.

Results

A slight but significant decrease in drinking behavior was demonstrated for those students whose perception of the norms of several significant reference groups changed in the desired direction. Correction of perception and reduction in drinking were found irrespective of treatment group. However, the values continuum component may have inadvertently mimicked the social norms presentation by constructing "visual" social norms that resulted in a norms correction effect. Although the evidence for the efficacy of this early form of the SGNM intervention was modest and equivocal, there were clear trends showing a correlation between correction of misperception of alcohol use norms and a decrease in alcohol consumption. That is, changes in drinking behavior were mostly correlated with changes in perception regardless of how those changes in perception were brought about. These findings were encouraging and led to further exploration of the SGNM.

Case Study Two: Greek System Interventions, Spring 1999 and 2000

Members of seven fraternities (n = 176) and two sororities (n = 95) took part in time 1 (T1) data collection approximately three weeks prior to the intervention in 1999. Beginning in January, Greek house presidents were recruited and trained as facilitators. In turn, they solicited the cooperation of their memberships. T1 data were collected in February. During March, trained house presidents facilitated SGNM interventions in their respective living groups, engaging their audience in lively, interactive discussion regarding the discrepancy between the actual norms and those estimated by the group. The intervention used in this study differed from that used in 1991. Instead of the posters described in study one, a series of overhead transparencies were used. The transparencies in this and subsequent studies contain explanation of social norms theory, media literacy, and comparison of campuswide and group-specific norms data using the norms reported by the targeted group. In addition, information about negative consequences of alcohol use was deleted from the presentation; instead, data were presented about instances of protective behaviors and fun students have when they are not using alcohol. T2 follow-up data were gathered three to four weeks after intervention. Focus groups were conducted with three fraternities and one sorority on the evening following the intervention. Unfortunately, the participation rate in the follow-up survey was too low to conduct a reliable evaluation.

In the following year (spring 2000), we again conducted the SGNM intervention with Greek organizations. Members of eight fraternities (n = 194) and four sororities (n = 140) took part in T1 data collection approximately three weeks prior to receiving the SGNM intervention. T2 follow-up data collection was conducted three to four weeks after intervention. A total of fifty fraternity and ninety-five sorority participants completed both T1 and T2 surveys and attended the SGNM presentation. A second follow-up data collection (T3) was conducted seven weeks after intervention. A total of twenty-four fraternity and fifty-three sorority participants completed both T1 and T3 surveys and attended the SGNM intervention. The intervention cycle was implemented as in 1999. T1 group-specific data collection was conducted three weeks prior to the delivery of the intervention. Two follow-up data collections were conducted, the first at three to four weeks after intervention, the second at seven weeks after intervention. Focus groups were not conducted during this study.

Results for Sororities

At T2, sorority members who attended the SGNM intervention demonstrated significant correction of their estimates (misperception) for these variables: (1) times per month most students drink (decrease of 1.97 times, $p < .0001$); (2) number of drinks most students have per occasion (decrease of .72 drinks, $p = .003$); (3) times per month students in their respective chapters drink (decrease of 1.43 times, $p = .001$); and (4) number of drinks students in their respective chapters have per occasion (decrease of 0.44 drinks, $p = .013$). Although T2 trends were in the desired direction for personal consumption, these sorority women did not demonstrate a statistically significant decrease in the frequency of their drinking (times per month decreased by 0.35 times, $p = .269$) or number of drinks per occasion (decrease of 0.22 drinks, $p = .231$).

Figures 7.1 and 7.2 present sorority members' change in perception of campus and chapter drinking norms over the longer assessment period. At T3, sorority members who had attended the SGNM presentation demonstrated significant correction of their estimates (misperception) for these variables: (1) times per month most students drink (decrease of 2.44 times, $p = .001$); (2) number of drinks most students have per occasion (decrease of 1.04 drinks, $p = .001$); and (3) times per month students in their respective chapters drink (decrease of 1.37 times, $p = .014$). At this time, their estimate of the number of drinks students in their respective chapters have per occasion (decrease of 0.25 drinks, $p = .311$) and the actual number of drinks they themselves consumed per occasion (decrease of 0.22 drinks, $p = .447$), though moving in the predicted direction, were not statistically significant. However, they demonstrated a significant decrease in the frequency of their own drinking (decrease of 1.38 times per month, $p = .010$). Only changes for quantity and frequency of actual drinking, and not absolute levels, are provided for this study as part of a participation agreement with the Greek chapters. This agreement enhanced participation by ensuring some degree of confidentiality.

FIGURE 7.1. SORORITY ESTIMATES OF PEER DRINKS PER OCCASION, WSU AND CHAPTER.

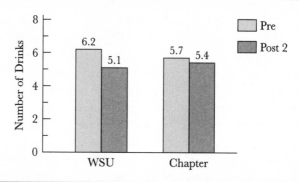

Notes: Spring 2000, n = 53.

Post 2 refers to post-intervention second measurement at T3 measure.

Sorority women's estimates of drinking quantity before and after intervention T3, spring 2000. Actual quantity of drinking decreased by 0.3 drinks following one intervention (specific numbers for actual quantity not reported for reasons of confidentiality).

FIGURE 7.2. SORORITY ESTIMATES OF PEER TIMES DRINKING PER MONTH, WSU AND CHAPTER.

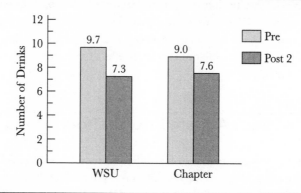

Notes: Spring 2000, n = 53.

Post 2 refers to post-intervention second measurement at T3 measure.

Sorority women's estimates of drinking quantity before and after intervention T3, spring 2000. Actual frequency of drinking decreased by 1.4 times per month following one intervention (specific numbers for actual frequency not reported for reasons of confidentiality).

Results for Fraternities

At T2, fraternity members who attended the SGNM intervention exhibited reduced misperception as predicted for all measures, but these measures did not reach a statistically significant level. The observed decrease in their estimates (misperception) were (1) times per month most students drink (decrease of 2.13 times, $p = .132$); (2) number of drinks most students have per occasion (decrease of .36 drinks, $p = .402$); (3) times per month students in their respective chapters drink (decrease of .77 times, $p = .387$); and (4) number of drinks students in their respective chapters have per occasion (decrease of 0.65 drinks, $p = .296$). They did not demonstrate a significant decrease in the frequency of their personal drinking (times per month decreased by 0.17 times, $p = .402$). However, they did demonstrate a marginally significant decrease in the number of drinks consumed per occasion (decrease of 0.91 drinks, $p = .067$).

Figures 7.3 and 7.4 present fraternity members' change in perception of campus and chapter drinking norms over the longer assessment period. Although most of the changes in perceived norms were in the predicted direction for fraternity members who attended the SGNM presentation, they were not statistically significant on the basis of the small number of men (n = 24) who responded at T3. Changes in their estimates (misperception) were (1) times per month most students drink (decrease of 2.65 times, $p = .180$), (2) number of drinks most students have per occasion (increase of .06 drinks, $p = .880$), (3) times per month students in their respective chapters drink (decrease of 0.25 times, $p = .830$), and (4) number of drinks students in their respective chapters have per occasion (decrease of 0.6 drinks, $p = .337$). Their personal drinking declined, but again not to a statistically significant degree: frequency of their drinking (times per month) decreased by .22 times ($p = .189$) and the number of drinks they consumed per occasion decreased by 0.78 drinks ($p = .189$).

Case Study Three: Athlete Intervention, Spring 1999

Members of three teams—one male, two female; two varsity and one junior varsity (n = 79 at T1)—were recruited to take part. Team captains received three hours of training as facilitators for their respective teams. At T2 follow-up data collection (six to seven weeks after intervention), thirty-nine team members attended the SGNM intervention and completed survey forms at T1 and T2. Data from male and female participants were not analyzed separately. Data collections and presentations were timed to coincide with each team's active playing season.

FIGURE 7.3. FRATERNITY ESTIMATES OF PEER DRINKS PER OCCASION, WSU AND CHAPTER.

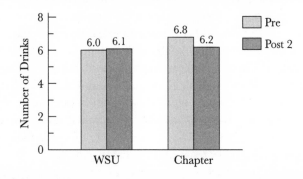

Notes: Spring 2000, n = 24.

Post 2 refers to post-intervention second measurement at T3 measure.

Fraternity men's estimates of drinking quantity before and after intervention T3, spring 2000. Actual quantity of drinking decreased by 0.5 drinks following one intervention (specific numbers for actual quantity not reported for reasons of confidentiality).

FIGURE 7.4. FRATERNITY ESTIMATES OF PEER TIMES DRINKING PER MONTH, WSU AND CHAPTER.

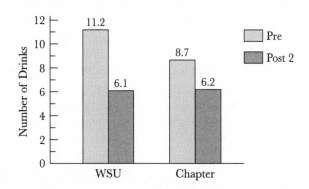

Notes: Spring 2000, n = 24.

Post 2 refers to post-intervention second measurement at T3 measure.

Fraternity men's estimates of drinking frequency before and after intervention T3, spring 2000. Actual frequency of drinking decreased by 2.2 times per month following one intervention (specific numbers for actual frequency not reported for reasons of confidentiality).

The SGNM intervention was delivered as described in study two. This study did not use a control group.

Regarding results, specific numbers for quantity and frequency of drinking are not provided for this study as part of a participation agreement with the WSU Athletic Department. This agreement enhanced participation by ensuring some degree of confidentiality. At T2, athletes who attended the SGNM intervention demonstrated significant correction of their estimates (misperception) for these dependent variables: (1) times per month most students drink (decrease of 3.67 times, $p < .0001$), (2) number of drinks most students have per occasion (decrease of 1.2 drinks, $p = .020$), (3) times per month their respective teammates drink (decrease of 3.5 times, $p < .016$), and (4) number of drinks their respective teammates have per occasion (decrease of 1.22 drinks, $p < .0001$).

These student athletes demonstrated no appreciable change in their own drinking, however. This is likely due to the finding that these particular athletic teams were not, in fact, high-risk groups to begin with. The quantity and frequency of their use was already at or below the campuswide norms. Having corrected their misperception, however, it was anticipated they would "carry" more accurate norm information to their peers.

Case Study Four: Curriculum Infusion, Fall 1999

A brief description of this study is included here. Further details can be found in Peeler, Far, Miller, and Brigham (2000).

Participants and Procedures

The SGNM intervention was presented in Psychology 106 classes, a one-credit self-management class for freshmen divided into fifteen sections ($N = 213$). Sections were randomly assigned to the treatment (seven sections, n = 145) or control (eight sections, n = 117) conditions. Presenters were trained and supervised "peer teacher" pairs who team-taught the classes; they were chosen to teach these classes because of their skill and competence with a facilitative teaching style.

During week one of the class, all students completed the Student Life and Health Behaviors survey (T1: preintervention survey). Then class sections were randomly assigned to conditions: treatment (seven sections, n = 145) or no-treatment control (eight sections, n = 117). During week nine, peer teachers facilitated the SGNM intervention for their respective sections in the treatment condition; the class curriculum was otherwise identical for both conditions. During week fifteen, all students again filled out the survey instrument (T2: post-intervention survey).

Results

The treatment group receiving the SGNM intervention demonstrated a significant increase in the accuracy of their perceptions at T2 with regard to the alcohol-use attitudes of students campuswide. They also reported at T2 a significant change in their own attitudes in the desired direction and in the amount of alcohol they consumed per occasion when compared to the control group. Treatment condition participants drank on the average 1.55 drinks less per occasion than control condition participants at the end of the semester ($p = .007$).

Participants did not demonstrate greater accuracy in several of their estimates of classroom peer attitudes (although all variables demonstrated change in the desired direction). This may reflect the greater saliency of campuswide norms to their own attitudes and behavior choices. Greek system members might be expected to have greater interest in their own group's norms as opposed to campuswide norms (a question for further research), but these classroom members are not likely to experience the "reference group" identification to their class felt by Greek members for their group (Far, 1984, 1998).

Overall Greek and Campuswide Findings

We have observed significant reduction in misperception of student drinking frequency (times per month) and quantity (drinks per occasion) associated with implementation of the Small Groups Norms-Challenging Model in the Greek population since 1995 (see Figure 7.5). All data are taken from the preintervention surveys of the particular year. The 1991 data reflect a small pilot project in several Greek chapters. Initiatives began in earnest in 1995–96. Since that time, actual drinking quantity among Greeks has decreased by 2.2 drinks per occasion. (Specific numbers are not reported here for reasons of confidentiality.) Furthermore, significant decreases in actual frequency have been documented in this population.

In addition, correction in misperception of quantity of drinking as well as decrease in actual drinking quantity have been demonstrated in the surveys of students campuswide over the years of the SGNM interventions (see Figure 7.6). Importantly, no ongoing campuswide campaign to reduce misperception (such as a social norms marketing campaign) was in place during the time these studies were conducted, which gives more credence to our claim that the various SGNM

FIGURE 7.5. GREEK ESTIMATES OF PEER DRINKING QUANTITY OVER TIME.

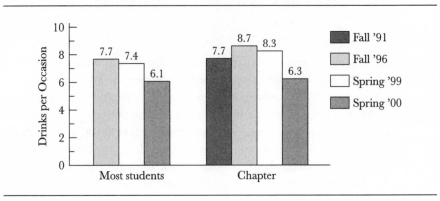

FIGURE 7.6. CHANGES IN CAMPUSWIDE MISPERCEPTION OF DRINKING QUANTITY OVER TIME.

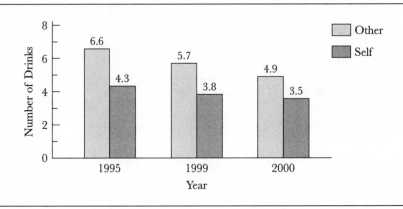

interventions have collectively made a difference in perception among students in general. Finally, we have observed a decrease in actual drinking quantity as well, on the basis of the surveys of students campuswide over the years of the SGNM interventions (see Figure 7.7).

A nearby university with similar characteristics and a similar Greek system acted as a control group comparison for our 1999 to 2000 Greek and campuswide data on actual consumption. Again, for reasons of confidentiality, actual alcohol consumption figures are not reported for that campus. Nevertheless, control-campus data indicated a slight increase in alcohol consumption campus-

FIGURE 7.7. CAMPUSWIDE DRINKING QUANTITY AND FREQUENCY OVER TIME.

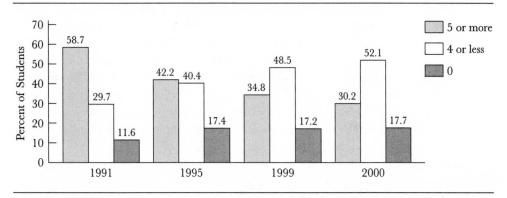

wide and in the Greek system, while a decline was observed at WSU during the same period.

Reflections on Strengths and Weaknesses of the Studies

The goal of the studies reported in this chapter is to establish the efficacy of the Small Groups Norms-Challenging Model as a viable delivery system for accurate social norms information. It is anticipated that this information, so delivered, will influence changes in alcohol-use behavior in groups perceived to be at high risk for alcohol abuse and related problems, and possibly the larger population for whom these groups may serve as highly visible models. Care has been taken to maintain rigorous experimental design and data analysis, and the strategy has been tested in a variety of settings. The Greek system studies, however, have suffered from a high rate of attrition from T1 to T2 and T3, resulting in a small number of participants taking part in the intervention and completing the postintervention surveys. As a result, it is difficult to interpret the findings. This problem and possible solutions are discussed in a following section.

Furthermore, the effects of this type of intervention may take some time to manifest as behavior change; a three-or-four-week follow-up may not be sufficient time for students to process their intervention experience. This may account for findings showing a significant difference in some of the studies using a longer postintervention assessment. Participants appear to hear the information, accept its accuracy conditionally, and start to closely observe the behavior of their peers. As they watch and keep track of other students' actual drinking behavior, rather than uncritically accepting the common misperception they hear from others and see in the media, they notice that most students drink moderately and responsibly. Like the developing independent thinkers they are, these young adults listen to the information and then seek to validate it with their own experience.

The studies to date have used a single intervention with three-to-fifteen-week postintervention data collection. Supplemental or complementary interventions might strengthen the SGNM's influence, and we need to examine the observed misperception correction and behavior change over a longer time span. We plan to study the effects of increasing social norms dosage in future studies, with multiple interventions in the same population (for example, a specific Greek chapter might receive the intervention for several consecutive semesters).

Strengths and Weaknesses of the Small Groups Norms-Challenging Model

Most delivery mechanisms for social norms information implemented to date, such as social norms marketing, expose students repeatedly to small bites of information (dosage) such as "The majority (70 percent) of WSU students consume 0–4 drinks when they party." Posters, ads, and other materials containing accurate social norms information are displayed frequently and changed often, keeping the messages fresh while increasing the information dosage. Students probably take in these bites of information without much discriminative awareness or processing of information content, much as we take in the multiple bites of advertising we are exposed to every day.

In contrast, SGNM gives students accurate norms data over a forty-five-minute exposure time, while engaging them in a voluntary, interactive, nonjudgmental discussion about norms and misperceptions, including how they are formed and perpetuated and how they influence alcohol-use behavior. During this process, students may consider how they interact with the social milieu, how the milieu affects their behavior choices, and how they might want to change those interactions. We believe these discussions give students an opportunity to experience, process, and begin resolving cognitive dissonance not available with delivery systems such as social norms marketing. We believe this facilitated, intensive processing is necessary to influence behavior change in a high-risk membership or reference group.

Other strengths of the Small Groups Norms-Challenging Model are that it is easy to replicate, adaptable, portable, and inexpensive. This model can be implemented simply using (1) a copy machine to reproduce surveys, (2) information from a one-page survey filled out by the target group prior to the intervention, (3) hand calculators to extract group norms data from the surveys, and (4) overhead transparencies to present the norms data. In addition, campuswide data may be gathered by surveying students in several large, dissimilar classes as an adequate and inexpensive substitute for a true random-sample survey. (When presenting these data to specific groups, participants should be told how the campuswide data were collected.)

Some weaknesses of the model must also be addressed. The SGNM could be considered time- and labor-intensive for the number of participants reached by each intervention, particularly if one is using campuswide data along with group-specific data (which is highly recommended). Data collection and statistical analyses to obtain the information for the overhead transparencies can be time-consuming, and random-sample mail surveying requires technical expertise if it is to be effective and accurate. In addition, recruitment of participant target groups can be a challenge. If high-risk groups are "in the misperception," they may be reluctant to become involved. Training of presenters, preferably done in a group, requires several hours and a good working knowledge of the model.

We believe that these apparent difficulties are outweighed by what we have experienced to be the positive gains from implementing the Small Groups Norms-Challenging Model. Two such gains are the richness and depth of the information presented, and the discussion generated during (and following) presentation. Another is the successful reduction of drinking behavior, albeit a small decrease at times, with just a single intervention among groups considered at high risk for alcohol abuse and related problems. In the experimental studies previously described, almost all groups demonstrated more accurate perception following the intervention. Most groups demonstrated a decrease in drinking behavior in the desired direction, and many times the decrease was significant. All in all, we believe the strengths of the model far outweigh the weaknesses.

Greek System: Lessons Learned

The members of the Greek system at WSU have, on the whole, been cooperative and willing project participants over the years. However, issues have surfaced as a challenge to maintaining good cooperation: recruitment and retention of participants; confidentiality agreements; and the perception that project staff were, at times, supplying the university administration with negative data.

Participant buy-in is vital to attaining sufficient numbers for meaningful outcomes and helpful information for future programming. This has been relatively easy to accomplish in the classroom or with an athletic team, where the group meets regularly and has adult authority figures (professors or coaches) to sanction the project and make the group available. This has been more difficult within the Greek system, where studies are hampered by difficulties with participant recruitment and retention.

Recruiting participants for the initial study in 1991 went smoothly (Barnett, Far, Mauss, and Miller, 1996). Chapter presidents received written and oral invitations to participate. Many Greek chapters agreed to take part after learning about the project and its potential for reducing alcohol abuse among Greek membership and enhancing the public image of the Greek system. However, a series of events took place during 1995 and 1996 that created barriers to further Greek participation.

A number of alcohol-related incidents at WSU and a nearby university campus crystallized public opinion against continued conspicuous alcohol abuse by college students in general, and by members of the Greek system in particular (where alcohol abuse was perceived to be the heaviest). During 1996, the vice-provost for student affairs formed a Campus Alcohol Task Force to review alcohol abuse and related problems campuswide, as well as the various prevention programs in place at the time. The task force included representatives from Student Affairs, Residence Life, campus police, Greek and non-Greek student leadership, and from the local community. In March 1996, the task force, with the support of the student representatives, strengthened the university's alcohol policy. Greek leaders asked for time to process the new policy with their membership to foster buy-in and support. However, the policy was made public before this could happen; the Greek membership believed they did not have a voice in these decisions and resented what appeared to them to be a top-down command.

During this time, the authors were implementing a study of the SGNM intervention in the Greek system and were involved in follow-up data collection when the policy announcement was made (Far, 1998). Some Greek members believed the Greek data generated by the project's activities had contributed to the new, more restrictive policy affecting how their chapters could socialize with alcohol. As a result, some chapters and members became reluctant to participate in future projects.

Recruitment efforts were intensified to overcome this resistance and to distance the project from any perceived involvement with university administration. The authors began attending meetings of the Panhellenic Council, the Inter-Fraternity Council, and fraternity and sorority presidents. In addition to explaining the project, a brief social norms intervention was facilitated for each group. The leaders were given project data demonstrating a decrease in drinking behavior for the Greek system as a whole. They were shown that most Greek students were making healthy and responsible choices about alcohol and were caring people willing to help each other and the campus community. They were told that the project was designed to focus on this positive reality and that the project staff was committed to publicizing this to the Greek membership, as well as to the campus community. In addition, focus groups and meetings with fraternity and sorority representatives were convened to devise strategies to enhance participation, reduce attrition, and focus on obstacles to leadership. These efforts have reestablished good working relationships between project staff and the Greek leaders, while correcting their own misperception of Greek drinking behavior. In turn, cooperation and participation have increased and better data are becoming available.

Assurance of Confidentiality

One specific source of resistance to participation has been concern about confidentiality. We describe here a strategy that has been implemented to address this concern. During recruitment meetings, the survey coding system is explained to prospective participants to assure them of individual anonymity. They are told that all project staff sign a confidentiality agreement as a condition of their employment. Further, the chapter coding system is explained to make it clear that data from individual chapters is identified only by a code number during data analysis. They are informed that only one person, the project codirector, ever knows which data presented on the overheads belong to which house. Finally, they are told that any publications resulting from the project will not report actual quantity and frequency of drinking figures for the WSU Greek system, or for individual Greek chapters.

Athletic team participants were also concerned about confidentiality. The Athletic Department was willing to allow team participation only if they were given absolute assurance that no specific teams would be identified by name and that actual consumption figures would not be published. The sports psychologist working with the athletes personally pledged to the department and the athletes that absolute confidentiality would be maintained.

The authors believe that this concern about confidentiality comes from the fact that, prior to involvement in the project, administrators, coaches, and other participants are in the misperception. Like students campuswide, they misperceive and exaggerate how much students in their group of interest drink and approve of drinking. In turn, they fear these misperceptions becoming public knowledge, making them appear unhealthy and irresponsible and drawing negative judgment. As each group learns that its average drinking is less than the members thought (and perhaps feared), we believe participant concerns will lessen and their willingness to continue with the project will increase.

Implications for Future Research

The decrease in drinking behavior demonstrated with the SGNM has resulted from participants' exposure to a single intervention. We believe that efficacy would be enhanced by increasing intervention dosage through multiple presentations, or by combining the intervention with other strategies such as social norms marketing. Future studies could be designed to examine this. For example, during the course of a semester, an SGNM intervention might be combined with (1) a second "booster" presentation delivered later in the semester to a specific Greek system target group; (2) Greek chapter-specific or Greek system-specific social marketing interventions, such as posters displayed within the privacy of chapter living quarters; (3) e-mail messages with Greek-specific data sent only to Greek system members; or (4) a self-monitoring alcohol-use exercise.

In addition, the intervention could be delivered to a wider variety of campus populations. We have chosen to target students considered to be at high risk for alcohol abuse and related problems, such as freshman classes, Greek students, and student athletes. Other populations that might benefit from these focused interventions are freshmen or entering students in a setting other than the classroom, students living in a residential area near campus where excessive drinking is known to occur, a specific ethnic or cultural group, and members of a recognized student organization such as a social or special interest club.

Another question raised by these studies concerns salience of norms. Which set of accurate drinking norms presented during the SGNM intervention are most potent in influencing drinking behavior for members of that particular group: campuswide or group-specific norms? Attitude or behavior norms? The possible variations in salience of norms could be tested by having each of several treatment groups receive a particular norm or combination of norms during the intervention. Further studies with a larger number of participants are needed to clarify these important theoretical and implementation issues.

We believe that social norms approaches may lend themselves to prevention work in many areas other than alcohol abuse. For example, we have implemented a small pilot study addressing tobacco-use prevention in some Greek chapters and in a classroom, and we have collected campuswide tobacco social norms data (not yet analyzed). In addition, we recently gathered social norms data (perceptions and behaviors) on sexual activity, sexual communication, and questions of social justice and diversity. We plan to use these data to develop, implement, and study SGNM interventions to address problems in these areas, including the reduction and prevention of violence.

References

Baer, J. S. "Effects of College Residence on Perceived Norms for Alcohol Consumption: An Examination of the First Year in College." *Psychology of Addictive Behaviors*, 1994, *8*, 43–50.

Barnett, L., Far, J. M., Mauss, A. L., and Miller, J. A. "Changing Perceptions of Peer Norms as a Drinking Reduction Program for College Students." *Journal of Alcohol and Drug Education*, 1996, *41*(2), 39–62.

Berkowitz, A. D. "From Reactive to Proactive Prevention: Promoting an Ecology of Health on Campus." In P. Clayton Rivers and E. R. Shore (eds.), *Substance Abuse on Campus: A Handbook for College and University Personnel*. Westport, Conn.: Greenwood Press, 1997.

Berkowitz, A. D., and Perkins, H. W. "Problem Drinking Among College Students: A Review of Recent Research." *Journal of American College Health*, 1986, *35*, 21–28.

Berkowitz, A. D., and Perkins, H. W. "Current Issues in Effective Alcohol Education Programming." In *Alcohol Policies and Practices on College and University Campuses* (National Association of Student Personnel Administrators, Inc., Monograph Series), 1987.

Borsari, B. E., and Carey, K. B. "Understanding Fraternity Drinking: Five Recurring Themes in the Literature." *Journal of American College Health*, 1999, *48*, 30–37.

Coggins, N., and McKellar, S. "Drug Use Amongst Peers: Peer Pressure or Peer Preference?" *Drugs: Education, Prevention, and Policy*, 1994, *1*, 15–26.

Dillman, D. A. *Mail and Telephone Surveys: The Total Design Survey Method*. New York: Wiley, 1978.

Far, J. M. "Membership Groups and the Self-Concept." Unpublished manuscript, Washington State University, Pullman, 1984.

Far, J. M. "Evaluating the Norms Challenging Model for Decreasing Alcohol Abuse in a University Greek System." Unpublished dissertation, Department of Educational Leadership and Counseling Psychology, Washington State University, Pullman, 1998.

Far, J. M., Thompson, R., and Miller, J. A. "Students and Alcohol at WSU: A General Survey." (Unpublished raw data.) Pullman: Washington State University, 1995.

Goodwin, L. "Explaining Alcohol Consumption and Related Experiences Among Fraternity and Sorority Members." *Journal of College Student Development*, 1989, *30*, 448–458.

Haines, M. P., and Spear, S. F. "Changing the Perception of the Norm: A Strategy to Decrease Binge Drinking Among College Students." *Journal of American College Health*, Nov. 1996, pp. 134–40.

Johannessen, K., Collins, C., Mills-Novoa, B., and Glider, P. *A Practical Guide to Alcohol Abuse Prevention: A Campus Study in Implementing Social Norms and Environmental Management Approaches*. Tucson: Campus Health Service, University of Arizona, 1999.

Lo, C., and Globetti, G. "A Partial Analysis of the Campus Influence on Drinking Behavior: Students Who Enter College as Non-Drinkers." *Journal of Drug Issues*, 1993, *23*, 716–734.

Lo, C., and Globetti, G. "The Facilitating and Enhancing Roles Greek Associations Play in College Drinking." *International Journal of Addictions*, 1995, *30*(10), 1311–1322.

Page, R. M., Scanlan, A., and Gilbert, L. "Relationship of the Estimation of Binge Drinking Among College Students and Personal Participation in Binge Drinking: Implications for College Health and Promotion." *Journal of Health Education*, 1999, *30*(1), 99–104.

Peeler, C., Far, J. M., Miller, J. A., and Brigham, T. A. "An Analysis of the Effects of a Program to Reduce Heavy Drinking Among College Students." *Journal of Alcohol and Drug Education*, 2000, *45*(2), 39–54.

Perkins, H. W. "College Student Misperceptions of Alcohol and Other Drug Norms Among Peers: Exploring Causes, Consequences, and Implications for Prevention Programs." In *Designing Alcohol and Other Drug Prevention Programs in Higher Education: Bringing Theory into Practice.* Newton, Mass.: Higher Education Center for Alcohol and Other Drug Prevention, Education Development Center, 1997.

Perkins, H. W., and Berkowitz, A. "Perceiving the Community Norms of Alcohol Use Among Students: Some Research Implications for Campus Alcohol Education Programming." *International Journal of the Addictions,* 1986a, *21,* 961–976.

Perkins, H. W., and Berkowitz, A. "Using Student Alcohol Surveys: Notes on Clinical and Educational Program Applications." *Journal of Alcohol and Drug Education,* 1986b, *27,* 146–53.

Salant, P., and Dillman, D. A. *How to Conduct Your Own Survey.* New York: Wiley, 1994.

PART THREE

EXPANDING SOCIAL NORMS INTERVENTIONS TO OTHER COLLEGE STUDENT APPLICATIONS

CHAPTER EIGHT

PERCEPTIONS, NORMS, AND TOBACCO USE OF COLLEGE RESIDENCE HALL FRESHMEN

Evaluation of a Social Norms Marketing Intervention

Linda C. Hancock, F.N.P., Ph.D.; Neil W. Henry, Ph.D.

Is social norms marketing (SNM) an effective strategy for tobacco-use prevention and cessation at the local campus level? In this chapter, we describe an SNM campaign and present the results of a pretest, posttest comparison group study conducted in the fall of 1999. This study assessed the impact of a campuswide nonsmoking SNM intervention on tobacco-use perceptions and behavior in residence hall freshmen during their first semester on campus. We discuss some of the practical lessons learned from creating the SNM campaign and from the ensuing research effort. Resources created during this tobacco-use prevention effort are free and available at www.smokefreeVCU.org. We begin with an overview of recent tobacco-use trends on college campuses and review studies documenting misperceptions of tobacco use.

The authors wish to thank Norma Pierce, the communications coordinator for the Division of Student Affairs, and Debbie Mulcahy for all of their incredible talent, expertise, and enthusiasm. Deep gratitude and appreciation is extended to the student creators of the SNM campaign: Jon Rosen, Jenna Hall, and Ashley Miles. Finally, thanks to all of the VCU students who have taught us so much about substances, health, and perception.

Campus Tobacco-Use Trends

Tobacco use is the leading cause of preventable morbidity and mortality in the United States (U.S. DHHS, 2000). In the past, college health educators, overwhelmed by more immediate student health issues such as alcohol abuse and HIV transmission, gave limited attention to tobacco use. A national survey of college students in 1995 found that only 27.8 percent reported receiving information on tobacco-use prevention from their college or university (CDC, 1997). A national survey of college health center directors in 1999 found that more than 40 percent of schools did not offer a smoking cessation program, and that the demand for cessation programs was low (Wechsler, 2001).

The resurgence of tobacco use by high school and college students in the 1990s was the impetus for college health educators to reconsider how much effort they devote to tobacco prevention, cessation, and policy improvement. Longitudinal data from the Monitoring the Futures Studies indicate that although past-month use by high school seniors fell in the late 1970s and stabilized in the 1980s, it rose steadily in the 1990s. Past-month use peaked in 1997 with the tobacco-use rate almost identical to that in 1975. In 2001, 25 percent of college males and 27 percent of college females reported smoking in the past month (Johnston, O'Malley, and Bachman, 2002).

A national cross-sectional study of college students found a 27.8 percent rise in the prevalence of current (thirty-day) cigarette smoking between 1993 and 1997, from 22.3 percent to 28.5 percent (Wechsler, Rigotti, Gledhill-Hoyt, and Lee, 1998). Another national survey in 1999 found that nearly half (45.7 percent) of college students had used tobacco in the past year and 32.9 percent within the past month (Rigotti, Lee, and Wechsler, 2000). Both studies concluded that a substantial number of college students are starting to smoke regularly and that many are trying to stop.

Misperception About Tobacco Use

Although this resurgence in tobacco use is cause for concern, the fact remains that *most college students do not smoke*. Research consistently shows that teenagers and college students misperceive and overestimate their peers' use of tobacco. Perkins and others (1999) analyzed data from 100 college campuses and found that more than three-quarters of the students believed the typical student used tobacco almost weekly; almost half believed that the typical student used it every day. Perkins and Berkowitz (1986) and others working with younger students (Sussman and others, 1988; Hansen and Graham, 1991) have developed theories and conducted research demonstrating that the misperception process may lead students to increase their substance-use behavior to fit false norms.

As mentioned in earlier chapters, correcting overestimation of alcohol use and related misperceptions through social norms marketing has been shown to decrease alcohol consumption (Haines and Spear, 1996; Gilder and others, 2001). More replication studies are under way to confirm the effectiveness of the SNM strategies with alcohol, but there is as yet no published data about the impact of SNM on tobacco use at the college level. Since misperceptions about smoking norms have been shown to exist among college students, however, it seems reasonable to believe that efforts to correct them may have a healthy benefit.

College Smoking Behavior: Research and Norms

In 1997, the Office of Health Promotion at Virginia Commonwealth University (VCU) decided to study the impact of a nonsmoking SNM mass media campaign on college students. We were aware that tobacco use had increased nationally and on the VCU campus, but our review of the literature revealed that little was known about smoking behavior in college students (Chassin, Presson, and Sherman, 1995). Up to that time, most prevention and research efforts had focused on "early-onset" smokers in middle and high school. Tobacco addiction was thought of as a "pediatric disease" (Kessler, 1997). We suspected that legislation changes in the 1990s and restrictions on cartoon advertising might tend to increase smoking in our population since tobacco advertisers were increasingly targeting the legal, eighteen-to-twenty-four-year-old potential smoker (Males, 1999).

The literature also added to our concern that college students might begin smoking while at school. There were data suggesting that late-onset smokers, who start smoking after the age of eighteen, are qualitatively different from early-onset smokers (Chassin, Presson, and Sherman, 1995). Late-onset smokers tend to be more academically oriented and less prone to rebellious behavior than early-onset smokers. They also tend to move much more quickly from experimentation to regular use than do early-onset smokers. In one study late-onset smokers had double the risk of progressing to established smoking relative to younger students (Choi and others, 1997).

Pierce and others (1996), who evaluated the California tobacco prevention media campaigns, found that not all nonsmokers are the same. They described some nonsmokers as "cognitively committed" to nonsmoking and others as "cognitively vulnerable" to smoking. We wanted to know if SNM could help strengthen the college student's cognitive commitment to nonsmoking.

We also wanted to know whether this prevention campaign might have an impact on cessation. When designing media interventions, one encounters difficulty in distinguishing between activities that are directed toward prevention and those that might influence cessation. Diffusion of innovation theory (Rogers, 1995) helped us conceptualize this overlap. A college population consists of potential late adopters of smoking as well as potential innovators for cessation (Redmond, 1999). According to diffusion theory, peer pressure is a necessary adjunct if late adopters are to begin a behavior. Since SNM deals with "imaginary peer pressure" by correcting misperception of peer norms, we hypothesized that the SNM might slow the diffusion of smoking initiation on campus and simultaneously hasten the diffusion of cessation.

The Nonsmoking SNM Campaign

We created the nonsmoking SNM campaign by following the guidelines pertaining to SNM strategies for alcohol-use reduction recommended by experts (Haines, 1996; Zimmerman, 1997). We began by collecting past-month smoking statistics from the national and local levels. VCU had conducted a random mail out survey in 1997 using the Centers for Disease Control's College Health Risk Behavior Survey and, during the 1997–98 school year, surveyed 537 residence hall freshmen. These data helped to document that misperception existed and were useful in developing the campaign and designing the associated assessment research.

The campaign was specifically designed to be campuswide rather than just in the freshman residence halls, even though the research assessment was conducted only on freshmen. Since most freshmen want to identify with upperclassmen and interact with them socially and academically, it made sense to have the intervention target all students at VCU.

The SNM media campaign consisted of several distinct components; it was funded in part by a grant from the Virginia Department of Health. The team that created the campaign comprised three graduate students in advertising, the communications coordinator for the Division of Student Affairs, and author Hancock. A series of posters and newspaper advertisements that varied slightly but retained the same normative message were planned (Figures 8.1 and 8.2 show examples). The campaign included media elements that addressed both cessation and prevention of smoking. The primary focus was the "True Facts of Modern Life" campaign, which promoted the message "Seven of ten college students don't smoke." The team decided that humor would help to deal with the sensitive issue of tobacco use by capturing students' attention and making the advertisements more positive and memorable. Once the various components of the campaign were created, pilot testing in focus groups was undertaken to further evaluate message impact.

FIGURE 8.1. CAMPAIGN POSTER:
TRUE FACTS ABOUT MODERN LIFE (TOILET PAPER).

Source: Used by permission of Office of Health Promotion, Virginia Commonwealth University.

FIGURE 8.2. CAMPAIGN POSTER: TRUE FACTS ABOUT MODERN LIFE ("DARTH VAPOR").

Source: Used by permission of Office of Health Promotion, Virginia Commonwealth University.

In working with the graduate team of advertising students and with students in focus groups, we found that students often tended to have ideas for strategies that were interesting and that might have turned out to be effective, but they were not norm-related. Conscious effort was required to remain faithful to norm setting as the primary message, since our primary research goal was to evaluate the effectiveness of social norm marketing.

Implementing the Campaign

The media intervention was launched the first week of school in the fall of 1999. The intervention relied primarily on the True Facts of Modern Life campaign. This was made up of a series of five posters, each with a funny graphic image and a related humorous statistic, followed by the true statement that "seven of ten college students don't smoke." Fine print cited credible national and local data sources on current smoking rates. Anyone interested in tobacco use reduction is permitted to use our campaign materials (available electronically at www.smokefreeVCU.org); simply delete our local data and school logo and replace it with your own information. Please let us know if you find the material useful and have any research findings to report.

In addition to the posters and campus newspaper advertisements based on them, table tents in dining halls and other public areas and a spokesperson named "Darth Vapor" were central to the campaign. Darth was a student volunteer who traveled around campus in costume five times during the first ten weeks of the semester giving a dollar or a key chain to those who could tell him that "seven of ten college students don't smoke." The grant funds were also used to purchase newspaper advertisement space and other promotional items such as T-shirts and mouse pads. See Table 8.1 for campaign components and cost.

To determine market saturation of the campaign, an intercept survey of residence hall freshmen (n = 70) was conducted early in the second semester. This survey showed that 94 percent of the freshman residence hall target audience could recall seeing at least one component of the campaign. The two components with the highest recall were the posters (77 percent) and the table tents (49 percent). Only 25 percent had seen the newspaper advertisements, only 15 percent had seen the T-shirts, and 5.7 percent had seen the mouse pads. Surprisingly, the cheapest interventions had the greatest impact on recall. The two most memorable campaign items (posters and table tents) were inexpensive black-and-white media pieces. The intercept survey found that the freshmen often did not read the campus newspaper and as a result did not see the relatively expensive advertisements. The promotional items produced limited recall and were expensive for the number purchased.

TABLE 8.1. NONSMOKING SNM CAMPAIGN COMPONENTS AND COST.

Campaign Components	Approximate Cost (Rounded to Nearest $10)
Print campaign	
Poster campaigns	
Primary "True Facts" posters, black and white (500)	$80
Color posters (150)	330
Table tents for dining facilities (250)	30
Newspaper advertisements	
Primary campus paper: 5 full-page, 2 half-page advertisements	1,200
Secondary paper: 3 full-page advertisements	270
Promotional items	
T-shirts (300, 100 of each type)	1,800
Key chains (250)	210
Mouse pads (100)	400
Nail files (500)	150
Darth Vapor dollars	40
Darth's costume	70
Total	$4,580

The Evaluation Study

The purpose of the research study was to assess the impact of the campuswide SNM campaign on residence hall freshmen's tobacco-use perception and behavior. In addition, the study assessed changes in nonsmokers' cognitive commitment to nonsmoking. The design was a straightforward before-and-after survey, over a one-semester period. The first wave of data was collected during the first week of the fall semester, before the media campaign began. The second wave was collected ten weeks later. We limited the time frame for the study to decrease attrition and to limit confounding environmental variables (such as a cigarette price increase). We also decided to match preintervention and postintervention responses to reduce sampling error that would be due to the natural variability of individuals.

It was obvious that a comparison sample was needed. Both the literature and our clinical experience had led us to believe that the smoking rate would increase as students spent time in college. As students grow older, they have more time to initiate smoking. As they transition from the parental supervision of their homes, they have more freedom to either start or escalate use. It was conceivable, therefore, that the smoking rate might increase in the VCU freshman population even if the SNM campaign turned out to be effective.

Characteristics of VCU and the Comparison Campus

Virginia Commonwealth University is a large, public, urban university. We selected a comparison campus that was also a large, public university in the same geographic region of the country. Both VCU and the comparison campus had approximately twenty-two thousand students, thirteen thousand undergraduates. All students at VCU were exposed to the campuswide, multichanneled, SNM media campaign during the first semester. No special activities took place at the comparison school, although the traditional amount of tobacco-related health information was given to freshman, consisting primarily of information about university cessation services. As happens on most campuses, the comparison school did *not* mention normative use.

There were some demographic differences between the campuses. According to campus enrollment data, VCU had relatively more females (61 percent compared to 55.9 percent) and more African Americans (16 percent compared to 8.5 percent). This difference is reflected in the sample. In other ways, they were quite similar. Both universities are primarily commuter schools where smoking is not permitted in the classroom or in most public buildings. As a result, smoking at both sites primarily occurred near the entrance and exit to buildings or in residence hall rooms.

VCU housed about twelve hundred freshmen on campus; the comparison campus housed about one thousand. Most students at each school lived in rooms where smoking was allowed in the room if all roommates agreed. At the comparison school, 34 percent of the residence hall floors were smoke-free (twelve of thirty-five floors), while at VCU 6.7 percent of the residence hall floors were smoke-free (two of thirty floors).

Data Collection Method

The week before freshmen arrived, residence hall assistants (RAs) at each campus were trained to administer the thirty-three-item preintervention survey instrument. The RAs distributed and collected the survey in their first hall meeting during orientation week. The freshmen were told that participation was optional and that responses would be kept confidential. Although the surveys were anonymous, respondents were asked to write in the last four digits of their social security number. This information, combined with three demographic variables, allowed accurate matching of the preintervention and postintervention responses. The follow-up survey took place ten weeks later, and the same data collection strategy was followed.

The study instrument was a thirty-three-item pencil-and-paper, self-report, multiple-choice questionnaire. Most of the behavioral items were modeled on questions from the CDC's College Health Risk Behavior Survey and the Teenage Attitudes and Practices Survey (TAPS). The questionnaire focused on four areas: perception of tobacco use, tobacco use behavior, cognitive commitment of non-smokers, and demographics. The three questions pertaining to vulnerability to future smoking were taken from the work of Pierce and others (1996) and Choi and others (1997) in California. Meta-analyses of the validity of self-reported smoking suggest that most respondents are honest if the behavior is legal (Patrick, 1994).

Matching Respondents

Table 8.2 summarizes by campus the number of surveys collected at each time. This table displays the total number of surveys collected and the residence hall occupancy rate. Approximately 60 percent of the residents participated in the first wave of the study. At VCU, participation at the second wave dropped off slightly, but on the comparison campus it fell by a factor of almost 50 percent. The follow-up instrument was scheduled to be administered in hall meetings ten weeks into the semester. At VCU, the RAs were required to hold hall meetings after ten weeks for a reason unrelated to this study. At the comparison campus, the follow-up hall

TABLE 8.2. SURVEY RETURNS: TOTAL RESPONDENTS AND MATCHED RESPONDENTS.

	VCU		*Comparison Campus*	
	Preintervention	**Postintervention**	**Preintervention**	**Postintervention**
Total number of surveys collected	765	683	585	334
Freshmen residence hall occupancy	1,171	1,158	1,053	1,049
Percentage of total population returning a survey	65.3	55.5	58.9	31.8
Matching Surveys	371		163	
Percentage of post-intervention surveys that could be matched	371 of 683 = 54.3%		163 of 334 = 48.8%	

meetings were encouraged but not required. This variation in procedures resulted in a lower number of advisors actually holding a meeting at the comparison campus. However, from the returns it appears that if the comparison site RAs did hold a hall meeting then the response rate was similar to that obtained at the intervention campus hall meetings.

About half of the postintervention surveys at each campus could be matched with preintervention responses, using the last four digits of the social security number. Responses were also checked for gender and race consistency. The mean age of both matched samples was eighteen. Other characteristics of the matched samples are in Table 8.3. The matched respondents were similar in gender distribution and ethnicity to the overall sample and to the university demographics at each site. Because of the gender difference in the two sites, further analysis by gender

TABLE 8.3. CHARACTERISTICS OF MATCHED RESPONDENTS AT PREINTERVENTION.

Variable	VCU Matched Sample (n = 371)		Comparison Matched Sample (n = 163)	
	f	%	f	%
Gender				
Male	103	27.8	72	44.2
Female	267	72.2	91	55.8
Missing	1	0.3	—	—
Race				
Caucasian	214	57.7	119	73.0
African American	98	26.4	20	12.3
Asian	30	8.1	9	5.5
Hispanic	14	3.8	3	1.8
Other	13	3.5	9	5.5
Missing	2	0.5	3	1.8
Major				
Undeclared	49	13.2	36	22.1
Art or performing arts	77	20.8	9	5.6
Biology, health, or phys ed	89	24.0	20	12.2
Other	153	41.7	97	59.5
Missing	3	0.8	1	0.6
Room policy				
Smoke-free	44	11.9	30	18.4
Smoking-optional	327	88.1	133	81.6

was undertaken (as described in Hancock, 2001). In general, controlling for gender did not affect our conclusions.

SNM Intervention and Control Group Results

The analysis examines the changes in individuals over time at each campus and the difference in these changes between campuses. The results discussed here include changes in perception, in tobacco-use rate, and in the cognitive predisposition of nonsmokers toward smoking. Two-tailed paired-sample t-tests were used to assess the statistical significance of changes in individuals over time. One-tailed independent-sample t-tests were used to test the difference between campuses, since the intervention was designed to cause changes consistent with reduced tobacco use. Cognitive predisposition was analyzed using chi-square. Table 8.4 shows the paired-sample and independent-sample t-test results.

Changes in Perception

We asked respondents to estimate what percentage of college students they thought had smoked cigarettes in the past month, forcing choices of 10 percent, 20 percent, 30 percent, and so on. Figure 8.3 graphically displays the pre- and post-SNM perception estimates. At the preintervention time, the distribution of responses is remarkably similar at both sites. Freshmen on both campuses at preintervention overestimated the percentage of college students who smoked. The mean perception at VCU was that 57.1 percent of college students smoked in the past month; at the comparison site it was 54.3 percent. The reality is that only 30–40 percent of college students had smoked in the past month.

Ten weeks later, the mean perception estimates at the comparison school showed no significant change (increasing from 54.3 percent to 55.9 percent). At VCU, the mean perception estimate became significantly more accurate as it decreased by more than 10 percent (from 57.1 percent to 46.9 percent). The sharp peak at 30 percent for the VCU sample is consistent with the primary media message (seven of ten college students don't smoke). The independent-sample t-test of difference in mean change between campuses was also statistically highly significant ($p < .0005$).

Perception change was the primary thrust of the SNM intervention. Common sense would lead one to expect that misperception might become even more pronounced as students leave high school and live at college. High school campuses prohibit all smoking by students, whereas smoking is legal at college and current indoor air policies tend to make smokers more visible. The results of this study indicate that respondents at both sites came to college with misperceptions leading them to overestimate tobacco use by college students. In the comparison sample,

TABLE 8.4. SUMMARY OF *t*-TEST STATISTICS: CHANGES IN SMOKING PERCEPTION AND BEHAVIOR.

Dependent Variables	VCU Matched Sample (n = 371)			Comparison Campus Matched Sample (n = 163)			
	Preintervention	Postintervention	Paired Samples	Preintervention	Postintervention	Paired Samples	Independent Samples
Mean perception of percentage who smoke	57.1	46.9		54.3	55.9		
t value			−9.23			1.25	
p value (two-tailed)			<.0005			.204	
t value							7.16
p value (one-tailed)							<.0005
Mean days smoked per month	6.81	7.47		7.36	8.94		
t value			2.07			3.23	
p value (two-tailed)			.039			.001	
t value							1.57
p value (one-tailed)							.055
Mean cigarettes smoked per day	2.91	2.95		2.47	3.33		
t value			.242			2.44	
p value (two-tailed)			.809			.061	
t value							2.07
p value (one-tailed)							.019
Mean cigarettes smoked per month	76.84	78.58		61.42	91.15		
t value			.355			2.80	
p value (two-tailed)			.723			.006	
t value							2.42
p value (one-tailed)							.008

FIGURE 8.3. PERCEPTIONS OF SMOKING BEHAVIOR BY CAMPUS.

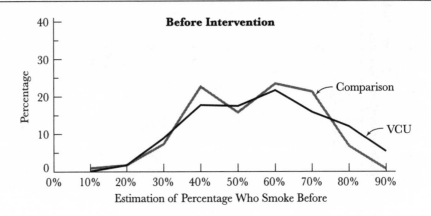

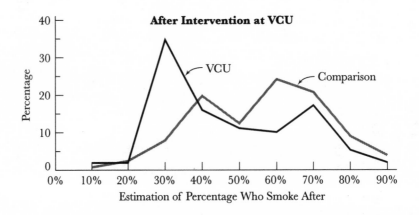

misperception persisted ten weeks into the semester and, as one might expect, even increased slightly. The VCU sample's perception estimates reflect a direction change opposite to what common sense suggests should happen. In other words, it appears that the SNM campaign was associated with VCU college freshmen's perceptions becoming more accurate despite the fact that they now lived on campus, where smoking was probably more visible than it was on their high school campus.

Change in Cigarette Use

Analysis of smoking behavior in young adults is complex and fraught with difficulties. The behavior of individuals as they move through the uptake continuum can be highly variable. For example, some students may try a puff or a cigarette and then never restart. Others may try smoking, stop, retry, stop, restart, and persist in this behavior for years. Still others rapidly escalate from first cigarette to heavy regular use in only a few weeks or months. Students also vary their use depending upon situations and stressors. Weekend or party smokers may smoke heavily for a day or two and then not smoke again for weeks. The process of quitting can also have an intermittent pattern. Students who are trying to quit may cut back or stop and then relapse partially or fully.

Since experimentation is common in young adults, researchers need to understand how crucial it is to clearly define and understand the terms used to describe smoking behavior. For example, in the past CDC studies have defined a "current smoker" as a respondent who has smoked even one cigarette in the thirty days preceding the survey. Experts caution against using just one variable, such as current smoking, to evaluate prevention interventions (Kovar, 2000).

In this study, cigarette smoking behavior was measured in three ways: (1) the number of days smoked in the past thirty days; (2) the number of cigarettes smoked on an "average" smoking day; and (3) the number of cigarettes smoked per month, calculated by multiplying the previous two answers. Because of the variation in smoking uptake patterns previously discussed, the decision was made to include both smokers and nonsmokers in the behavioral analysis. The sample was too small to conduct statistical analysis for only the new onset smokers or for quitters.

The paired t-statistics show that the mean number of days smoked per month increased in both samples but was higher in the comparison sample. The VCU sample increased use by about two-thirds of a day per month ($p = .039$) while the comparison sample increased use by roughly one and a half days per month ($p = .001$) The independent-sample t-test for difference in change between sites approached, but did not reach, the conventional limit for statistical significance ($p = .055$).

The mean number of cigarettes smoked per day when smoking did increase, though by only 0.04 in the VCU sample but by almost a full cigarette (0.87) per day in the comparison sample. The paired-sample t-test was not significant for VCU but approached statistical significance for the comparison sample ($p = .061$). The independent-sample t-test for difference in change between sites was significant ($p = .019$). The increase in cigarettes per day was significantly lower at VCU.

The number of cigarettes smoked per month by the VCU sample remained relatively stable, increasing by only 1.7 cigarettes. In the comparison sample, on the other hand, use increased by about a pack and a half (thirty cigarettes) per month. The latter change was statistically significant ($p = .006$). The difference in mean change between sites was highly significant ($p = .008$).

Smoking behavior remained relatively unchanged in the students exposed to SNM at VCU, while it increased substantially at the comparison site. This shows how important a comparison site is when evaluating a media campaign. The natural history of smoking in youth and young adults leads one to expect increased onset and rate of use in the teens and early twenties (U.S. DHHS, 2000). The expected increase in smoking behavior did not occur at VCU. In this study, the lack of increase in smoking behavior supports the belief that the SNM was effective, even though it was not associated with a decrease in tobacco use.

Cognitive Commitment to Nonsmoking

The concept of cognitive commitment to nonsmoking is an important one because nonsmokers vary in their susceptibility to future smoking. John Pierce and colleagues (1996), who work on evaluating the effectiveness of the tobacco prevention program in California, have studied this issue in depth. They have adapted three questions from the Teenage Attitudes and Practices Survey (TAPS) for use in the California Tobacco Survey (CTS). These three questions are given to nonsmokers. To be categorized as cognitively committed to nonsmoking, a youth has to choose the most definitely negative response to all three questions. If any less emphatic response is chosen, the student is categorized as cognitively vulnerable. These three questions were included as survey items for this study.

At preintervention, 58.4 percent of the VCU nonsmokers met the criterion of cognitive commitment to nonsmoking. At the comparison campus 53.5 percent met the criterion. Ten weeks later at the comparison campus, the percent of cognitively committed nonsmokers had decreased to 49.1 percent while at the same time the cognitive commitment of nonsmokers to nonsmoking at VCU increased to 63.5 percent. The difference in change of cognitive vulnerability to smoking between sites was statistically significant ($X^2 = 2.78$, $p = .047$). VCU nonsmokers were more likely to change toward becoming cognitively committed to nonsmoking, whereas the comparison campus nonsmokers were more likely to become cognitively vulnerable.

It is crucial to understand the concept of cognitive commitment to nonsmoking when assessing a tobacco prevention campaign. The vast majority of students are nonsmokers, and they need support to persist in their healthy behavior. Students don't decide just once if they are going to smoke and then never reconsider the issue. Many students need to rethink their commitment to nonsmoking each time they go to a party or sit outside with friends on a break between classes. Evaluation of SNM interventions should use survey questions related to cognitive commitment to assess their effectiveness and not simply focus on actual smoking behavior.

Study Implications and Work in Progress

The findings of this study are consistent with the theoretical work of Perkins and Berkowitz (1986) and the applied research of Haines (1996). As expected, this study documented that a difference exists between college students' perceptions of the smoking rate and the actual smoking rate. This study has further demonstrated that once the "true" norms were advertised through an SNM campaign, perception became more accurate. In addition, this study supports use of SNM in decreasing cigarette-smoking behavior. Finally, this study demonstrated that a SNM campaign was associated with increasing the number of nonsmokers who were cognitively committed to nonsmoking.

Even without the use of a comparison site, the association of healthier changes in individuals could be found related to perception and cognitive predisposition. However, documenting a positive impact on actual smoking behavior in such a short time span would have been jeopardized if a comparison site had not been used. Without a comparison campus, the lack of change in the smoking rate at the intervention site would have been more difficult to interpret as beneficial.

Results suggest that some students resist change in perception. Even though 94 percent recalled seeing the campaign, not all students changed their misperceptions. Further study is needed to discern what type of student is resistant to correction of norms about tobacco. Some interesting qualitative data were uncovered in the intercept survey at VCU. On the one hand, although many nonsmoking freshmen knew the accurate campaign statistics, they expressed the opinion that the numbers were not believable. On the other hand, several of the smoking students commented that they found the statistics entirely believable because when they tried to "bum a light or a cigarette" most students didn't have one.

This study has several limitations. Selection bias is a threat to validity in this study given nonrandom sampling. Increased participation, especially at the second wave at the comparison school, would have increased the credibility of our findings. Future studies of this type should explore better methods of matching respondents to the preintervention and postintervention surveys. This study was too small to assess the effect of the intervention on quit attempts, although the data do suggest that regular smokers tended to moderate their use. The effect of an SNM campaign on students who are addicted to tobacco is an issue left in question and one that needs further study.

VCU has since continued its efforts in nonsmoking social norms marketing. The market saturation survey in the fall of 1999 indicated that the least expensive media had the greatest recall. So, in the fall of 2000, the SNM campaign was continued at VCU using only the black-and-white posters and table tents. Because of limited staffing and time, no comparison group was used. Instead of collecting data through the residence halls, a freshman orientation class (VCU 101) was used to gather information. These freshmen completed the same thirty-three-item instrument used in the previous study. The first wave of data was collected during the first week of class and the second during the tenth week of class. As before, the survey was anonymous, with matching accomplished using the last four digits of the social security number. The matching process produced a sample of 310 students.

Initially, the mean smoking perception was that 55.1 percent of college students had smoked in the past month. After the intervention, this estimate became more accurate, falling to 45.7 percent ($p < .0005$). This finding is almost identical to the perception change in fall 1999 with the campaign that cost almost $5,000. The intervention in the fall of 2000 cost less than $300. The behavior change in this sample was also almost identical to what we found in 1999. The smoking rate did not increase and in fact held amazingly constant.

A related campaign is currently under way to make nonsmokers more visible. Nonsmoking and ex-smoking students have agreed to share their stories about why they are nonsmokers in order to help to break down the misperception that "everybody smokes" (this information has been published at www.smokefreeVCU.org). A new poster campaign has been developed using qualitative data from focus groups and intercept surveys; see the optical illusion campaign at the Website.

It is difficult to say from our small samples what impact SNM has on cessation. The intervention did seem to keep smokers from increasing their smoking behavior. Anecdotally, however, we have noted a large increase in students seeking cessation services at the university's Student Health Clinic. More than 140 VCU students were given "Quit Kits" in the fall semester of 2001. Part of this may be due to all of our SNM media advertising where to obtain cessation services. It may also be the case that smokers are becoming more aware of how nonnormative their behavior is. Although our studies are small and have some limitations, they also indicate that SNM may be quite a cost-effective tool at the local level.

References

Centers for Disease Control and Prevention (CDC). Youth Risk Behavior Surveillance: National College Health Risk Behavior Survey. *Morbidity and Mortality Weekly Report*, 1997, *46*(SS-6), 1–54.

Chassin, L., Presson, C. C., and Sherman, S. J. "Social-Psychological Antecedents and Consequences of Adolescent Tobacco Use." In J. L. Wallander and L. J. Siegel (eds.), *Adolescent Health Problems: Behavioral Perspectives*. New York: Guilford Press, 1995.

Choi, W. S., and others. "Which Adolescent Experimenters Progress to Established Smoking in the United States?" *American Journal of Preventive Medicine*, 1997, *13*(5), 385–391.

Gilder, P., and others. "Challenging the Collegiate Rite of Passage: A Campus-Wide Social Marketing Media Campaign to Reduce Binge Drinking." *Journal of Drug Education*, 2001, *31*(2), 207–220.

Haines, M. P. *A Social Norms Approach to Preventing Binge Drinking at Colleges and Universities.* (Department of Education ED/OPE/96–18.) Newton, Mass.: Higher Education Center for Alcohol and Other Drug Prevention, 1996.

Haines, M. P., and Spear, S. F. "Changing the Perception of the Norm: A Strategy to Decrease Binge Drinking Among College Students." *Journal of American College Health*, 1996, *45*(11), 134–140.

Hancock, L. C. "Perceptions of Cigarette Smoking and Tobacco Reduction in College Students: A Social Norms Marketing Intervention." Unpublished doctoral dissertation, School of Education, Virginia Commonwealth University, 2001.

Hansen, W. B., and Graham J. W. "Preventing Alcohol, Marijuana and Cigarette Use Among Adolescents: Peer Pressure Training Versus Establishing Conservative Norms." *Preventive Medicine*, 1991, *20*, 414–430.

Johnston, L. D., O'Malley, P. M, and Bachman, J. G. *Monitoring the Future: National Survey Results on Drug Use, 1975–2001.* (NIH publication no. 02-5107.) Bethesda, Md.: National Institute on Drug Abuse, 2002.

Kessler, D. A. "Nicotine Addiction: A Pediatric Disease." *Journal of Pediatrics*, 1997, *130*, 518–523.

Kovar, M. G. "Four Million Adolescents Smoke: Or Do They?" *Chance*, 2000, *12*(2), 10–14.

Males, M. *Smoked: Why Joe Camel Is Still Smiling.* Monroe, Maine: Common Courage Press, 1999.

Patrick, D. L, and others. "The Validity of Self-Reported Smoking: A Review and Meta-Analysis." *American Journal of Public Health*, 1994, *84*(7), 1086–1093.

Perkins H. W., and Berkowitz, A. D. "Perceiving the Community Norms of Alcohol Use Among Students: Some Research Implications for Campus Alcohol Education Programming." *International Journal of Addictions*, 1986, *2*, 961–976.

Perkins, H. W., and others. "Misperceptions of the Norms for the Frequency of Alcohol and Other Drug Use on College Campuses." *Journal of American College Health*, 1999, *47*(5), 253–258.

Pierce, J. P., and others. "Validation of Susceptibility as a Predictor of Which Adolescents Take up Smoking in the United States." *Health Psychology*, 1996, *15*, 355–361.

Redmond, W. H. "Product Disadoption: Quitting Smoking as a Diffusion Process." *Journal of Public Policy Market* 1999, *15*, 87–97.

Rigotti, N. A., Lee, J. E., and Wechsler, H. "U.S. College Students Use of Tobacco Products: Results of a National Survey." *Journal of the American Medical Association*, 2000, *284*(6), 699–705.

Rogers, E. M. *Diffusion of Innovations* (4th ed.). New York: Free Press, 1995.

Sussman, S., and others. "Adolescent Nonsmokers, Triers and Regular Smokers' Estimates of Cigarette Smoking Prevalence: When Do Overestimations Occur and by Whom?" *Journal of Applied Social Psychology*, 1988, *18*(7), 537–551.

U.S. Department of Health and Human Services (U.S. DHHS). *Reducing Tobacco Use: A Report of the Surgeon General.* (S/N 017–001–00544–4.) Atlanta: Office of Smoking and Health, Centers for Disease Control and Prevention, 2000.

Wechsler, H., Rigotti, N. A., Gledhill-Hoyt, J., and Lee, H. "Increased Levels of Cigarette Use Among College Students: A Cause for National Concern." *Journal of the American Medical Association*, 1998, *280*(19), 1673–1678.

Wechsler, H., and others. "College Smoking Policies and Smoking Cessation Programs: Results of a Survey of College Health Center Directors." *American Journal of College Health*, 2001, *49*(3), 205–211.

Zimmerman, R. *Social Marketing Strategies for Campus Prevention of Alcohol and Other Drug Problems.* Newton, Mass.: Higher Education Center for Alcohol and Other Drug Prevention, 1997.

CHAPTER NINE

A SOCIAL NORMS APPROACH TO BUILDING CAMPUS SUPPORT FOR POLICY CHANGE

William DeJong, Ph.D.

The University Hill section of Boulder, Colorado, was the scene of two successive nights of student riots in early May 1997 as hundreds of inebriated students from the University of Colorado (CU) smashed windows, set fires, and threw rocks and bottles at police. Several people were injured, while local businesses suffered more than $100,000 in property damage. Boulder police arrested about thirty-five people, including fourteen CU students (McPhee, 1997).

The Boulder riots occurred after a two-year effort by city and university officials to enforce tighter rules against student drinking. In 1995, Boulder police cracked down on underage drinking at fraternity houses. As a self-defensive measure, the fraternities voted to ban alcohol from their premises but later revoked

I am grateful to several colleagues for their helpful comments on earlier versions of this chapter: Tom Colthurst, Joel Epstein, Patricia Fabiano, Michael Haines, Koreen Johannessen, Jeff Linkenbach, Beverly Mills-Novoa, Rich Lucey, and H. Wesley Perkins. I also thank Linda Langford and John Pryor for their help in conducting the student survey reported here. Preparation of this article was supported by U.S. Department of Education contract ED-99-CO-0094 to Education Development Center, Inc. The opinions expressed here are those of the author and do not necessarily reflect the official position of the U.S. Department of Education.

the ban after deciding it was not working. In 1996, university officials banned beer at football games, thus ending a long-standing tradition (Bormann and Stone, 2001). Another new policy allowed university officials to discipline a student for breaking the law off campus.

This get-tough approach provoked the idea among some CU students that they were being treated "as a nuisance rather than as valued members of the community," according to a postriot statement issued by the CU Student Union (McPhee, 1997). Despite widespread public disapproval, some students remained defiant, justifying the riots as a "protest."

CU officials harbored no doubts they were on the right track with their tougher stance against student drinking. The point of the stricter policies was to create a safer campus community. CU officials recognized that students who abuse alcohol hurt not only themselves but those around them, even those who do not engage in heavy drinking. Even so, CU officials still had to wonder what they could have done differently to avoid a violent student protest against the new policies. Students themselves pointed to the lack of student involvement in either fact finding or the policy development process.

In recent years, student riots have occurred on other campuses as well, among them Michigan State University, Ohio University, and Pennsylvania State University. Officials from these schools have responded in ways similar to their colleagues at the University of Colorado. On the one hand, these officials remain firm about the need for tougher measures to control alcohol problems, which the alcohol-fueled riots only served to reinforce. On the other hand, these officials still second-guess whether those new policies could have been introduced differently to avoid student overreaction.

This is an important issue. Witnessing these events on other campuses, officials at some schools may now hesitate to act for fear of provoking strong student protests or even riots.

In this chapter, I explore how college presidents and other top administrators can best present the case for new policies and programs to stem student alcohol problems. I begin by reviewing the environmental approach to prevention, which calls for new policies to change the campus and community environment in which students make decisions about alcohol consumption. Next, I consider how college presidents and other top administrators usually try to build a climate of support for new policies and the pitfalls of those traditional approaches. I then outline an alternative strategy, which is grounded in the social norms approach. I conclude with general recommendations for how college officials can most effectively build student support for environmental change strategies, including policy change.

Environmental Management

The environmental management framework expands the range of strategies for alcohol and other drug (AOD) prevention in higher education to include policy change at the institutional, community, state, and federal levels. Research has shown that community coalitions can affect policy change to reduce alcohol consumption (Hingson and Howland, 2002). What is new is application of this strategy to reduce alcohol problems in higher education.

Application of this approach first requires thoughtful analysis of the physical, social, economic, and legal environment that affects substance use. With that assessment in hand, college officials, working both on campus and in partnership with others in the community, can give shape to new policies and programs that change the environment, thereby reducing the incidence of heavy drinking and the harm it causes (DeJong and Langford, 2002).

The need for environmental change is evident when we consider the types of mixed messages about heavy alcohol consumption now abundant in college communities:

- Many liquor stores, bars, and Greek houses fail to check for proof-of-age identification.
- Local bars and restaurants offer "happy hours" and other low-price promotions or serve intoxicated patrons.
- On-campus advertising for beer and other alcoholic beverages "normalizes" heavy alcohol consumption.
- With too few alcohol-free social and recreational options, heavy drinking can become the default option for students who seek spontaneous entertainment.
- Some faculty make minimal demands on students and take little interest in their well-being.
- Lax enforcement of campus regulations, local ordinances, or state and federal law teaches students to disregard the law.
- A general failure to intervene with students who are in trouble with alcohol creates the impression that the college is indifferent to alcohol-related problems.

Until these mixed messages are changed, college officials face an uphill battle in reducing alcohol consumption and the harm it can cause.

On campus, an AOD task force should conduct a broad-based examination of the college environment, looking not only at AOD-related policies and programs but also at the academic program, the academic calendar, and the entire college infrastructure. The objective is to identify key points of leverage—that is, ways in which the environment can be changed to clarify the school's expectations for its students, better integrate students into the intellectual life of the school, change student norms away from alcohol and other drug use, or make it easier to identify students in trouble with substance use.

Campus-Community Coalitions

Work in the surrounding community can be best accomplished through a campus and community coalition. Community mobilization, involving a mix of civic, religious, and governmental agencies, is widely recognized as a key to successful prevention of alcohol and other drug problems (Walter, 1997). Essential to making community-based programming work is the formation of coalitions and interagency linkages that lead to a coordinated approach, with adequate planning and a clear division of responsibility among coalition members. Where such programs are lacking, higher education officials, especially college and university presidents, can take the lead in forming these citizen-led coalitions and moving them toward an environmental approach to prevention (Presidents Leadership Group, 1997). The chief focus of a campus-community coalition should be to curtail youths' access to alcohol and to eliminate irresponsible alcohol sales and marketing practices by local bars, restaurants, and liquor outlets.

An association of colleges and universities can be the organizational mechanism for college presidents and other top administrators to speak out on matters of state or federal policy. There are several potentially helpful laws and regulations that can be considered, notably a distinctive and tamper-proof license for drivers under age twenty-one; increased penalties for illegal service to minors; prohibition of happy hours and other reduced-price promotions; restricted hours for alcohol sales; reduced density of retail outlets; and increasing the excise tax rate on alcohol (DeJong and Langenbahn, 1996; Toomey and Wagenaar, 2002).

The key to developing and implementing new policies is a participatory process that includes all major sectors of the campus and community, including students. College presidents and other top administrators on many campuses have grappled with the problem of how to involve students as real partners in this process. Which student leaders should be involved? How should they be selected? What is a meaningful role for them to play? These are difficult questions. What is self-evident, however, is that the participation of any group of student leaders will not be accepted by the student body at large absent broad student support for policy change. The paramount question, then, is how such support can be generated.

Focusing on the Severity of the Problem

Whatever the issue, getting public attention and building support for policy change usually begins with a presentation of facts that underscore the nature and scope of the problem. Through experience, policy advocates have learned that statistics alone are usually insufficient to move the public. One option is to repackage statistical information in a form that is attention-getting, newsworthy, and memorable, a technique called "creative epidemiology" or "social math." Another option is to convey the seriousness of the problem through the story of a single individual, preferably one whose plight dramatizes the need for action (Wallack, Dorfman, Jernigan, and Themba, 1993).

Policy advocates concerned about the problem of student drinking have tried all of these strategies. Biennial reports from the Harvard College Alcohol Survey (CAS) have received a great deal of national and campus attention. Most often, news accounts of this work focus on the reported incidence of so-called binge drinking. For men, this has been defined as having five or more drinks in a row, and for women as having four or more drinks in a row. According to the 2001 Harvard survey, 44.4 percent of undergraduate students at four-year institutions engaged in binge drinking during the two weeks prior to the survey (Wechsler and others, 2002). Press accounts of this survey and earlier ones at Harvard usually recite these findings with great alarm. Similarly, college presidents and other top administrators, wishing to make the case for new policies, have pointed to the Harvard surveys or have cited comparable findings from their own campus surveys.

Stories that illustrate the dangers of alcohol have emerged as a common feature of campus educational programs. For years, college students died from alcohol-related causes with little public notice. That changed in 1997 with the alcohol-poisoning deaths of Benjamin Wynne at Louisiana State University and Scott Krueger at the Massachusetts Institute of Technology. Both deaths made national headlines. These cases did not signal that the problem was suddenly worse than it had been, because that is not the case. Yet this was the impression created by suddenly interested news media. Since that time, college presidents and other top administrators have cited these students' deaths in their messages to several constituencies, including students, not only to sound a word of warning but also to build the case for new policies and programs for dealing with student alcohol problems.

Student Reactions

College presidents, administrators, and faculty might find these presentations compelling and highly motivating, but can we expect students to be moved by them? We first need to understand that, for the most part, the standard educational messages are being targeted to heavy drinkers, an approach consistent with the common belief that arming students with good information will enable them to make better choices about alcohol consumption. Unfortunately, only a relatively small number of college students absorb this information and make a decision to reduce their alcohol consumption. It is important to understand why this is the case.

College administrators and prevention educators seem to believe that the best way to motivate students to change their alcohol consumption is to give them hard-hitting, even scary factual information about the negative consequences of drinking. Such appeals have long been a staple of public service announcements on substance abuse, alcohol-impaired driving, AIDS and other sexually transmitted diseases, and a range of other social issues. In general, however, scare tactics do not work and can even backfire. Most health communications experts have concluded from the body of available research that fear-based campaigns, despite their intuitive appeal, are extremely difficult to execute, rarely succeed, and may be counterproductive (DeJong and Winsten, 1998; Hale and Dillard, 1995).

Students involved in heavy drinking can easily distance themselves from information about the negative consequences of drinking, no matter how compelling it might appear to be. Regarding long-term consequences, most young people take good health for granted, and many view the dire, long-term consequences of their behavior as too distant and too unlikely to be of concern to them. Moreover, many young people do not understand the probabilistic nature of risk, and this uncertainty is an opening for denial. Finally, many young people overestimate their own capacity to change their behavior before long-term consequences are an issue (DeJong and Winsten, 1998).

Regarding short-term consequences, students involved in heavy drinking already know that alcohol can lead to serious injury and death. Today's students have been taught this from their earliest years in elementary school. As noted before, those lessons have been underscored by recent national headlines. Today's students also know from their own experience that these dire consequences, though common enough to be noteworthy, are still rare, especially when considered against the fact that 80.7 percent of college students consume alcohol (Wechsler and others, 2002).

When students who drink heavily learn about a peer who has died or suffered a serious injury, they are likely to find fault in that individual's particular actions, rather than see those consequences as the predictable result of heavy alcohol consumption. The questions students raise reveal a strong desire to avoid generalizing beyond the particular case at hand. Why did Scott Krueger allow himself to be bullied into drinking so much alcohol? How could Benjamin Wynne not know that "funneling" hard liquor was potentially lethal? By blaming the victim, students invested in heavy drinking can put aside the possibility of harm coming their way (Ryan, 1976).

This same mind-set can affect how students react to public policy proposals. Logically, if one believes that injury, death, or other problems due to alcohol consumption are rare events, and if one believes there are special factors at work in each case to explain what happened, then there would appear to be no legitimate basis for supporting new policies or toughened enforcement. By extension, it would seem unfair that the irresponsible actions of a few should lead to policies that impose new restrictions on everyone.

This is the fundamental debate at the center of many public health controversies: Should prevention efforts be targeted to those at greatest risk, or should they be applied instead to the population as a whole (Rose, 1992)? In the case of alcohol, the research literature suggests that the most effective means of reducing alcohol-related problems is to reduce average alcohol consumption in the general population (Edwards and others, 1994). Population-based strategies target all drinkers through environmental change—not just alcoholics and problem drinkers, but even moderate drinkers who may drink excessively only on occasional. Few college administrators, and even fewer students, know this research literature, a fact that impedes progress toward a population-based prevention strategy, including policy change.

Reinforcing the Misperception of the Norm

Trying to build student support for policy change by focusing on the nature and scope of the problem can present other pitfalls. Whether and how heavily students drink partly depends on their perception of campus drinking norms (Perkins, 1997). News accounts and other messages about student drinking that are designed to underscore the seriousness of the problem can have the unintended consequence of reinforcing the misperception that heavy drinking is the norm. Ironically, the very information that is designed to motivate corrective action may instead bolster a set of beliefs that make the problem more resistant to change. A related concern is that a focus on "bad news" can lead to a myopic dismissal of "good news" that could potentially be used to denormalize heavy alcohol consumption or to reinforce positive trends in student behavior that are already under way, which could then stimulate even further positive change.

This problem is evident in news coverage of alcohol problems on campus. According to the nation's newspapers, the 1997 Harvard student survey was bad news for America's colleges and universities. "Binge Drinking on Campus Rising," read the *Boston Globe* headline on September 11. "'Drunk 101' Still the Norm for College Students," said the Associated Press. "Survey Shows Campus Drinking Crackdown Had Little Effect," added CNN in its Website report (DeJong, 1998). Actually, the results of the study were more complex. Although the binge drinking rate in 1993 was 44.1 percent, it was 42.7 percent in 1997—not a meaningful drop, but certainly no increase. It was also true, unfortunately, that the percentage of frequent binge drinkers (those who drink at this level three or more times in a two-week period) increased slightly, from 19.5 percent in 1993 to 20.7 percent in 1997 (Wechsler and others, 1998).

The Harvard study also had two pieces of good news that the press largely ignored. First, the survey found that 19.0 percent of college students abstained from drinking in 1997, up from 15.6 percent in 1993, a nearly 22 percent increase. Second, the so-called binge drinking rate decreased at 64 of the 116 colleges participating in both surveys, while 44 saw an increase and 8 stayed the same. Nine schools saw a statistically significant decrease, while only 3 saw a statistically significant increase (Wechsler and others, 1998). Also noteworthy is that both the 1993 and 1997 surveys found that the majority of college students had not consumed alcohol heavily during the two weeks prior to the survey. All of these facts mean that the national headlines could just as easily read "Proportion of College Students Who Abstain from Alcohol Jumps 22 Percent" or "'Responsibility 101' Still the Norm for College Students."

An additional issue is that the Harvard survey definition of binge drinking magnifies an exaggerated view of the problem. Critics have noted that the definition does not specify a time period over which the alcohol is consumed on a single occasion. Four or five drinks "in a row" over a period of several hours does not conform to the popular notion of a binge, or even to the clinical definition (DeJong, 2001; Schuckit, 1998). Total daily alcohol consumption is a legitimate concern, but with a focus on college students the more acute worry is whether students are drinking at a rate that can lead to impairment or, in more dramatic instances, severe alcohol poisoning (Perkins, DeJong, and Linkenbach, 2001).

Focusing on Positive Social Norms

Researchers have found that whatever the true level of heavy drinking is on campus, college students tend to greatly overestimate the percentage of their peers who engage in dangerous alcohol consumption. In many instances, the disparity between reality and perception is enormous (Perkins and others, 1999). This pattern of misperception can have critical repercussions. If college students believe that most students drink heavily, then the rate of heavy drinking will be sustained or may even rise in response (Perkins, 1997).

As explained elsewhere in this volume, prevention experts have demonstrated that this dynamic can be turned around through a campus-based media campaign that informs students about how much drinking is really going on, as opposed to what they think is the case (DeJong and Linkenbach, 1999). Another way to think about a social norms marketing campaign is that it puts students, faculty, and administrators in touch with the positive social norms embraced by the majority of students on campus.

A critical point here is that policy reforms cannot go too far beyond the existing social norms without provoking resistance. It follows, then, that support for policy change is less forthcoming if students have an exaggerated view of current norms regarding alcohol. Later—once students are made to realize that the majority of their peers are already practicing safe, moderate behavior—college administrators can more easily enlist the student support they need to advance policy reforms.

This basic outline is consistent with the natural progression of most public health campaigns (Chin and Benne, 1976). Early on, there is typically a focus on providing the public with information about the problem, which is intended to help people act as individuals to protect their health. The common experience is that some people (but usually far from all) respond to this information by making changes in their behavior.

The success of these "early adopters" can then become the basis for convincing still others. Once a critical mass of people are taking the necessary steps to protect their health, the typical public health campaign then goes into a second phase, when normative pressures are brought to bear. In essence, the smart thing to do becomes the right thing to do. Additional people respond to these normative pressures and change their behavior.

Over time, a group of community leaders, supported by a growing majority, begin to focus on the late adopters who have failed to change their behavior. It is at this point that the typical public health campaign goes into its third and final phase, when policies are implemented and enforced to compel this resistant minority to change their unhealthy or dangerous behavior. In an important sense, the new policies represent an affirmation of the majority's values and behavioral norms.

The U.S. antismoking campaign, among others, has followed this sequence (DeJong and Winsten, 1998). First, in 1964, the Surgeon General's widely publicized report alerted the public to the health dangers of smoking. Over time, as more and more smokers quit, normative pressure came into play. What had once been viewed as a sexy, glamorous habit now was seen as a sign of poor self-discipline. Next, growing concerns about the financial burden to society caused by smoking, coupled with new awareness of the dangers of secondhand smoke, led to public support for excise taxes on tobacco, restrictions on tobacco advertising, and policies to ban smoking in public places.

In sum, the majority of students are responsible in their use of alcohol yet are still negatively affected by the minority of students who choose to drink irresponsibly. Greater awareness of this basic truth can then set the stage for pursuing policy reforms that change the campus and community environment driving alcohol consumption.

Misperception of Policy Support

This analysis makes clear that new policies to combat student alcohol problems can be more quickly and effectively enacted if the campus community sees those policies as a means of affirming its values. As noted, this is one reason it is vital to provide students, faculty, and administrators with accurate feedback about the true level of student drinking. Absent this information, the community is not fully aware of the positive values and behavioral norms that are in effect.

Equally critical is to provide evidence of substantial support for new policies that are consonant with those values and norms. Misperception is likely to come into play here, too. If people have an exaggerated view of how many students are engaged in heavy drinking, then it follows that they are also likely to greatly underestimate the level of student support that exists for policy reform.

Evidence on this point comes from a recent Website-based student survey conducted at Dartmouth College. The survey instrument was sent via electronic mail to 1,200 randomly selected undergraduates. A total of 496 students completed the survey, for a response rate of 41.3 percent. The survey asked students to what extent they supported or opposed each of several policies and procedures designed to reduce student alcohol problems and underage drinking. The survey also asked to what extent they thought other students at their institution supported or opposed those options.

The pattern of results was clear (see Table 9.1). Whatever percentage of students indicated support for a policy, a smaller percentage reported that other students also supported it. For example, 72.6 percent of the students favored the current prohibition against kegs in residence halls, yet only 34.0 percent stated that they thought other students support this policy. Stated differently, 66.0 percent misperceived the normative opinion of their peers. Similarly, a majority of 54.3 percent supported using stricter disciplinary sanctions for repeated violations of campus alcohol policies, yet only 25.7 percent indicated other students support this policy. In this case, 74.3 percent were out of touch with the majority's preference. Finally, 94.0 percent supported using stricter disciplinary sanctions for students who engage in alcohol-related violence. In this case, 72.3 percent said that other students would support this policy. This means that 27.7 percent did not know the majority's preference, a still sizeable percentage.

Obviously, not all policy proposals receive majority backing, and the level of actual support for any particular option varies from campus to campus. Nevertheless, college administrators everywhere should be able to count on having a

TABLE 9.1. SELF-SUPPORT VERSUS PERCEIVED OTHER STUDENT SUPPORT FOR ALCOHOL CONTROL POLICIES (DARTMOUTH COLLEGE, 1999).

Alcohol Control Policy	Student Support	
	Self[a] (Percentage)	Others[b] (Percentage)
Alcohol-free residence halls		
Offer alcohol-free residence halls	95.1	87.7
Make all residences on campus alcohol-free	10.0	2.3
Reduction in alcohol availability		
Prohibit kegs in residence halls	72.6	34.0
Enforce legal age restrictions on alcohol use	31.7	13.4
Prohibit delivery of alcohol to campus	12.0	3.8
Prohibit kegs in fraternities and sororities	8.8	1.0
Make all Greek houses on campus alcohol-free	5.1	0.0
Application of stricter penalties		
Use stricter disciplinary sanctions for students who engage in alcohol-related violence	94.0	72.3
Use stricter disciplinary sanctions for students who repeatedly violate campus alcohol policies	54.3	25.7
Apply stricter penalties for use of false ID to purchase alcohol illegally	45.2	15.9
Use suspension or expulsion as a sanction for alcohol-related policy violations	32.6	13.9
Use stricter disciplinary sanctions for violation of underage laws at room parties	20.9	7.7
Restrictions on advertising and promotion		
Restrict advertising that promotes alcohol consumption at parties or events	32.0	15.0
Eliminate "happy hours" and other low-price alcohol promotions targeted to college students	12.8	3.8
Local and state public policy		
Increase taxes on alcohol to help pay for programs to prevent minors from drinking	44.9	20.9
Conduct sting undercover operations at liquor stores to increase compliance with underage laws	32.9	9.2
Conduct sting undercover operations at bars and restaurants to increase compliance with legal age restrictions on alcohol use	21.2	7.5
Limit the number of alcohol outlets near campus	12.9	2.9

Notes: [a]Percentage of survey respondents (n = 496) indicating support (question: "To what extent do you support or oppose the following possible policies or procedures?"; response options: "strongly support," "support," "oppose," or "strongly oppose")

[b]Percentage of survey respondents (n = 496) indicating other students' support (question: "To what extent do you think other students at your institution support or oppose the following possible policies or procedures?"; response options: "strongly support," "support," "oppose," or "strongly oppose")

majority of students who will support at least some of the policies being considered. The 2001 Harvard survey showed that 54.7 percent of undergraduate students nationwide supported efforts at their college to "crack down on underage drinking" (Wechsler, Lee, Nelson, and Kuo, 2000). Similarly, an earlier Harvard survey revealed there is widespread student support for various measures to reduce heavy drinking, including strict enforcement of the rules (65 percent), prohibiting kegs on campus (60 percent), cracking down on Greek organizations (60 percent), and banning on-campus advertisements from local alcohol outlets (52 percent; Wechsler, Nelson, and Weitzman, 2000).

Moving forward, then, the key is for college officials to identify where student support for stricter policies exists and to correct any misperception about that support. In this context, administrators can more successfully advance their policy agenda. Over time, as the new policies take hold and the rate of heavy drinking declines, student support may next be found for even tougher policies that protect the rights of the majority to a safe campus and reaffirm the campus community's positive values.

I am not suggesting that college administrators should never install a policy that a majority of students does not want. Clearly, there is always the possibility of competing political or financial concerns that may dictate that choice. Rather, my point is that whenever they can do so, administrators should consider working from the basis of what students themselves support. There is far more support for tougher policies and stricter enforcement than most college administrators realize.

Secondary Effects of Heavy Drinking

Another type of information useful in building the case for policy change concerns the secondary effects of heavy drinking—that is, the negative consequences students experience as a result of other students' misuse of alcohol. The Harvard surveys have found that a majority of college students experiences these consequences, which include interrupted study and sleep; having to take care of a drunken student; being insulted or humiliated; having a serious argument or quarrel; having property damaged; unwanted sexual advances; being pushed, hit, or assaulted; and being a victim of sexual assault or date rape (Wechsler and others, 1998). In 2001, 55.2 percent of abstainers and nonheavy drinkers who lived in a residence hall, fraternity, or sorority experienced two or more such secondary effects (Wechsler and others, 2002).

These findings underscore the need for college presidents and other top administrators to give greater emphasis to stemming student alcohol consumption and fostering a safe campus environment. Defenders of the status quo might argue that most students who drink heavily, if left alone, will learn from their mistakes. In the meantime, however, the majority of students who drink in moderation or abstain must fend for themselves against the inconsiderate, insulting, intimidating, and criminal behavior of the students around them who engage in irresponsible heavy drinking. What gave new momentum to the antitobacco movement was the realization that secondhand smoke puts nonsmokers at risk. What can give momentum to the growing movement for new policies to fight student misuse of alcohol is awareness that heavy drinking by a minority of students also hurts the majority of students who themselves are not abusive drinkers.

Developing Campus Support for Policy Change

What I have outlined here can be thought of as a social norms approach to building campus support for policy change. The inclination of college students to exaggerate the incidence of heavy drinking among their peers can feed their belief that stricter alcohol control policies are unreasonable and unfair. As a corollary, this misperception also results in students (and others on campus) underestimating the true level of student support for new policies and stricter enforcement. In some cases, a majority of students will support certain policy or enforcement options yet believe that only a small minority of students shares their opinion.

Advancing a policy agenda can go more smoothly if efforts are made to correct misperceptions of drinking norms, reinforce the positive values held by the majority of students, and demonstrate majority student support for certain reforms. Absent these efforts, students are more likely to think that most of their peers oppose rather than support those reforms, which in turn may provoke noncompliance and even open defiance.

This analysis suggests specific actions that college presidents and other top administrators can take to build student support for policy change.

First, administrators should collect and report survey data that correct misperceptions of student drinking norms. As noted, students tend to hold an exaggerated view of how much other students are drinking. Correcting misperceptions can have a positive effect on behavior, both directly and by helping build support for policy changes that reflect the health-protective values and behavioral norms of the majority.

Second, administrators should publicize positive trends to help reinforce further changes in behavioral norms. A narrow focus on the severity of student alcohol problems often causes good news to become obscured or disregarded. In fact, there are positive changes under way on many campuses. Letting students know this helps strengthen the resolve of abstainers and moderate drinkers to stay that course, while also motivating still other students to moderate their alcohol consumption.

Third, college administrators should define the problem in a way that motivates behavior change. This means focusing on the secondary effects of heavy drinking rather than the incidence of negative consequences experienced by the drinkers themselves. When describing the problem in this way, administrators should take care to avoid inadvertently reinforcing misperceptions of student drinking norms (DeJong and Linkenbach, 1999).

Fourth, coupled with a sincere effort to give students a meaningful role in reviewing, developing, and implementing campus policies, administrators should collect information on student opinion about various policy options. If a majority of students favors certain alcohol control measures, that fact should be made known to the community. It is vital to correct misperceptions about the level of support, which is commonly assumed to be less than it actually is.

Fifth, whenever feasible, administrators should consider implementing a program of environmental change by starting with those policies that enjoy majority student support. When students know that the new policies are consonant with the values and behavioral norms of the community, protests from opponents are less likely, and if they occur they can be more easily contained.

Finding the Right Balance

Will this social norms approach to building campus support for policy change work on every campus? No. On some campuses, administrators find only tepid student support for the kind of policy reform needed to reduce heavy drinking. Adhering to student preferences is the safer route in terms of avoiding open conflict, but if followed strictly this may lead to only slow, evolutionary change in student behavior. A slow rate of change may not satisfy administrators, faculty, parents, private donors, legislators, and other key constituencies (including many students). In the short run, it may also fail to satisfy the legal requirement that institutions of higher education take reasonable protective measures to guard against foreseeable hazards and risks in the school environment (DeJong and Langenbahn, 1996).

When necessary, then, higher education administrators must also be prepared to move forward even if most students stand opposed. This prospect is made somewhat easier by the fact that today's students will eventually graduate and leave campus, while tomorrow's students will have applied to a school being fully aware of its policies. But this only lessens the difficulty; it does not eliminate it.

In essence, this is the burden of college leadership: to negotiate the difference between what the majority of students might prefer and what college presidents and other administrators believe is the right thing to do. Either choice can lead to criticism. Leaders who do only what the majority of students want run the risk of failing to do what is necessary. Leaders who ignore the wishes of the majority run the risk of open protest and defiance.

There is no formula for how to find the right balance, which depends on the history of the institution, the exact views of competing constituencies, outside pressures, and many other factors. Given this complexity, presidents and other top administrators must continue to foster a campus environment where the majority of responsible students who want policy reform and stricter enforcement of the rules are emboldened to speak out and be heard. This can happen more easily if a social norms marketing campaign is in place to dispel the myths about drinking on campus and replace them with the facts.

References

Bormann, C. A., and Stone, M. H. "The Effects of Eliminating Alcohol in a College Stadium: The Folsom Field Beer Ban." *Journal of American College Health*, 2001, *50*, 81–88.

Chin, R., and Benne, K. K. "General Strategies for Effective Change in Human Systems." In W. Bennis and others (eds.), *The Planning of Change* (3rd ed.). Austin, Tex.: Holt, Rinehart, and Winston, 1976.

DeJong, W. "Some Good News on Campus." *Prevention Pipeline*, 1998, *11*(6), 6–7.

DeJong, W. "Finding Common Ground for Effective Campus-Based Prevention." *Psychology of Addictions*, 2001, *15*, 292–296.

DeJong, W., and Langenbahn, S. *Setting and Improving Policies for Reducing Alcohol and Other Drug Problems on Campus: A Guide for Administrators*. Washington, DC: Higher Education Center for Alcohol and Other Drug Prevention, U.S. Department of Education, 1996.

DeJong, W., and Langford, L. M. "A Typology for Campus-Based Alcohol Prevention: Moving Toward Environmental Management Strategies." *Journal of Studies on Alcohol*, 2002, Supplement no. 14, 140–147.

DeJong, W., and Linkenbach, J. "Telling It Like It Is: Using Social Norms Marketing Campaigns to Reduce Student Drinking." *American Association of Higher Education Bulletin*, 1999, *52*(4), 11–13, 16.

DeJong, W., and Winsten, J. A. *The Media and the Message: Lessons Learned from Past Public Service Campaigns*. Washington, D.C.: National Campaign to Prevent Teen Pregnancy, 1998.

Edwards, G. and others. *Alcohol Policy and the Public Good*. New York: Oxford University Press, 1994.

Hale, J. L., and Dillard, J. P. "Fear Appeals in Health Promotion Campaigns: Too Much, Too Little, or Just Right?" In E. W. Maibach and R. L. Parrott (eds.), *Designing Health Messages: Approaches from Communication Theory and Public Health Practice*. Thousand Oaks, Calif.: Sage, 1995.

Hingson, R. W., and Howland, J. "Comprehensive Community Interventions to Promote Health: Implications for College-Age Drinking Problems." *Journal of Studies on Alcohol*, 2002, Supplement no. 14, 226–240.

McPhee, M. "CU Rioters Grouse About Cops." *Denver Post On-Line*, May 6, 1997. (www.denverpost.com/news)

Perkins, H. W. "College Student Misperceptions of Alcohol and Other Drug Norms Among Peers: Exploring Causes, Consequences, and Implications for Prevention Programs." In U.S. Department of Education, *Designing Alcohol and Other Drug Prevention Programs in Higher Education: Bringing Theory into Practice.* Newton, Mass.: Higher Education Center for Alcohol and Other Drug Prevention, U.S. Department of Education, 1997.

Perkins, H. W., DeJong, W., and Linkenbach, J. "Estimated Blood Alcohol Levels Reached by 'Binge' and 'Non-Binge' Drinkers: A Survey of Young Adults in Montana." *Psychology of Addictions,* 2001, *15,* 317–320.

Perkins, H. W., and others. "Misperceptions of the Norms for Frequency of Alcohol and Other Drug Use on College Campuses." *Journal of American College Health,* 1999, *47,* 253–258.

Presidents Leadership Group. *Be Vocal, Be Visible, Be Visionary: Recommendations for College and University Presidents on Alcohol and Other Drug Prevention.* Newton, Mass.: Higher Education Center for Alcohol and Other Drug Prevention, 1997.

Rose, G. *The Strategy of Preventive Medicine.* New York: Oxford University Press, 1992.

Ryan, W. *Blaming the Victim.* New York: Vintage, 1976.

Schuckit, M. A. "The Editor Responds." *Journal of Studies on Alcohol,* 1998, *59,* 124.

Toomey, T. L., and Wagenaar, A. C. "Environmental Policies to Reduce College Drinking: Options and Research Findings." *Journal of Studies on Alcohol,* 2002, Supplement no. 14, 193–205.

Wallack, L., Dorfman, L., Jernigan, D., and Themba, M. *Media Advocacy and Public Health: Power for Prevention.* Thousand Oaks, Calif.: Sage, 1993.

Walter, C. L. "Community Building Practice: A Conceptual Framework." In M. Minkler (ed.), *Community Organizing and Community Building for Health.* New Brunswick, N.J.: Rutgers University Press, 1997.

Wechsler, H., Lee, J. E., and Kuo, M. "Trends in College Binge Drinking During a Period of Increased Prevention Efforts: Findings from Four Harvard School of Public Health College Alcohol Study Surveys, 1993–2001." *Journal of American College Health,* 2002, *50*(5), 203–217.

Wechsler, H., Lee, J. E., Nelson, T. F, and Kuo, M. "Underage College Students' Drinking Behavior, Access to Alcohol, and the Influence of Deterrence Policies: Findings from the Harvard School of Public Health College Alcohol Study." *Journal of American College Health,* 2000, *50,* 223–236.

Wechsler, H., Nelson, T., and Weitzman, E. "From Knowledge to Action: How Harvard's College Alcohol Study Can Help Your Campus Design a Campaign Against Student Alcohol Abuse." *Change,* Jan.–Feb. 2000, pp. 38–43.

Wechsler, H., and others. "Changes in Binge Drinking and Related Problems Among American College Students Between 1993 and 1997." *Journal of American College Health,* 1998, *47,* 57–68.

PART FOUR

YOUNG ADULTS AND
SOCIAL NORMS WORK
BEYOND THE CAMPUS

CHAPTER TEN

MISPERCEPTIONS OF PEER ALCOHOL NORMS IN A STATEWIDE SURVEY OF YOUNG ADULTS

Jeffrey W. Linkenbach, Ed.D.; H. Wesley Perkins, Ph.D.

Most young adults under the age of twenty-one in the United States report consuming alcohol. Nationally, somewhere between 70 and 80 percent of young adults report drinking alcohol at least once in the past year, and over half report doing so in a given month (Johnston, O'Malley, and Bachman, 2001). Young people in Montana are no different, and the deadly consequences of drinking alcohol and driving are well documented. People under the age of twenty-one engaging in this behavior accounted for approximately 40 percent of all of Montana's licensed drivers who died in alcohol-related fatal crashes in 1997 (Montana Department of Transportation, 2001). Although by the mid-1990s Montana had experienced a reduction of approximately 60 percent in alcohol-related crashes in the preceding fourteen years among the overall driving population, the percentage of young adults in the eighteen-to-twenty-four-year-old age group continued to be overrepresented (Montana Department of Transportation, 2001). Montana young adults made up only about 12 percent of all licensed drivers, but they accounted for more than 26 percent of all alcohol-related crashes—a trend that remained relatively constant throughout most of the 1990s. It was from this

We would like to acknowledge the innovation and support of leaders in the Montana Department of Transportation, Traffic Safety Bureau—namely, Albert Goke, Kent Mollohan, Pricilla Sinclair, and Jack Williams.

173

context that traffic safety officials in Montana turned to national research on college campuses for possible clues on how to reverse this troubling trend with regard to Montana's young adult population.

In 1998, Montana State University was contracted by the Montana Department of Transportation's Traffic Safety Bureau to embark upon the mission of reducing the incidence of impaired driving among Montana's young adults by using environmental prevention approaches from a social norms framework. The challenges associated with applying the social norms model to a statewide population were many, but initially they all hinged upon collection of formative data and whether the result would demonstrate the existence of widespread misperception about young adult drinking. Although misperceived drinking norms was emerging as a characteristic finding among the nation's college students (Perkins and others, 1999), the question still remained of the prevalence of such misperception outside of the campus setting. It was from this context that we engaged in the process of exploring the new frontier for applying social norms across the state of Montana.

Our background research about what lessons could be adapted from leaders in the college substance abuse prevention field revealed a striking pattern of success. Even though a large number of colleges were engaged in administering comprehensive substance abuse programs, only a few campuses across the country (such as Northern Illinois University, the University of Arizona, Hobart and William Smith Colleges, and Western Washington University—all of which were implementing the social norms approach to prevention) were achieving a significant reduction in heavy drinking and associated consequences among their undergraduate students (Haines, 1996; Johannessen, Collins, Mills-Novoa, and Glider, 1999; Perkins and Craig, 2002). Most striking about the results was the fact that these campuses were measuring an 18–21 percent reduction in heavy drinking among their college student population within two years, compared with a national backdrop of heavy drinking in college students that remained virtually unchanged at around 44 percent of students reporting such behavior (Perkins, 2002).

The foundation of the social norms approach to prevention is data that demonstrate a disparity between the actual and perceived norms for alcohol use among college students and their peers (Perkins and Berkowitz, 1986; Perkins, 1991). Across the nation, irrespective of demographic differences in the campus environment, students tend to perceive much more permissive norms and a higher level of alcohol abuse among their peers than is actually the case (Perkins and others, 1999). On the basis of these data, practitioners at the aforementioned institutions were able to develop interventions using strategic communication, marketing, and environmental management techniques to correct misperception by promoting greater awareness of the actual moderate alcohol-use norms practiced by the majority of students. Clearly, the social norms approach to prevention held tremendous promise for achieving similar results for young adults across an entire state if some significant challenges associated with launching such an effort could be overcome—the first of which was obtaining data from a group of young adults who are difficult to access.

From Research Questions to Survey Methodology

The root of any social norms effort is quantitative (survey) data demonstrating a disparity between what the target group reports as their actual norms compared to their perception of what they view as being typical (normative) of others in their reference group. From this scientific orientation, any attempt to achieve a reduction in alcohol-related crashes using the social norms model would require data demonstrating a gap between what Montana's young adults reported as their perception of the frequency of drinking and driving as compared to what they reported as their actual alcohol use norms. Since data about patterns of misperception of alcohol-use norms had never been gathered for young adults beyond the college context, we needed to think outside of the box and explore some possible survey methodologies.

From the beginning, we wondered how we might develop an efficient and cost-effective tool for assessing the perceptions and reported behavioral norms of young adults across the state. We questioned whether the patterns of perceiving exaggerated abuse of alcohol as the norm among young adult peers, and the consistent underperceiving of peers' protective behaviors, would exist throughout a statewide population of young adults, most of whom were not college students. Would there be a significant difference in the patterns of misperception among subpopulations (such as college students versus other young adults) indicating specialized social norms strategies or marketing approaches? The answers to these and other questions would determine the efficacy of using a social norms campaign for targeting a statewide population of young adults.

On college campuses, the convenience of mailing lists, the classroom setting, and wide access to computers creates an environment for obtaining data through use of pencil-and-paper and Web-based survey methods of administration. However, once we looked beyond the college campus, the process of gathering information from those adults in the eighteen-to-twenty-four-year-old range who were not enrolled as college students became much more complex. Gathering reliable and valid data across a rural state presented unique challenges owing to a variety of demographic factors: part-time or full-time college enrollment; marital and parental status; and type of residence, including living on a military base or one of Montana's seven Native American reservations. The heterogeneous nature of our would-be target population was just the first of many challenges that we encountered when we began to focus on gathering data.

Additionally, we were not certain how many people actually existed in the target group because various data sources produced only partial information. We answered some of the questions associated with defining the young adult target population by comparing Montana Department of Commerce data with what we obtained from the Office of Montana's Commissioner of Education. By extrapolating from these databases, we were able to estimate that most (approximately two-thirds) of the target population of Montana's eighteen-to-twenty-four-year-olds were not enrolled as students in the state's institutions of higher education. The remaining third (about thirty thousand) of Montana's eighteen-to-twenty-four-year-olds were attending institutions of higher education. Of these students, most were attending school at Montana's two largest universities, while the remainder were scattered around the state and attending one of Montana's twenty-one other institutions of higher education.

Phone Survey of Statewide Sample

In March 1998, we contracted with an independent market research group to conduct a statewide random phone survey of five hundred young adults across the state of Montana between eighteen and twenty-four. Phone numbers were drawn at random from a database of residences within Montana representing each of the fifty-six counties in proportion to their population size. The survey contained questions concentrating on personal drinking patterns, perceived alcohol-use norms, and reported protective behaviors concerning alcohol use and related driving issues. Some of the questions were taken from current national instrumentation, while we developed other survey items as new measures for this study. The marketing group that was contracted to conduct the survey carried out the training of phone survey staff and the final pilot testing of the survey instrument. After completing the survey, we hired an independent research group to randomly select 10 percent of the phone survey respondents from the list of participants to validate their participation.

The resulting sample was a diverse group of 497 young adults (three cases were eliminated from the database because of an insufficient or unreliable response) from across the state of Montana, with about half (47 percent) being under the legal drinking age of twenty-one. Ninety percent of the sample were Caucasian, 5 percent were Native American, and 5 percent were of other races. Fifty-seven percent were female. About three-quarters (74 percent) were currently employed, and 85 percent owned a vehicle. About one-third of the sample (32 percent) were living with a spouse, 42 percent were living with parents, and 27 percent had children living with them. One-third (33 percent) of these eighteen-to-twenty-four-year-olds were attending college, while two-thirds (67 percent) were not. This proportion closely reflects the statewide proportion of young adults who were college students (30 percent of eighteen-to-twenty-four-year-olds in Montana). Among those who were students, about half (52 percent) had a car on campus.

Actual Versus Perceived Norms for Alcohol Use

Moderation in drinking or abstinence was clearly the predominant reported behavior for personal drinking patterns of young adults in this sample. A large majority (81 percent) reported typically consuming four or fewer drinks when they drank or did not drink at all. About two-thirds of the males (66 percent) and three-quarters of the females (76 percent) typically consumed three or fewer drinks or reported not drinking at all. Forty-five percent of the men and 51 percent of the women were abstainers, with 59 percent of young adults under twenty-one abstaining and 40 percent of those twenty-one and older abstaining. Comparing the actual patterns of personal use with what these young adult Montanans believed to be the practice among their peers, however, reveals a highly distorted perception of common drinking behavior.

Average Number of Drinks

The average number of drinks consumed among all men per occasion was three (or five if men who usually drink no alcohol are excluded from the average). The average number for women was two drinks (or four if women who usually drink no alcohol are excluded from the average). When respondents were asked what they thought was the average number of drinks that Montanans their age consumed per occasion, the average perception among all respondents was that males had seven drinks and females five per occasion.

Heavy Episodic Drinking

When males were asked how often during the past two weeks they had consumed five or more drinks at one time, 29 percent indicated they had done so at least once. Thus a clear majority of young Montana males (71 percent) did not exhibit heavy episodic drinking during that time period. Almost everyone sampled (including females and males, 99 percent), however, estimated when asked about "the average Montana male" that he had done this type of drinking at least once during that time. Perhaps even more remarkable, more than three-quarters of the sample (76 percent) thought that the average male had been drinking at this level at least three times during the past two weeks. The pattern was similar for females, using a measure of four or more drinks at one time as an indicator of heavy episodic drinking. Only 18 percent of females had consumed alcohol at this level during the last two weeks prior to the survey, and yet almost the entire sample of men and women (97 percent) thought that the average Montana female had done so at least once in that time period. Over half of the sample (56 percent) estimated that the average female consumed this amount at least three times in the previous two weeks.

Frequency of Consumption

Among respondents who consume alcohol, they reported drinking on an average of four days in a typical month. (The average days per month for all young adults in the sample including abstainers was one day per month.) In contrast, all of these Montanans, on average, estimated that peers in their state typically drank eight days per month.

Drinking and Driving

Thirty percent of drinkers (15 percent of all respondents) reported that within the past month they had driven within one hour after consuming two or more drinks. Almost all respondents (96 percent) said yes, however, when asked whether or not they thought the average Montanan their age had done so. Although 36 percent of male drinkers (20 percent of all males) drove within one hour of having two or more drinks, the average estimate by all respondents of the percentage of males their age doing so was 57 percent. Likewise, although 24 percent of female drinkers (12 percent of all females) reported such drinking and driving, the average perception was that 42 percent of female peers behaved this way.

Protective Interventions

All respondents were asked whether or not they had intervened to stop a person from driving the last time they were out and saw someone they knew who was going to drive after drinking two or more drinks within an hour. Although not all respondents were in a drinking situation to carry out an intervention, 61 percent of the young adults in this sample had done so. Nevertheless, this same sample estimated that only 17 percent of their peers would have intervened.

College Versus Noncollege Patterns

The overarching pattern of exaggerated perception of drinking norms included inflated perception of the frequency and level of alcohol use, inflated perception of drinking and driving, and underestimation of actual protective interventions in drinking and driving situations among young adults. This pattern was replicated for both college students and other eighteen-to-twenty-four-year-olds in these data. In fact, there was little difference between the college students and other young adults in comparison of actual behavior or perception considering all the measures examined. Only one item about personal drinking behavior produced a statistically significant difference ($p < .05$) between the subpopulations of college students and other adults. College females were more likely to report heavy episodic drinking (four or more drinks in a row in the last two weeks) than were other Montana females of the same age (25 percent as compared to 15 percent respectively). Also, only one item about perceived norms produced a statistically significant result. Although both college and other young adults perceived a higher average number of drinks as typically consumed at one sitting by male peers than was the actual norm among the sample, the young adults who were not current college students reported, on average, a more exaggerated perception of typical male consumption (7.2 drinks) than did college students (6.4 drinks).

Framing the Problem in the Context of Actual Norms

We were able to draw several conclusions as a result of this formative survey research:

1. The pattern of misperceptions frequently noted in college populations was found to be virtually the same, whether looking at college students and their sense of statewide peers or young adults not in college and their view of peers. In both cases, the reference group was seen to be consuming much more alcohol than was actually the case.

2. The data demonstrate that most young adults in Montana are either relatively moderate and safe drinkers or abstain from alcohol use. This finding does not minimize the harmful consequences incurred by those young adults who do engage in alcohol abuse, or the fact that it is illegal for young people under the age of twenty-one to drink. The data do, however, serve as an accurate framing of the true context of the young adult drinking culture. This culture can easily become distorted if only negative occurrences are emphasized, to the near exclusion of these "mundane" but overwhelmingly positive norms.

3. Misperception found in this research demonstrates two consistent and interrelated patterns: (1) young adults tend to overexaggerate the amount of alcohol-related *risk taking* among peers (such as heavy episodic drinking or driving while impaired), and (2) at the same time they also underestimate the prevalence of *protective action* (such as intervening to keep friends from driving while impaired) that were the norm, and that serve to reduce the risks associated with alcohol use. In both cases, these coexisting patterns of misperception serve to create a distorted view of young adult drinking by implying that there is more acceptance for harmful behavior and less approval for safety than is actually the case.

4. Although differences in the perception of men's and women's alcohol-related behavior as well as their actual behavior exist, the general pattern of misperception remains for both men and women.

5. Finally, engaging in the high-risk behavior of driving while alcohol impaired is an infrequent behavior of young adults, but its prevalence is substantially overperceived. Once again, the fact that this behavior does not normally occur among most young adults does not minimize the seriousness of this deadly behavior. Instead, it serves to underscore the importance of accurately framing the context of the issue in which impaired driving occurs. The data clearly indicate that the minority of young adults who do recklessly choose to drive under the influence of alcohol typically do so believing that they are no different from most young people their age. Moreover, they do so with the tacit, albeit unintended, support of most other young people who think that those who drink and drive are in the majority. In a sense, the many young adults who hold and convey the misperception of drinking and driving as normative are perversely "enabling" the drinking driver with the erroneous notion that his or her "commonplace" behavior does not warrant serious concern. Thus, challenging this illusion of DUI prevalence and acceptability among young adults with credible data about actual peer norms is likely to be a crucial element of success in any broad-based prevention initiative.

References

Haines, M. P. *A Social Norms Approach to Preventing Binge Drinking at Colleges and Universities.* Newton, Mass.: Higher Education Center for Alcohol and Other Drug Prevention, 1996.

Johannessen, K., Collins C., Mills-Novoa, B. and Glider, P. *A Practical Guide to Alcohol Abuse Prevention: A Campus Case Study in Implementing Social Norms and Environmental Management Approaches.* Tucson: Campus Health Service, University of Arizona, 1999.

Johnston, L., O'Malley, P., and Bachman, J. *National Survey Results on Drug Use from the Monitoring the Future Study, 1975–2000, College Students and Young Adults.* (NCADI no. BKD422.) Bethesda, Md.: National Institute on Drug Abuse, 2001.

Montana Department of Transportation. *Traffic Safety Problem Identification (FY 2002)*. Helena, Mont.: Engineering Division, Traffic and Safety Bureau, 2001.

Perkins, H. W. "Confronting Misperceptions of Peer Drug Use Norms Among College Students: An Alternative Approach for Alcohol and Drug Education Programs." In *Peer Prevention Program Implementation Manual*. Fort Worth: Higher Education Leaders/Peers Network, Texas Christian University, 1991.

Perkins, H. W. "Social Norms and the Prevention of Alcohol Misuse in Collegiate Contexts." *Journal of Studies on Alcohol*, 2002, Supplement no. 14, 164–172.

Perkins, H. W., and Berkowitz, A. D. "Perceiving the Community Norms of Alcohol Use Among Students: Some Research Implications for Campus Alcohol Education Programming." *International Journal of the Addictions*, 1986, *21*, 961–976.

Perkins, H. W., and Craig, D. W. *A Multifaceted Social Norms Approach to Reduce High-Risk Drinking: Lessons from Hobart and William Smith Colleges*. Newton, Mass.: Higher Education Center for Alcohol and Other Drug Prevention, U.S. Department of Education, 2002.

Perkins, H. W., and others. "Misperceptions of the Norms for the Frequency of Alcohol and Other Drug Use on College Campuses." *Journal of American College Health*, 1999, *47*(6), 253–258.

CHAPTER ELEVEN

THE MONTANA MODEL

Development and Overview of a Seven-Step Process for Implementing Macro-Level Social Norms Campaigns

Jeffrey W. Linkenbach, Ed.D.

With evidence accumulating on the effectiveness of applying the social norms approach to prevention of heavy episodic drinking at individual college campuses (Perkins and Berkowitz, 1986; Perkins, 1997; Haines, 1996; Johannessen, Collins, Mills-Novoa, and Glider, 1999; Perkins and Craig, 2002), a next question for social norms work concerns the possibility of expanding this promising approach into larger statewide populations and other health issues. Because such a wide-scale, macro-level application of the social norms approach had never been attempted beyond the college campus setting, a model for an expanded adaptation of these successful strategies would need to be developed. To implement and operate a statewide social norms intervention targeting a variety of health issues, the Montana Model of Social Norms Marketing (Linkenbach, 1999) was developed. This chapter presents an overview of the model itself as well as the context

In addition to providing technical assistance to the project, I would like to recognize Michael Haines for developing the term MOST of Us®, which has become the registered Montana trademark brand for all efforts associated with the Montana Social Norms Project. I would also like to thank Jamie Cornish of the MSNP for assisting with ideas and editing of this chapter. Special thanks go to Alison Govi of the MSNP for graphic images.

in which it was created. Additionally, key insights gained from practical application of this seven-step social norms template are discussed.

Emergence of a Statewide Social Norms Project

Throughout the 1980s, officials in the Traffic Safety Bureau of the Montana Department of Transportation (MDOT) were following national trends by implementing common prevention approaches to reducing the incidence of impaired driving. These approaches included raising the minimum legal drinking age to twenty-one and creating statewide community-based prevention coalitions. Nationally, such efforts were deemed to be successful in reducing impaired driving among young people. This accomplishment was marked in part by the fact that the greatest percentage drop in alcohol-related traffic fatalities during the early 1990s occurred among drivers under the age of twenty-one (National Highway Traffic Safety Administration, 1993).

By the mid-1990s, however, even though officials in the Montana Traffic Safety Bureau had witnessed a reduction of approximately 60 percent in alcohol-related crashes over the past fourteen years among the overall driving population, they realized that their work in preventing this deadly behavior was far from finished. The percentage of young adults in the eighteen-to-twenty-four-year-old age group continued to be overrepresented in the statistics for alcohol-related crashes. Data revealed that Montana young adults made up only about 12 percent of all licensed drivers, but they accounted for more than 26 percent of all alcohol-related crashes. People under the age of twenty-one still constituted approximately 40 percent of all of Montana's licensed drivers who had died in alcohol-related fatal crashes (Montana Department of Transportation, 2001). The director of traffic safety was concerned with these statistics and resolved to explore Montana-based solutions to realize even greater gains in reducing impaired driving among young adults.

In the early 1990s, I was contracted by the Montana Department of Transportation to conduct a statewide study to gather data on the perception of alcohol servers for the purpose of exploring how to reduce underage drinking and impaired driving (Linkenbach, 1995). One of the key implications of this study was that to reduce impaired driving among Montana's young adults, any successful intervention would need to address the perception of target audiences from Montana-specific perspectives. Through this initial statewide study, I developed a partnership with the bureau chief and other key staff members in the Montana Traffic Safety Bureau that evolved into ongoing, strategic planning discussion related to exploring possible solutions to this complex societal problem of impaired driving.

The Search for Effectiveness

At the same time that the strategic discussions hosted by the Montana traffic safety officials were increasingly turning toward program effectiveness, various government agencies in the prevention field (such as the Centers for Disease Control and Prevention, and the Center for Substance Abuse Prevention) were gravitating toward a focus on science-based approaches to prevention. These agencies sought to answer the question, "What works in prevention?" With a strong commitment toward achieving maximum reduction in DUI trends, state officials at the bureau were also engaged in a seemingly endless search for those programs that might be most effective at reducing the rate of impaired driving in both youths and adults in Montana.

Although much of the responsibility for the nation's positive gains in reduced impaired-driving crashes among young people during the 1980s and early 1990s was attributed to introduction of the twenty-one-year-old minimum legal drinking age (Ross, 1992), Montana officials were asking questions about what additional interventions might enhance these favorable trends.

Discussion led us to explore the possibilities of new and potentially effective practices that might serve to complement social policies such as the minimum legal drinking age law. One concern that we raised was that of using traditional "health terrorism" (Linkenbach, 1999) strategies that sought to reduce harm by continually raising individual awareness of the negative consequences associated with health choices. Although this type of approach was extremely popular at the time, our discussion group surmised that if negatively oriented public information and education campaigns had indeed been responsible for any positive outcomes, these gains would be short-lived at best.

A primary concern centered on whether Montana's young adults would soon become desensitized to the emotionally laden, deterrent-based messages. To continue engaging the attention of the target population, such messages would need to become increasingly more graphic and disturbing. By moving away from being a purveyor of objective factual information, traffic safety officials were beginning to express concerns about how these negatively focused tactics might actually backfire by tarnishing the public's high regard for the credibility of their agency. From these factors, the stage was set for Montana to explore the possibilities of a new approach to prevention: one that would operate from a positive perspective.

Lessons Learned from College Prevention Programs

Since I was working in the field of college health during the time period of this series of traffic safety meetings, I had the opportunity to introduce information into the discussion about how colleges across the United States were also engaged in a parallel process of seeking practical solutions to the seemingly intractable problem of preventing DUI-related (driving under the influence) behaviors among college students (DeJong, 1995). Our planning discussion then reviewed lessons being learned in college substance abuse prevention efforts. We sought clues as to what might work for reducing DUI behavior with young adults, and improving other healthy behaviors across Montana.

Throughout the 1990s, the field of substance abuse prevention in higher education was undergoing a radical transformation. It was moving from the traditional approach to prevention that focuses on reducing substance abuse behaviors by educating individuals about the harmful consequences associated with abuse, toward proactively addressing the broader social environment in which substance abuse occurs (Berkowitz, 1997). Central to this change was the emergence of three interrelated views: (1) the environmental approach to prevention (DeJong and others, 1998); (2) the recognition of the importance of the campus-community relationship (Gebhardt, Kaphingst, and DeJong, 2000); and (3) the social norms approach to prevention (Perkins and Berkowitz, 1986; Perkins, 1991).

Although the trend toward focusing on comprehensive programs from a broad-based environmental context was clearly gaining momentum, what was even more striking to us was the pattern of success seen at those few college campuses that were employing social norms strategies to effect change in the drinking culture. The social norms approach to prevention is based upon data that demonstrate a disparity between the actual and perceived norms for alcohol use among college students and their peers (Perkins and Berkowitz, 1986; Perkins, 1991). Working from these data, practitioners at various institutions such as Northern Illinois University, the University of Arizona, Hobart and William Smith Colleges, and Western Washington University were able to develop interventions that communicated actual moderate alcohol use norms practiced by the majority of students. (See previous chapters in this book.) These interventions were implemented by using strategic communication, marketing, and in some cases environmental management techniques to correct misperceptions and therefore promote greater awareness of the actual alcohol norms.

This handful of campuses that were implementing the social norms approach to prevention were at various stages of reporting a significant reduction in heavy drinking and associated consequences among their undergraduate students (Haines, 1996; Johannessen, Collins, Mills-Novoa, and Glider, 1999; Perkins and Craig, 2002). Most impressive however, was the fact that those colleges that were employing the social norms approach to prevention were measuring an 18–21 percent reduction in heavy drinking among their college student populations within two years, against a national backdrop that remained virtually unchanged. We determined that the social norms approach to prevention held tremendous promise for achieving similar results among young adults and other populations across the state of Montana. However, at that point, the use of social norms marketing had not been attempted on the broad macro level, as with a statewide campaign. It was unclear whether or not the strategies used on the college campus could actually be applied in a larger community population.

The Montana Social Norms Project

The Montana Social Norms Project was first created in 1998 with the intention of expanding social norms marketing for use in contexts much larger than a college campus. The Montana Department of Transportation provided funding to Montana State University's Department of Health and Human Development to develop our research group. The primary aim of this endeavor was to conduct research and apply the social norms approach toward the issue of reducing alcohol-related crashes across Montana's statewide population of eighteen-to-twenty-four-year-old young adults.

The basis of any social norms effort is quantitative survey data that demonstrate a disparity between what the target group reports as their actual norms, as compared to their perception of what they view as being typical (normative) of others in their reference group. Yet in 1998, it was not certain whether the same pattern of misperception that was documented on certain college campuses existed among nonstudents of the same age. Therefore, all efforts toward developing this statewide project hinged upon survey data that could demonstrate that misperception about DUI-related behavior was also prevalent in a statewide population of young adults.

To address this primary social norms question, we developed the Montana Young Adult Alcohol Phone Survey and administered it to a sample of Montana's eighteen-to-twenty-four-year-olds. The results of this survey demonstrated that a gap did indeed exist between what Montana's young adults reported as their perception of the frequency of drinking and driving, compared to what they reported as their actual alcohol-use norms (Linkenbach and Perkins, Chapter Ten in this volume).

Equipped with data, the Montana Social Norms Project was officially launched in an effort to correct these misperceptions and the influence they were having on the actual rate of impaired driving. I then faced the pragmatic challenge of whether or not embarking upon this macro-level application of social norms was even possible and what sort of infrastructure could successfully support such an effort. Fueling the necessity of answering this and many other questions was the fact that during this same time frame, other state agencies in Montana were beginning to express an interest in using the social norms approach to address their agency-specific health and safety prevention needs.

A need existed for developing a core model that could be adapted to a variety of possible health topics and target populations. Validation of this need came through the data from subsequent Montana surveys, which demonstrated that the same pattern of statewide misperception of norms compared to actual behaviors seen with regard to young adults and alcohol use was also prevalent with regard to other issues and target populations such as youth tobacco use (Linkenbach and Perkins, Chapter Thirteen), parenting behaviors (Linkenbach, Perkins, and De-Jong, Chapter Fifteen), and adult seatbelt use (Floyd and Linkenbach, 2000).

From these survey findings, it was apparent that this pattern of misperceiving the social environment regarding health and safety issues was extremely widespread and pervasive, even reaching across health issues and subpopulations. The significance of this insight was that a culture existed in which the people of Montana, including youths, were making crucial perceptual errors when it came to some of their most important health and safety decisions—a pattern I later came to define as "cultural cataracts" (Linkenbach, 2001). Exaggerated perception of risk-taking behaviors, as well as underestimation of protective factors and true health norms, was adversely influencing the public's actions and attitudes. There was a great need to reshape the cultural environment by correcting these misperceptions across our state.

Development of the Montana Model

With the creation of the Montana Social Norms Project, I began to devise the Montana Model of Social Norms Marketing. This model became the foundation of several MOST of Us® campaigns, including interventions to reduce DUI behavior among eighteen-to-twenty-four-year-old young adults, delay the onset of first-time tobacco use among teenagers, increase support for parent-child communication concerning nonuse of alcohol and drugs, and increasing adult seatbelt use.

The Montana Model (see Figure 11.1) is based upon a core seven-step framework. It serves as a blueprint of a data-driven process for all campaigns operated by the Montana Social Norms Project, ranging in scope from a single junior high school up through a multiyear statewide campaign. All components of this model interact to turn social science into social action by correcting misperceptions and building upon the positive attitudinal and behavioral norms that already exist in the culture.

Rather than developing all of the components of this model from scratch, I incorporated components from the practical experiences and models of leading practitioners in the areas of social marketing (Kotler and Andreasen, 1996; Siegel

FIGURE 11.1. MONTANA MODEL OF SOCIAL NORMS MARKETING.

Source: Used by permission of Montana Social Norms Project, Montana State University.

and Doner, 1998; U.S. Center for Substance Abuse Prevention, 1998) and the social norms approach to prevention (Perkins and Berkowitz, 1986; Fabiano and others, 1999; Haines, 1996; Johannessen, Collins, Mills-Novoa, and Glider, 1999). Early
development of this model was greatly influenced by the work of Michael Haines
at Northern Illinois University, who pioneered the combination of joining social
marketing principles with social norms theory to introduce social norms marketing.

After pilot testing and experimenting with numerous versions of campaign brands, I chose MOST of Us. This brand worked best because it communicated the normative concept of the majority ("MOST") as seen from the perspective of the target population ("Us"). The selection of this identity was crucial because it would serve as a unifying concept to connect the various campaigns targeting numerous health and safety issues. However, even more important was the fact that the MOST of Us brand was also the main message that needed to be communicated to the people of Montana regarding their various health issues. By creating MOST of Us as brand and message, our project would not have to waste precious resources establishing both a brand identity as well as market a separate health message; they were in essence one in the same.

By the late 1990s, it became apparent that there were many increased complexities involved with implementing social norms campaigns across our entire state, as opposed to implementation on a more homogeneous campus-only setting. Primary among these complexities was attempting to limit the number of contradictory campaign messages being delivered to the target audience by other prevention efforts. The macro-level focus of statewide audiences was much more diverse and the campaign environment more complex. Therefore, the emerging model must have an ability to address this larger cultural landscape. The early version of the model created in 1998 would need to be adjusted to better incorporate influences from the larger culture that were affecting the perceptual environment—such as state and national media, economic factors, and conflicting health messages from state and local prevention programs.

At the same time, the substance abuse prevention field in higher education was gravitating toward environmental management strategies. These strategies involved analysis of the contextual features that increase the risk of substance abuse, followed by a consensus-building initiative to change those factors in the environment and reduce those risks (DeJong and others, 1998; Green, Lucie, and Potvin, 1996). It would be natural, then, for me to incorporate this perspective into this new Montana Model by combining social norms theory with other environmentally focused strategies.

However, a challenge emerged at the time that still continues today in the process of joining these differing approaches. The difficulty was that in the process of implementing many of the environmentally oriented approaches, it was common practice to solely emphasize the policy and enforcement domains of the culture while neglecting or paying only partial attention to the culture as seen in the predominant social norms. It was all too common at that time, as it is today, to hear prevention professionals state that their goal was to "change" social norms through tighter policies and enforcement. The environmental prevention approach and social norms marketing can work symbiotically, but not when the environmental approach is based on the theory of changing norms solely through legislation and enforcement.

Occasionally, proponents of environmental approaches misguidedly assume that new norms can be decreed through mechanisms such as policies and sanctions (Skiba, 2000). Such a practice all too often results in forming autocratic relationships between the prevention professionals and the target audience they intended to "serve." Backlash has occurred with students in riots and demonstrations (Zimmerman, 1999). Environmental approach advocates occasionally overlook the more effective strategy of working in concert with the target population to support behavioral changes or policy changes by raising awareness of norms that already exist.

Social norms marketing operates from a data-based, asset-focused perspective recognizing the fact that the already existent social norms (majority behavior) represent health, protection, and lowered health risks. For example, our statewide surveys have demonstrated that most (85 percent) of Montana's young adults reported not drinking and driving in the previous month (Linkenbach and Perkins, Chapter Ten); most (73 percent) Montana teenagers had not smoked cigarettes in the previous month (Montana Department of Public Health and Human Services, 2000); and most (74 percent) of Montana's adults are observed to be using their seatbelts when driving a vehicle (Montana Department of Transportation, 2001). This context of focusing on the already existent social norms does not minimize the seriousness and the need to change the risk-taking behaviors of those individuals outside of this health majority, but instead it establishes a platform from which to address such issues.

Social norms strategies can also be used to catalyze policy change. Misperception about public support for changed laws or enforcement is common. Making people aware that it is acceptable and typical to support a specific policy can harness the most powerful social change agent: the people the policy intends to serve. People are often surprised to find that the majority of the target population has attitudes or behaviors already aligned with a desirable new policy.

Montana data, for example, showed that more than 60 percent of young adults supported changing the existing law to lower the legal blood-alcohol concentration (BAC) limit from .10 BAC for legally being able to drive, down to .08 (Linkenbach and Perkins, 2001). Survey data also demonstrated nearly overwhelming support (over 94 percent) by Montana adults for increasing the efforts of law enforcement to reduce problems of impaired driving (Montana Department of Transportation, 2001). The majority of the target group already was practicing health and safety, and in support of strengthening environments to promote more of the same. Therefore, the type of model that was needed for addressing the statewide issues in Montana was one that would focus on the social environment and operate from the positive, asset-based orientation that is the hallmark of the social norms model.

At the University of Arizona, Koreen Johannessen and her staff at the Campus Health Service had successfully pioneered a bridge between these seemingly incongruent approaches. They were using the social norms approach within an overall environmental prevention framework focusing heavily on enlisting stakeholder support for communicating the positive normative messages (Johannessen, Collins, Mills-Novoa, and Glider, 1999). Most important, however, was that the Arizona project was demonstrating positive outcomes in reducing heavy alcohol use in their large campus setting of approximately thirty-five thousand, whereas those campuses focusing only on the top-down environmental strategies were not reporting such outcomes. For these reasons, the Arizona model held tremendous potential for use in Montana. By drawing from the broad-based work at the University of Arizona, I was then able to adapt other components designed to affect the larger cultural landscape of Montana's varying health goals and develop the seven-step process known as the Montana Model.

An Overview of the Seven Steps of the Montana Model

Let us turn to a basic overview of the core components of the Montana Model of Social Norms Marketing, as well as some key insights associated with its implementation (see Figure 11.1). Although the steps are presented linearly, the actual day-to-day implementation is a dynamic process that typically involves operating among many of these steps simultaneously. This model serves as a blueprint for all of the Montana MOST of Us campaigns irrespective of the particular project goals or target population. All of these elements serve to shift perceptions of individuals and change structures in the sociocultural environment with the desired aim of measuring and reinforcing healthy norms.

Step One: Planning and Environmental Advocacy

Step one consists of strategic planning and environmental advocacy, both of which guide the scope and direction of the campaign. The planning is an ongoing process throughout each project to ensure that all efforts are aligning with the overall program goals. We begin by first conducting research on any previous interventions or campaign efforts that have attempted to address the targeted behavior. In examining previous efforts, we pay particular attention to any data that may be used as baseline measures and that may have been gathered on program effectiveness. We often find that if any evaluation has been conducted, it lacks the rigorous design needed for measuring outcome effectiveness. Evaluations are in general limited to formative and process data that may simply reflect a possible awareness of previous campaign efforts. One of the first conversations that we have with a potential funding agency often deals with the costs and time needed to create a rigorous research design able to measure campaign effectiveness.

Our strategic planning then focuses on developing a time line that is based upon key elements of the seven steps. Typically, it takes more than one year to go through the entire process of all seven steps and report impact data from our efforts. Therefore, at the beginning of a campaign it is necessary to begin planning ways to sustain the efforts of the program beyond the cyclical nature of short-term grant projects. One way to do so is by creatively partnering with and building upon existing networks. During this initial planning phase, we also assess training needs and provide education to various stakeholders on the social norms approach. This type of stakeholder training is a crucial element toward promoting a consistent framing and communication of issues from a positive social norms perspective at all levels of the press.

Our overall goal with environmental advocacy is to create a political, economic, and social atmosphere conducive to supporting the goals of the campaign. Since the traditional health communications model focuses on increasing awareness of the problem to motivate people toward solving the problem, it is an ongoing challenge to train professionals in this new approach of focusing on the positive elements of already existing norms.

One of the most important elements of environmental advocacy is ensuring that the intervention area is free of other prevention efforts that may conflict directly with the campaign or cause confusion among the target audience. An example of this type of environmental advocacy occurred when we were operating the MOST of Us Are Tobacco Free campaign for teenagers in the western counties of our state. We pilot tested a TV commercial in a middle school by showing the students the ad once and then asking them to answer questions. This ad had been tested in several other schools where students had no problem understanding the main message of the ad ("Most, 70 percent, of Montana teens are tobacco free"). However, at the middle school referred to here, the students had just been though an intensive drug prevention program. Of the 203 students who viewed the commercial, 24 percent thought that the ad was about not doing drugs and that the main message was "just say no and walk away."

These students were so indoctrinated with the other prevention program that they projected its central messages onto our ad. This served as an indication that in the children's minds there was confusion or overlap between prevention messages. Thus when trying to evaluate the effectiveness of a campaign it is critical to maintain an environment where only one type of prevention strategy is being used, or else there could be significant contamination of the study. This is particularly important when dealing with social norms interventions. If students are told one day that most of their peers are tobacco-free, and the next day that hundreds of teens start smoking every week, the students will receive conflicting messages. To work toward a statewide media environment where all health communications reflect clear, consistent, pervasive messages that accurately depict social norms, ongoing advocacy is required.

Step Two: Baseline Data

The second step of the model is to establish baseline data. All campaign efforts are driven by data that demonstrate a disparity between perceived and actual norms. For operating a new campaign, we begin by examining any previously existing data to establish a baseline related to the program goals of affecting behavior, attitudes, or perceived norms. However, even if a program does have data related to its particular issue (tobacco, impaired driving, parenting, and so on), we typically find that the data lack required measurements related to precise pairing of perceptions of norms with the actual norms. Therefore, it is usually necessary to conduct an additional baseline survey (Web, phone, or mail) to establish a solid benchmark to be used for evaluation purposes. Developed in partnership with Wesley Perkins as a social norms consultant, our baseline data-gathering efforts focused upon three primary components: (1) awareness of the campaign message, (2) the perception of the norm for attitudes and behaviors, and (3) the actual reported norms.

The matched pairing of reported norms (actual) with the perceived norms (others) is a crucial component needed for developing messages and evaluating the effectiveness of social norms campaign efforts. In fact, a large disparity between the actual and perceived norms suggests a tremendous amount of potential for shifting personal behaviors or attitudes through correcting misperception.

Whenever possible, we seek to triangulate the data from one survey with those of other sources. For example, after obtaining data from the initial young adult phone survey (Linkenbach and Perkins, Chapter Ten), we were able to validate the statewide nature of misperceptions in Montana's college students by coordinating administration of the Core Alcohol and Drug Survey in thirteen participating Montana institutions of higher education. Both of these survey efforts revealed statewide misperception of alcohol norms in Montana's college students and became a basis for a statewide social norms initiative specific to college students.

Additionally, qualitative data are gathered through such means as focus groups and structured interviews. These data are used to produce rich description of the changing environment. For example, key stakeholders from across the state are often trained in how to collect and e-mail anecdotal stories that demonstrate examples of a campaign's reach or possible impact. On the recommendation of qualitative evaluation consultant Beverly Mills-Novoa, we primarily seek data that focus on key incidents or shifts in the public conversation related to the objectives of the program. An example of such a shift in conversation is seen when key stakeholders write opinion editorials after a local crisis, such as a crash related to impaired driving. The focus and content of the opinion editorial articles move from a traditional platform that communicates an epidemic of DUI behaviors— toward a true framework and context where such behaviors are presented as extreme, unacceptable, and outside the normal range of risk-reducing behavior practiced by the majority of citizens.

Step Three: Message Development

Once baseline data have been gathered and rigorously analyzed, coherent and easy-to-understand messages are derived. Message development should be undertaken with caution and sensitivity because the message is one of the most critical elements of a social norms campaign. It is the primary mechanism for setting the record straight with a target population regarding their misperception of the social environment. The message must clearly communicate information in a manner that is appealing and credible to the target group. The specifics of the message are determined, in part, by the target population's readiness for change, the constituents' current behavioral practices, and their perception or misperception of norms as compared to actual attitudes and behaviors.

It is critical that there be a consistent portrayal of the majority norm. Multiple messages can be confusing, so it is helpful to focus on one main campaign goal. There should be one unifying message for a campaign. For example, if the campaign goal is DUI prevention, there could be one unifying message ("MOST of Us prevent drinking and driving") and then localized statistics that reflect what percentage of people in various communities do not drink and drive. Segments of the target group may benefit from more localized messages, but the basic framework is consistent portrayal of the majority norm that is often supported by a statistic.

Overall, the main difference between a social norms message and formation of a traditional health promotion message is best described as the difference between communicating what is versus what should be. The social norms message seeks to communicate an objective statement of fact by mirroring back to the target group an affirming reflection of those behaviors or attitudes that just so happen to be most typical. Traditional health promotion messages tend to intensify or exaggerate the public's focus onto those individuals whose attitudes and behaviors are outside of the normal range of acceptance.

The statistic or message used in a social norms campaign is not an end point. In other words, it does not convey what should be happening, but rather what is happening. The message that "four out of five young adults do not drink and drive" does not imply that we have attained a satisfying level of DUI prevention. Any amount of drinking and driving that occurs is a problem. The message serves to reinforce the fact that the vast majority do not drink and drive; through raising this awareness in the public, the message should ultimately assist in reducing the risk-taking behavior of the minority (see Figure 11.2).

A common false assumption about social norms marketing is that it only deals in secondary prevention. Social norms messages are developed on the basis of the level of prevention the campaign is attempting to achieve: primary, secondary, or tertiary. Primary prevention is the general prevention that targets the population at large and seeks to address people before they engage in a high-risk behavior. Secondary prevention targets people who are already engaging in a certain risky behavior and attempts to have them reduce risks. Tertiary prevention deals with intervention or cessation. Here are examples of each message type:

- "Most (70 percent) of Montana teens are tobacco free" (primary)
- "Most (81 percent) of Montana college students have four, fewer, or no alcoholic drinks each week" (secondary)
- "Most (70 percent) of Montanans who have successfully completed substance abuse treatment reported no substance abuse after one year" (tertiary)

As a guideline for developing social norms campaigns, Haines (1997) suggests crafting a message that is positive, inclusive, and empowering. The positive element of the message is one informing the target population that, for the most part, they are engaging in healthy behavior. The message is beneficial, constructive, affirmative, hopeful, and optimistic; it leaves the target population feeling good about themselves. The inclusive element of the message is one that seeks to incorporate everyone in the target population by being embracing, involving, and comprehensive. The empowering part of message development seeks to energize and strengthen the target group by communicating to them their competence in making healthy decisions.

One of the key lessons that we have learned in applying social norms at a statewide level has been the importance of developing the message with the knowledge that it will be viewed and interpreted differently by varying audiences. In an ideal setting, we would like to be able to tailor a message to a subgroup within the target population on the basis of profession, interest, local region, and so forth, and ensure that only those materials specifically intended to reach a certain demographic group do so. However, in the practical reality of operating a

FIGURE 11.2.   MONTANA SOCIAL NORMS PROJECT POSTER:
MOST OF NORTHWESTERN MONTANA'S YOUNG ADULTS
DON'T DRINK AND DRIVE.

Source: Used by permission of Montana Social Norms Project, Montana State University.

statewide campaign, there are too many variables to maintain such control. Therefore, when crafting a campaign message it is critical to seek input from the various elements of the target population to make certain that the message appeals to them and does not alienate them.

Step Four: Market Plan

When people think of social norms marketing, they typically recall the media materials that deliver the campaign message. Yet behind those colorful posters and engaging television commercials are well-designed market plans. The overall goal of any social norms campaign is to sustain the exposure, or dosage, of the campaign message so as to create a shift in perception of what is normative. A high level of exposure is accomplished by maximizing the reach (percentage of target population), the frequency (average of how often individuals are exposed to the message), and the duration (length of the media flight) of the media and communication strategies.

Creation of any marketing plan begins by seeing things through the eyes of the target population and designing strategies to place the product in front of the consumer. Mass media (radio, television, and print) and grassroots strategies (contests, events, promotional items) are assessed for their potential to reach the target population within the limitations of the project budget. The results of these assessments are incorporated into the campaign-specific plan.

The field of social marketing is well equipped with materials on how to best segment a population and deliver messages that reach and appeal to them. The (ever expanding) five P's of the market mix (Siegel and Donner, 1998) break the process down into specific components:

1. Product (the specific behavior to be measured)
2. Price (the cost of performing the behavior, such as changing a misperception)
3. Promotion (the message and strategies used to sell the normative message)
4. Place (where the messages are placed to reach the target population)
5. Partners (people who will team up the campaign to assist with implementation)

We have learned that the most powerful market plans contain a mix of paid mass media advertising and strong grassroots efforts. Paid media advertising allows the campaign message to be broadcast to a large number of people in an undiluted and clear manner. Using donated airtime to broadcast public service announcements simply does not reach the target audience at a high enough frequency.

Grassroots efforts are extremely time-consuming and labor-intensive, but they can achieve effective results. The main caution to keep in mind about grassroots efforts is that in a local area a campaign is only as strong as its weakest link. For example, if we ship educational materials and promotional items to local schools and are not able to visit the schools ourselves, we must depend upon the teachers to distribute the materials to the students. If the teachers leave the items in their closet, then our campaign is nonexistent in those schools. Additionally, the teachers may distribute the items but undermine the campaign by questioning its message or effectiveness. Teachers may also be using the campaign materials in conjunction with lessons or other prevention campaigns that are contradictory. For these reasons, a campaign is most likely to achieve results if it comprises both extensive paid media time and well-organized grassroots efforts.

Step Five: Pilot Test and Refine Materials

It is critical to the success of any social norms campaign to assess how the target audience is receiving the campaign message, materials, and methods. Step five consists of pilot-testing and refining the significant elements and strategies of the campaign to maximize their effectiveness in shifting perception and strengthening behaviors and attitudes. This refinement process is dynamic and ongoing. It relies on formal and informal feedback measures.

Focus groups, in particular, are a key resource for gathering input from the target audience. Social norms researchers have identified special advantages associated with using this qualitative feedback process in a number of ways, including pinpointing strengths and weaknesses of a particular photo or message (Fabiano and Lederman, 2002). We typically use focus groups to guide our materials development by gathering new ideas or testing new concepts with the target population.

However, through our campaign administration experience we have come to develop a cautious attitude in how we use data that we obtain from the focus groups. Rather than viewing focus groups as an "objective source of truth" for guiding our efforts, we have become selective in how we use the opinions of focus group participants.

Focus groups have become an invaluable tool for us to test materials for their cultural appropriateness, believability, and appeal among the target group. Additionally, we use focus groups to identify any possible conflict, bias, or subtle prejudice that may be imbedded in our materials. For example, focus groups may indicate that minorities are being left out of the campaign images. We also test materials with people outside the target group, such as stakeholders who can provide important reactions to materials or messages. Focus groups are invaluable for helping us see our campaign through the eyes of our target group rather than filtering everything through our own values and set of experiences.

One example of the value of focus groups occurred when we were developing a campaign slogan for tobacco use prevention with Native American youth. After much testing and design we developed the slogan, "Most Montana Native American teens keep tobacco sacred." This message is significant because it honors the fact that for many of Montana's Native American tribes tobacco is seen as a sacred gift from the creator rather than a toxic substance that demands abstinence—a very different perspective from that of the mainstream culture (see Figure 11.3). We were able to develop this message only through the wisdom of the youths and elders of Montana's Native people.

The perceptions of focus group participants reflect their own legitimate perspectives, but there is an inherent caution here as well. Misperception is pervasive across various subpopulations; therefore it is likely that misperception permeates the statements of the focus group members as well. Specifically, it is quite common for the focus groups to reflect a commonly held misperception rather than the desired goals of the social norms campaign.

Focus group participants typically believe that the majority of people are engaging in harmful behaviors, and they typically express a proclivity toward the use of fear-based approaches when we ask them how we might encourage greater health ("Show us blood, gore, and negative consequences to get our attention"). Mass media have been saturated with this type of prevention for decades. Therefore, it is not surprising that the public is so indoctrinated into accepting this type of approach that they commonly refer to it as a powerful means of engaging their attention. However, as outlined throughout this book, social norms marketing has demonstrated dramatic results by focusing on positive normative messages, rather than on health terrorism techniques.

We have therefore learned to use discretion with focus groups and pilot testing of our materials and messages. Focus groups are invaluable for fine-tuning materials and messages, and for helping us to see through the eyes of cultures other than our own. We do not use them however, to direct the scientific efforts of reshaping misperception of the social environment.

After we have received a saturation of feedback where no new information is coming forth regarding our materials, we make a decision to terminate the refining process and go with our best concepts into the implementation phase of the campaign.

Step Six: Implement Campaign

Campaign implementation consists of all the elements necessary to run the campaign on a daily basis—including media flight, promotional item distribution, and training. During implementation, the campaign staff follows the strategic marketing

FIGURE 11.3. MONTANA SOCIAL NORMS PROJECT POSTER:
MOST NATIVE AMERICAN TEENS KEEP TOBACCO SACRED.

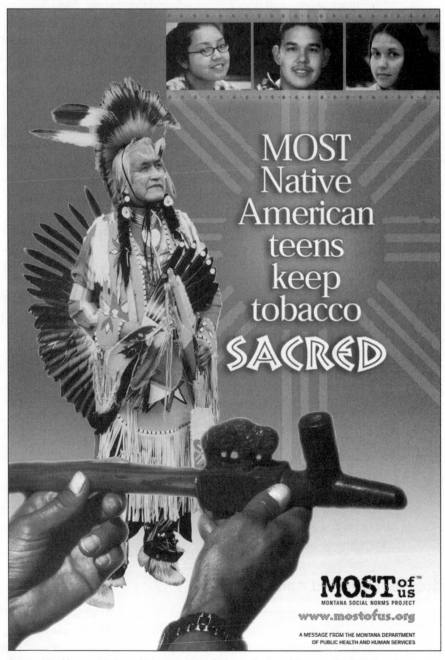

Source: Used by permission of Montana Social Norms Project, Montana State University.

plan and makes whatever adjustments are necessary to adhere to the data-driven fidelity of the Montana Model of Social Norms Marketing. Through practical experience, our staff have found that it is necessary to go beyond implementing campaign fundamentals—such as distributing promotional items, organizing locally developed activities, and placing print and broadcast media messages—to proactively seek out opportunities where we can advocate for enhancing cultural conditions that promote an accurate framing of health norms. In this way, our campaign staff functions as brokers who are constantly seeking to build upon environmental assets that are supportive of communicating consistent normative messages.

To reach the various target groups, we have used a combination of radio and television commercials, posters, newspaper advertisements, billboards, theater slides, and promotional items. We have also incorporated the use of electronic and computer-based marketing approaches that were modeled after the work at Hobart and William Smith Colleges (Perkins and Craig, 2002). Our campaigns have been implemented on several levels (public schools, colleges, various regions of the state). Recently, we have also been increasing the use of media advocacy strategies. When survey results are analyzed, we create strategic news making thorough use of press releases, opinion editorials, and letters to the editor.

From feedback in our various campaign efforts, we have learned the importance of constantly educating stakeholders about anticipating and reframing initial disbelief from the target audience (or other audiences) regarding the campaign message. We typically hear stories, have disbelieving comments scribbled onto our posters, or read letters to the editor basically challenging the fact that *most* of the group could actually be that healthy. We are constantly informing our stakeholders of the fact that a social norms campaign is developed because widespread misperception of true health norms exist. It is expected that a social norms campaign will catalyze public discussion and disbelief precisely because it is designed to counter these common, but inaccurate, beliefs about the exaggeration of risk-taking behaviors or attitudes. Because misperception is so greatly entrenched and reinforced by the culture, a campaign message that seeks to promote a view challenging dominant public opinion is commonly rejected. Implementing a social norms campaign is the process of systematically promoting a paradigm shift.

From a marketing perspective, our campaign implementation is about seeking to strategically capture market share (correct perception) from a highly competitive rival that seeks to maintain the dominant share (misperception). We document all feedback as data and channel it back into our planning process. Implementation involves constant monitoring of the public's reactions. Public feedback and interaction with the campaign process are documented so that any changes that occur over time can be tracked.

In this way, the campaign implementation process actually becomes one of "piloting on the run," where all data are used for shaping future generations of messages, materials, or strategies. Campaign implementation is about maintaining a proactive focus and trusting that the process will align perception with true health norms, and ultimately result in measuring even stronger health norms.

Step Seven: Evaluation

Step seven is a continuous evaluation of campaign effectiveness that ultimately drives the entire campaign process toward the desirable end goal of strengthened health and protective norms in the target population. Qualitative and quantitative data are gathered, analyzed, and fed back into the campaign to refine the goals and process of implementation.

The current environment of increased accountability for prevention programs to demonstrate effectiveness necessitates a higher level of evaluation rigor. One of the best ways to demonstrate a program's success is to compare treatment and control groups. When possible, we now advocate operating all projects by using a preintervention, postintervention, quasi-experimental design that allows comparison between intervention and control groups. The basic evaluation follows the logical progression of the social norms process. Ideally, three stages are documented in the campaign evaluation efforts. First, the target population demonstrates a high level of awareness of the campaign message; second, their perceptions undergo a measurable change; and third, their behaviors or attitudes change.

The evaluation must first establish a difference in awareness of the campaign message between the treatment and the control groups after operating the campaign, whereas no such difference should be present prior to the intervention. To be effective, any marketing or communications effort must penetrate its intended audience with enough saturation to achieve a change in the target audience's level of awareness. A social norms effort is no different. We have found that adequate message exposure is the fulcrum point that determines the difference between a campaign that successfully measures changes in behavior and one that does not. If a statistically significant difference in campaign awareness does not exist between the intervention and the control sites, then change in perception or behavior cannot be expected.

If the intervention area demonstrates a higher level of awareness of the campaign message, we then look to see if a difference also exists with regard to perception of norms. If enough time has lapsed (approximately eight months to one year), then it is anticipated that we should be able to measure more accurate views of the normative environment among the intervention group, as compared to the control group. As misperception of the norms is corrected and a more accurate view of the social environment is established, then the intervention group is also expected to report, or be observed to change, their behavior or attitudes to gravitate toward this norm. Essentially, the data reflect behavior being subject to perception. It also implies the importance of reshaping the environment to accurately frame health, protection, and safety norms.

The Montana Blueprint

Building upon the success of several colleges in lowering their rate of harmful drinking, the Montana Model of Social Norms Marketing was created to establish a foundation from which larger macro-level campaigns could be planned, implemented, and evaluated. The Montana Model is a work in process. It is always being systematically refined so that it can achieve its maximum potential to affect social change in Montana and the nation. Although the examples cited in this chapter have focused on health promotion, we are continuing to broaden application of the model to realms unexplored by traditional social norms marketing, such as social justice and community development.

Within the Montana Model, all media, communications, and campaigns start from a framework accurately reflecting clear, consistent, engaging messages that strengthen the public's perception of healthy and safe lifestyles as the norm. The innovative approach of the social norms model, as seen through the application of the Montana Model, has demonstrated that a focus on shifting perception of norms can cultivate healthier public norms by turning social science into social action with measurable results.

Adhering to the fidelity and rigor of the Montana Model has been critical for the Montana Social Norms Project in attaining successful campaign results. The model was initially devised in 1998, yet it has already demonstrated its effectiveness in several areas. Evaluation data associated with our efforts have demonstrated reduced risks of DUI behavior in a statewide population of eighteen-to-twenty-four-year-olds (Linkenbach and Perkins, 2001); delayed first-time use of tobacco by teenagers in an eight-month, seven-county pilot project (Linkenbach and Perkins, Chapter Thirteen); and increased seatbelt use among Montana's adult population (Linkenbach and Perkins, 2001).

It is hoped that the Montana Model can serve as a guide to other practitioners. However, it is important to note that designing and implementing a social norms campaign is a challenging process that requires specialized knowledge. Social norms marketing is still a young field, and there are many unanswered questions. For example, to have impact, what is the minimum threshold at which the public must be exposed to campaign messages? Could several social norms campaigns occurring simultaneously and targeting different issues have a synergistic effect on the overall culture of health? When engaging in grassroots effort, could more significant results be obtained by going beyond merely exposing people to messages and educating them about social norms theory? These and many other questions merit further research and understanding. It is certain that the Montana Model will continue to develop as answers to these questions become known.

References

Berkowitz, A. D. "From Reactive to Proactive Prevention: Promoting an Ecology of Health on Campus." In P. C. Rivers and E. Shore (eds.), *A Handbook on Substance Abuse for College and University Personnel.* Westport, Conn.: Greenwood Press, 1997.

DeJong, W. *Preventing Alcohol-Related Problems on Campus: Driving Impaired Prevention.* (Publication no. ED/OP95-14.) Washington, D.C.: Higher Education Center for Alcohol and Other Drug Prevention, U.S. Department of Education, 1995.

DeJong, W., and others. *Environmental Management: A Comprehensive Strategy for Reducing Alcohol and Other Drug Use on College Campuses.* Washington, D.C.: Higher Education Center for Alcohol and Other Drug Prevention, U.S. Department of Education, 1998.

Fabiano, P. M., and Lederman, L. C. "Top Ten Misperceptions of Focus Group Research—The Report on Social Norms." (Working paper #3.) Little Falls, N.J.: PaperClip Communications, 2002.

Fabiano, P. M., and others. "LifeStyles, 1998: Patterns of Alcohol and Drug Consumption and Consequences Among WWU Students—An Extended Executive Study." *Focus: A Research Summary.* Bellingham, Wash.: Western Washington University, The Office of Institutional Assessment and Testing, 1999.

Floyd, J. W., and Linkenbach, J. W. *Montana Adult Seatbelt Norms Survey.* Bozeman: Montana Social Norms Project, Montana State University, 2000.

Gebhardt, T. L., Kaphingst, K., DeJong, W. "A Campus-Community Coalition to Control Alcohol-Related Problems Off Campus: An Environmental Management Case Study." *Journal of American College Health,* 2000, *48,* 211–215.

Green, L. W., Lucie, R., and Potvin, L. "Ecological Foundations of Health Promotion." *American Journal of Health Promotion,* 1996, *10*(4), 270–281.

Haines, M. P. *A Social Norms Approach to Preventing Binge Drinking at Colleges and Universities.* Newton, Mass.: Higher Education Center for Alcohol and Other Drug Prevention, 1996.

Haines, M. P. "Spare the Rod and Get Results: A Wellness Approach to Health Promotion Media." *Wellness Management,* 1997, *13*(3), 1, 4.

Johannessen, K. J., Collins, C., Mills-Novoa, B. M., and Glider, P. *A Practical Guide to Alcohol Abuse Prevention: A Campus Case Study in Implementing Social Norms and Environmental Management Approaches.* Tucson: Campus Health Service, University of Arizona, 1999.

Kotler, P., and Andreasen, A. *Strategic Marketing for Nonprofit Organizations* (5th ed.). Upper Saddle River, N.J.: Prentice Hall, 1996.

Linkenbach, J. W. "Behind the Big Sky Bar." Unpublished doctoral dissertation, Montana State University, Bozeman, 1995.

Linkenbach, J. W. "Application of Social Norms Marketing to a Variety of Health Issues." *Wellness Management,* 1999, *15*(3), 1, 7–8.

Linkenbach, J. W. "Cultural Cataracts: Identifying and Correcting Misperceptions in the Media—The Report on Social Norms." (Working paper #1.) Garfield, N.J.: PaperClip Communications, 2001.

Linkenbach, J. W., and Perkins, H. W. "Going Big: Key Findings and Lessons Learned from Statewide Applications of the Social Norms Approach to a Variety of Issues." Presented at National Conference on the Social Norms Model, Anaheim, Calif., July 19, 2001.

Montana Department of Public Health and Human Services. *Montana Prevention Needs Assessment Community Student Survey.* Helena, Mont.: Addictive and Mental Disorders Division, 2000.

Montana Department of Transportation. *Traffic Safety Problem Identification (FY 2002).* Helena, Mont.: Engineering Division, Traffic and Safety Bureau, 2001.

National Highway Traffic Safety Administration. *Traffic Safety Facts.* Washington D.C.: U.S. Department of Transportation, 1993.

Perkins, H. W. "Confronting Misperceptions of Peer Drug Use Norms Among College Students: An Alternative Approach for Alcohol and Other Drug Education Programs." In *Peer Prevention Program Resource Manual.* Fort Worth: Higher Education Leaders/Peers Network, Texas Christian University, 1991.

Perkins, H. W. "College Student Misperceptions of Alcohol and Other Drug Norms Among Peers: Exploring Causes, Consequences, and Implications for Prevention Programs." In *Designing Alcohol and Other Drug Prevention Programs in Higher Education: Bringing Theory into Practice.* Newton, Mass.: Higher Education Center for Alcohol and Other Drug Prevention, U.S. Department of Education, 1997.

Perkins, H. W., and Berkowitz, A. D. "Perceiving the Community Norms of Alcohol Use Among Students: Some Research Implications for Campus Alcohol Education Programming." *International Journal of the Addictions,* 1986, *21,* 961–976.

Perkins, H. W., and Craig, D. *A Multifaceted Social Norms Approach to Reduce High-Risk Drinking: Lessons from Hobart and William Smith Colleges.* Newton, Mass.: Higher Education Center for Alcohol and Other Drug Prevention, U.S. Department of Education, 2002.

Ross, H. L. *Confronting Drunk Driving: Social Policy for Saving Lives.* New Haven: Yale University Press, 1992.

Siegel, M., and Donner, L. *Marketing Public Health: Strategies to Promote Social Change.* Gaithersburg, Md.: Aspen, 1998.

Skiba, R. "Zero Tolerance, Zero Evidence: An Analysis of School Disciplinary Practice." (Policy research report no. SRS2.) Bloomington: Indiana Education Policy Center, 2000.

U.S. Center for Substance Abuse Prevention. *Technical Assistance Bulletin: Evaluating the Results of Communication Programs.* Rockville, Md.: Substance Abuse and Mental Health Services Administration, Department of Health and Human Services, 1998.

Zimmerman, R. "Alcohol and Student Disruptions on Campus." *Catalyst,* 1999, *5*(1), 6–7.

PART FIVE

THE SOCIAL NORMS APPROACH IN MIDDLE AND HIGH SCHOOL POPULATIONS

CHAPTER TWELVE

THE IMAGINARY LIVES OF PEERS

Patterns of Substance Use and Misperceptions of Norms Among Secondary School Students

H. Wesley Perkins, Ph.D.; David W. Craig, Ph.D.

By the late 1990s, several researchers and prevention specialists were reporting significant success in reducing alcohol and other substance abuse problems in college populations using a social norms approach (Perkins, 2002). This success lead us to consider expanding research and possible interventions to high school and middle school populations. The phenomenon of misperceived norms was observed in some research on high school students (Beck and Treiman, 1996); earlier controlled experiments demonstrated that providing accurate peer norm information to students in these age categories could indeed reduce use and that this strategy was effective when other traditional approaches such as education about consequences of use and resistance skill training were not having an impact (Evans and Bosworth, 1997; Hansen, 1993; Hansen and Graham, 1991).

Yet as social norms interventions began to spread among college populations, there was no comparable movement in this direction in secondary education. One obvious explanation for the lack of social norms initiatives in secondary education, compared to the growth of the strategy in higher education, is simply the fact that virtually all the researchers and prevention specialists implementing this approach were employed in colleges and universities; thus their work tended to remain in their own backyard. It was simply easiest to experiment with college students, something that is frequently done in many areas of research, and much of the research and resource support could be quickly acquired in these settings.

Another possible explanation accounting for the difference is that initiatives demonstrating norms of moderate use of alcohol in college would not be a viable message in high school, where abstinence is the only publicly acceptable position to promote for adolescents. But this assumes, of course, that abstinence was not the norm in middle and high schools, which itself was a possible misperception that needed to be empirically tested. Indeed, we found in our workshop interactions and informal conversations with secondary education teachers and administrators in many schools that they often believed the majority of their students were smoking cigarettes and drinking and perhaps using other drugs.

Credible and up-to-date data would be needed by schools that might be interested in the social norms approach, for two reasons: first, to find out if the majority were abstinent—a norm that could be presented to students without controversy; and second, to find out if students in a range of secondary schools also exhibited exaggerated misperceptions of peer use, thereby supporting as a worthwhile effort the use of a social norms approach to correct misperception. If students at a younger age did not misperceive their peers in such a distorted fashion as found in a college population, then perhaps the approach would not be as useful. Theory about what creates the misperception (Perkins, 1997; Perkins, 2002) led us to expect otherwise, however.

We surmised, on the basis of conversation with several school administrators, counselors, and teachers, that an important stumbling block to answering this question about the extent of misperception was the ability of schools to effectively gather the data needed to address these questions. Schools often do not have the staff with research methodological skills to design and administer a survey and analyze the data. They may not have the budget necessary for costly private agency surveys. Also, some schools reported that the lengthy turnaround time frame required to get back scanned survey data was often discouraging as well. Thus we decided to design and make available to middle and high schools a Web-based survey that would be (1) modest in cost, (2) efficient in gathering responses from potentially the entire student body, (3) fast in terms of permitting a short turnaround time for the return of data, and (4) include questions on perceived norms about peer attitudes and behaviors as well as personal attitudes and behaviors that could be compared.

Web-Based Surveys for Collecting Social Norms Data

Web-based surveys can (1) improve student response rates, (2) improve the accuracy of student responses, (3) promote the flexibility of adding customized questions for a particular school project or concern, (4) reduce data collection costs,

(5) greatly increase the rapidity with which data can be made available back to schools, (6) increase the integrity and efficacy of a social norms media campaign, and (7) facilitate an ongoing program assessment strategy.

The Web surveys we designed for collecting data in secondary schools were typically completed in ten to twelve minutes with a student sitting at a computer. This means that groups of students could be scheduled in fifteen-to–thirty-minute intervals for a computer laboratory throughout the school day. Most schools were able to survey all of their students present at school in less than one week.

Web-based surveys can dramatically improve the accuracy of data entry. Automatic validation can be incorporated into Web survey forms to ensure consistency of response and valid ranges of data entry. Anonymity can be ensured using Web-based survey procedures (described later) to improve the integrity of the responses and satisfy human subject review board requirements.

Surveys can be customized to meet the program needs of a participating school. Questions were added and references made to specific school programs to make the survey more responsive to the needs of a particular school. This also helped connect students to the survey, showing them that this survey was for their school.

There are no printing costs or paper distribution costs associated with these Web-based surveys, and customized surveys do not require costly reprinting. Students can correct mistyped entries without ambiguity or the need to start over on a new survey form. This strategy is also environment-friendly. Coding is completed automatically by a Web server as students complete their forms online. Automated reports can be generated from Web-based survey data, further reducing costs.

The sooner that data from a survey can be reported back to a school community, the more closely connected students feel to the information being reported. They have a better understanding of where the information came from, and they are naturally curious about the results of the survey right after they have taken it. These benefits are maximized when all students participate, rather than a subsample. With a Web-based survey, it does not matter how large or small the sample. Since coding is instantaneous and automatic, once the surveys have been administered a report can be generated and returned by electronic mail—the next day, if necessary.

By reducing costs and administrative overhead for survey administration, it was possible for some school systems to plan for ongoing data collection at regular, repeating intervals. As frequently noted in social norms studies, ongoing data collection is a crucial element of prevention work. It ensures the latest and most positive norms for messages, a student body that is closely connected to the source of information, and ongoing assessment of the success of the prevention programming in place.

Achieving Anonymity

The accuracy and integrity of survey responses are improved when respondent anonymity is ensured. At the same time, it is also critical to control the survey sample and data integrity, to be certain that individuals do not submit multiple surveys and that other individuals with the survey Web address but who are outside a survey sample (or school district) do not submit contaminating data. We have developed a timed username-password classroom strategy that can satisfy both of these objectives while simultaneously maintaining anonymity.

Usernames and passwords to a survey, active only for a selected time period, may be assigned to each group of students taking the survey in a participating school district. Time-limited usernames and passwords do not allow access to the survey before or after a class period. Neither students nor staff can use a username or password outside of the designated time period. During the period for survey administration, a class is collectively given the username and password for the survey. All students in the class have the same username and password, to ensure anonymity. Since the usernames and passwords expire at the end of a session, students may not return to the survey and make additional submissions. Each class period has its own username and password. This may seem complicated at first, but each student or teacher is really only confronted with a single username and password for a given period. To accelerate this process, many school districts have a monitor preenter the session username and password just prior to student arrival at the computer facility. Students can randomly choose the specific computer they use in the classroom or lab, so they realize they are not personally identified by the username or the computer they use.

Procedure for Survey Administration

The procedures for conducting a Web-based survey can be divided into four stages. First, the school works with consultants to design custom questions that it may need for additional data collection or local program assessment. As part of this process, the school enters into a data disclosure agreement with the hosting institution that defines the confidentiality of the data and to whom and how it is to be released. Second, the school creates a schedule of time periods for survey administration so that usernames and passwords can be defined and returned to the appropriate administrative officer. Instructions for technology staff or computer laboratory monitors are distributed. Third, students using the group username and password for each session take the survey. Fourth, a data report of response frequencies is returned to the designated school official.

Middle and High School Survey Participation

We discovered several schools were eager to collect data on their students using our Web-based survey methodology. They agreed to participate in our research, allowing us to report their data with only the stipulation that the specific school name not be identified without permission. The data reported in this chapter comes from all twenty-eight middle schools (grades six through eight) and high schools (grades nine through twelve) that used a version of our Web survey during the academic years of fall 1999 through spring 2002. A total of 8,860 students participated. (See http://alcohol.hws.edu for example surveys.) For schools that repeated the survey, only data from their first survey are reported here. Participation ranged geographically from East Coast to West Coast, including schools in Massachusetts, New York, Colorado, Montana, and Washington state. The smallest schools in rural areas had a total student population of fewer than one hundred students, and the largest schools using the survey had enrollments of more than one thousand. In most instances, a school attempted to have all students in attendance participate, while a few schools chose to survey a representative sample of students within the school. Response rates ranged from a low of 55 percent to total participation (100 percent of enrollment).

Comparing Actual Behavior and Perceptions of Peers

In each middle school and high school, we compared students' actual norms regarding substance use for each grade (determined by the distribution of personal behaviors) with the perception students held of their peers in that grade, from a variety of measures available in each survey.

In ten of the fourteen middle schools and eleven of the fourteen high schools, questions about the frequency of personal tobacco use and the perceived frequency of typical peer use were included that allowed us to compare actual and perceived norms for each grade. In each of the middle schools providing data, the majority of students in each grade reported never using any tobacco during the year. The rate of abstaining from tobacco ranged from 100 percent of sixth graders in one Montana school down to 71 percent of eighth graders in another Montana school. In the high schools, abstaining from tobacco was also the norm (greater than 50 percent) in every class in ten of the eleven schools and in two of the four grades in the remaining high school. The abstinence rate ranged from 94 percent among ninth graders in one Massachusetts school and one New York school down to 43 percent of seniors in one Montana school. Thus, for our data on seventy-one grade-level peer groups collectively drawn from twenty-one schools, in all but two of these groups, the majority abstained entirely from tobacco use. Overall, only 12 percent of the middle school students and 35 percent of the high school students had ever used tobacco within the year (see Table 12.1).

In each school, students were also asked to estimate the incidence rate of tobacco use and nonuse among students in their grade. Their estimates of use among their same-grade peers were then compared with the actual rate in their grade at their school. Students, on average, at every school (middle and high school) overestimated the actual rate of use in their grade. Middle school students typically overestimated (misperceived) the use rate in their grade by 16 percent and high school students by 17 percent.

TABLE 12.1. SUBSTANCE USE AND DRUNKENNESS RATES IN MIDDLE AND HIGH SCHOOLS OVERALL AND AVERAGE MISPERCEPTION OF PEER RATES.

	Middle Schools (Grades 6–8)	High Schools (Grades 9–12)
Percentage ever using tobacco within year	18	35
Mean overestimate of percentage of peers in grade ever using tobacco within year	16	17
Total *n* of students surveyed	2,747	4,218
Number of schools	10	11
Percentage using marijuana or illicit drugs within year*	10	33
Mean overestimate of percentage of peers in grade using illicit drugs within year	19	20
Total *n* of students surveyed	3,530	4,785
Number of schools	14	14
Percentage who have been drunk in the past month	7	29
Mean overestimate of percentage of peers in grade who have been drunk in the past month	23	26
Total *n* of students surveyed	2,591	3,976
Number of schools	10	11

Note: * In four middle schools and four high schools the survey question asked explicitly about marijuana; in ten middle schools and ten high schools the survey item asked about "marijuana or other illicit drugs."

In all twenty-eight schools, questions about personal and perceived use of marijuana and other illicit drugs (or in some schools marijuana only) were included that again allowed us to compare actual and perceived norms for each grade. (In twenty schools, the survey question asked about "marijuana and other illicit drugs"; in the other eight schools the question was more circumscribed by simply asking about marijuana, which is by far the most pervasive illicit drug used by students.) In all but one school, the majority in every grade never used marijuana (or marijuana and other illicit drugs). The percentage using marijuana (or marijuana and other illicit drugs) fell just below half (49 percent) in only two of the four grades in just one high school. Overall, 90 percent of the middle school students and 67 percent of the high school students never used marijuana (or marijuana and other illicit drugs). As was the case with tobacco, in each of these schools students were also asked to estimate the percentage of students in their grade who never used marijuana (or marijuana and other illicit drugs). When we compared their estimates of the rate among their same-grade peers with the actual rate in their grade at their school, substantial misperception was again revealed. In every school, students typically overestimated the actual rate of use in their grade. Middle school students, on average, overestimated the use by 19 percent—a perception of use almost triple the overall actual use rate. High school students overestimated the actual use rate by 20 percent.

We also asked students in ten middle schools and eleven high schools if they had gotten drunk within the last month. Only 7 percent of middle school students and 29 percent of high school students had done so. We found substantial overestimates of this behavior in all grades in all twenty-one schools. Middle school students' estimates of the percentage of peers drunk within the month, on average, were about four times the actual rate, with a mean overestimate of 23 percent. High school students' estimates of peer drunkenness roughly doubled the actual rate on average, with a mean overestimate of 26 percent.

Imaginary Norms of Peers in Grade and Older Peer Norms

Using another set of questions in the surveys, we were able to examine student perception of a wider grade range of peers. Specifically, we examined respondents' perceived norms for the frequency of substance use, with regard to perception not only of one's own grade but also of eleventh and twelfth graders for those respondents who were in tenth grade or lower. We wanted to see what students anticipated to be the norm as they looked up or ahead to future years as a junior or senior in their high school. To compare perceived norms with actual norms across an extended grade range, we examined seventh and eighth graders' as well as ninth and tenth graders' perceptions of their older peer group of high school juniors and seniors. This meant we needed data on juniors and seniors in the same school district as the younger students surveyed, to directly compare actual norms with the imagined norms of juniors and seniors held by younger students.

Among the twenty-eight middle and high schools participating in this research, twelve schools could be paired in this regard. Three middle schools and three high schools were structurally paired in a central school configuration that physically incorporated the middle and high school students. In the other instances, three participating middle schools were each the feeder school to a high school that also participated in the survey. Two of the middle school and high school sets were located in New York, two were located in Montana, and two were located in the state of Washington. Three were small school districts in terms of the number of students in each grade level, one was of intermediate size, and two were school districts with a relatively large student enrollment.

In each of the six school districts providing data on middle school and high school students, we conducted identical analyses. First, we grouped the student data into two-year segments: seventh and eighth graders, ninth and tenth graders, and eleventh and twelfth graders (excluding sixth graders). We then identified the most common (median) frequency of substance use for tobacco, illicit drugs (or marijuana specifically, depending on the survey used in the particular school district), and alcohol for each grade-level grouping. We compared that result with the most typical (median) perception students held of peers' frequency of use for the same grade level and also their most common (median) estimates of the frequency of use among juniors and seniors (if they were themselves in a lower grade). Actual use, as well as perception of what was most typical among peers, was measured using the response categories of never, one or two times per year, once a month, twice a month, once a week, twice a week, and daily.

Figure 12.1 presents the median responses (actual and perceived) for tobacco use along with the specific percentage that never used tobacco in each grade level in each of the six school districts, ordered by size. Clearly, no use of tobacco was the norm in each of the school districts and across all grades. Smoking was simply never normative (abstinence rates ranged from 58 percent to 91 percent). Student perception of norms (most often misperception of norms) would lead one to think otherwise, however. In every instance except the seventh and eighth graders of school district A, students on average estimated that peers in their same grade most typically used tobacco at least once or twice a year and more commonly thought their peers were using tobacco at least once a month. Furthermore, in most cases younger students believed that high school juniors and seniors typically used tobacco even more frequently (and never less frequently than same-grade peers), which was also a gross misperception, given that the actual norm for these eleventh and twelfth graders, as already stated, was one of abstinence.

FIGURE 12.1. ACTUAL TOBACCO USE AND PERCEIVED PEER/OLDER PEER USE BY GRADE (MEDIAN FREQUENCIES).

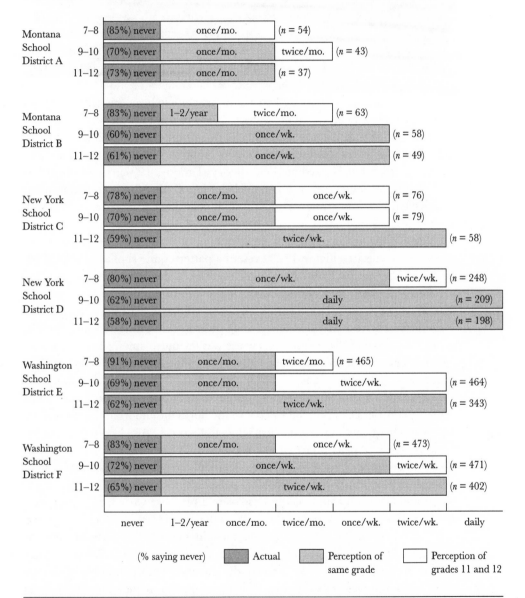

Note: Overlapping bars within grade level represent the median actual use, median perceived use by same grade years, and median perceived use by grades 11–12. Perception of same grade use is hidden if the median is the same as the actual use median; perception of grade 11–12 is hidden if the median is the same as the median for same grade perception. Only actual use and same grade perception are reported for grades 11–12.

Although abstinence remained the norm across grade levels, results also re-vealed a decline in these rates when moving from middle school, where the rate ranged between 80 percent and 91 percent, to the older grades of high school (with rates ranging between 58 percent and 73 percent). This decline should be expected from the point of view of social norms theory because students in the younger grades are already experiencing the simultaneously pernicious pull of both their exaggerated perception of peer norms in their seventh and eighth grade classes and their exaggerated perception of what older students do. Thus there are multiple levels of misperceived normative pressure to begin smoking: one from their own grade and one from the distorted view of what lies ahead.

Finally, in Figure 12.1 we see that the distortion of perceived norms com-pared to actual norms is larger when the peer group as a whole is larger. This find-ing is exactly what is predicted by theory (Perkins, 1997), suggesting that psychological attribution errors about the behavior of others become greater when perceiving the characteristics of more distant peers (that is, larger classes) as well as older cohorts.

Findings for student reports of the frequency of marijuana or marijuana and other illicit drugs (see Figure 12.2) present a pattern quite similar to that of to-bacco use already described. Abstinence was always the norm for all school dis-tricts and all class years, though the rate declined for older students in most districts. Again, students most commonly believed that at least some use of illicit drugs during the year was the norm among peers in their grade. In some districts, most students even believed that weekly use was the norm among peers their age. Again, younger students' perceptions of the norms for use among the juniors and seniors were even more exaggerated in some districts or otherwise equally dis-torted with their same-grade perceptions. (In only one case, ninth and tenth graders in district D, did students perceive the norm for juniors and seniors to be slightly less frequent than that of their same-grade peers.) Also like the pattern for tobacco, distorted perceptions of same-grade and older peer use of illicit drugs tended to be more extreme in the larger districts compared to small ones, where almost everyone would know each other personally.

Student data on actual alcohol use were a bit more varied, as seen in Fig-ure 12.3. Complete abstinence throughout the year is less common compared to tobacco and illicit drug use. Although abstinence was the norm for seventh and eighth graders in four of the six districts, abstinence rates declined to under half of high school students. Even so, the norm was most commonly to con-sume alcohol once or twice a year (which presumably included many students who would simply consume some alcohol at a family holiday celebration or re-ligious occasion and include that in their report of personal use). More impor-tant is the stark pattern of large misperception made obvious in Figure 12.3, just as found in the previous figures displaying misperception of other substance

FIGURE 12.2. ACTUAL ILLICIT DRUG USE AND
PERCEIVED PEER/OLDER PEER USE BY GRADE (MEDIAN FREQUENCIES).

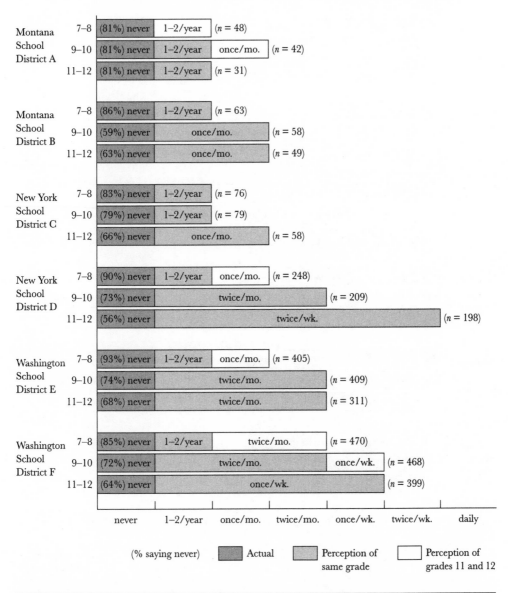

Note: Overlapping bars within grade level represent the median actual use, median perceived use by same grade years, and median perceived use by grades 11–12. Perception of same grade use is hidden if the median is the same as the actual use median; perception of grade 11–12 is hidden if the median is the same as the median for same grade perception. Only actual use and same grade perception are reported for grades 11–12.

FIGURE 12.3. ACTUAL ALCOHOL USE AND PERCEIVED PEER/OLDER PEER USE BY GRADE (MEDIAN FREQUENCIES).

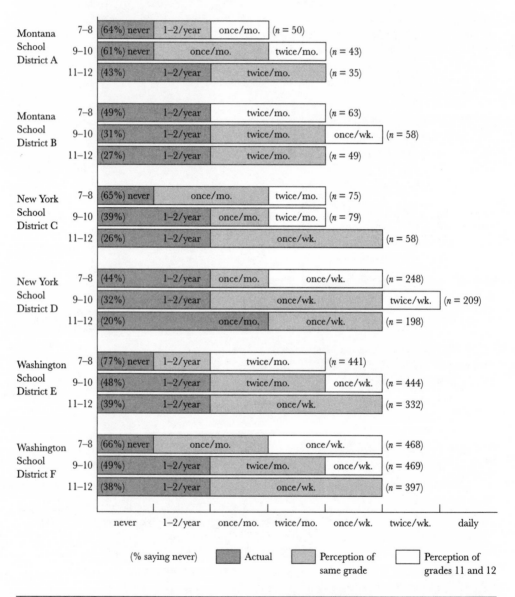

Note: Overlapping bars within grade level represent the median actual use, median perceived use by same grade years, and median perceived use by grades 11–12. Perception of same grade use is hidden if the median is the same as the actual use median; perception of grade 11–12 is hidden if the median is the same as the median for same grade perception. Only actual use and same grade perception are reported for grades 11–12.

use. At every grade level and in every school district, students most commonly believed that peers in their grade were typically drinking much more frequently than was the case. In every instance, middle school students and ninth and tenth graders held an even more exaggerated notion of how frequently juniors and seniors would drink.

Lessons Learned

Secondary school administrators and students participated in a Web-based assessment of alcohol, tobacco, and other drug norms and perceptions and were able to achieve a high level of participation in all grades. The short time required for survey administration, the low cost, the rapid return of data, and the broad availability of World Wide Web access were important factors ensuring the success of this project. The consistency of results across schools and across grades within a school district clearly demonstrates the reliability of this strategy for measuring norms and perceptions, as well as the transportability of this strategy to a broad range of institutional contexts. Moreover, the high level of participation afforded in a Web-based survey gives a greater degree of connection and credibility to the data reported in a social norms media campaign.

We found that abstinence was the norm for tobacco and illicit drugs for all schools and all grades in this study. Regarding alcohol use, abstinence was the most typical norm among the fourteen middle schools and the overall norm among middle school students who responded to our survey. Rare use of alcohol or abstinence (one or two times per year or not at all) was most typical across the fourteen high school settings and was the response of the majority of high school students overall participating in this study.

The data presented in this chapter also show clearly the pervasive nature of misperception across substances, across grades, across small and large schools, and across geographical regions. Moreover, although exaggerated misperception of same-grade peer norms was seen for all substances across all grades, even greater misperception of eleventh and twelfth grade norms was held by many younger students who ultimately aspire to become juniors and seniors. Thus, at least two levels of misperception create imaginary peer pressure toward greater use of tobacco, illicit drugs, and alcohol. Misperception was generally greater in larger schools than in smaller ones. If students are less familiar with most other peers as in a larger school, they make more distorted attributions about the character of peers around them. Likewise, they tend to make more distorted judgments about the norms of less familiar students in older grades in their school system. Finally, a declining rate of abstinence across grades shows the erosion that occurs as students evaluate their actions and make decisions on the basis of gross misperception of what their peers are doing.

All of these data suggest that secondary school students exhibit the fundamental pattern of misperceptions on which the social norms prevention strategy can work to reduce substance use. Data-based messages conveying the truth about the norm of peer abstinence for tobacco and illicit drugs for all grades can be used. Credible nonuse messages about alcohol norms can also be used for middle schools, and even for high schools when one considers time periods shorter than a full year. Although we cannot say that the majority of high school students have never used alcohol, we can say they rarely do, if ever. For example, the number of students who consume alcohol in a typical month can be computed from the survey data. A clear data-based message challenging misperception can state that the majority have not consumed alcohol in the last month, or simply that most students in one's grade, or most juniors and seniors, were not drinking last weekend—a reality that runs contrary to many high school students' image of their peers' social lives.

In closing, we offer an anecdotal account of student responses to the Web survey results from one school in this study as they were presented in a group meeting with student representatives and local educators. This could be the story of countless schools, but in reality it is the story of one particular school district where we conducted this research.

Several incidents, including a drug-overdose death and parties where heavy drinking occurred, were heavily publicized in the local newspaper. The majority of students involved were from one of the two high schools in the town. There were many letters to the editor and editorials expressing concern about drug and alcohol use in this particular school. The local police department, out of desperation and with the help of a government grant, decided to fund a social norms project for the high school to assess the degree of substance abuse and to use the information to mount a prevention program. Parents, teachers, and student groups were all fearful that results would confirm their entrenched notions that problem behavior was commonplace among the teens of the school.

In a presentation where students learned that 67 percent of them rarely or never drank alcohol and that the overwhelming majority did not use illicit drugs, one could see the relief on many of their faces. In a group session with student leaders, with tears in their eyes, students shared their relief to know that most of them "were good kids" after all, and that it was good to hear a positive message of support after so many negative and scolding messages from the community, police, and school staff. Although they were often surprised by the survey results, these findings gave them encouragement to continue their healthy behavior and promote it among peers.

References

Beck, K., and Treiman, K. A. "The Relationship of Social Context of Drinking, Perceived Social Norms, and Parental Influence to Various Drinking Patterns of Adolescents." *Addictive Behaviors,* 1996, *21,* 633–644.

Evans, A., and Bosworth, K. "Building Effective Drug Education Programs." *Research Bulletin,* 1997, no. 19.

Hansen, W. B. "School-Based Alcohol Prevention Programs." *Alcohol Health and Research World,* 1993, *17,* 54–60.

Hansen, W. B., and Graham, J. H. "Preventing Alcohol, Marijuana, and Cigarette Use Among Adolescents: Peer Pressure Resistance Training Versus Establishing Conservative Norms." *Preventive Medicine,* 1991, *20,* 414–430.

Perkins, H. W. "College Student Misperceptions of Alcohol and Other Drug Norms Among Peers: Exploring Causes, Consequences, and Implications for Prevention Programs." In *Designing Alcohol and Other Drug Prevention Programs in Higher Education: Bringing Theory into Practice.* Newton, Mass.: Higher Education Center for Alcohol and Other Drug Prevention, U.S. Department of Education, 1997.

Perkins, H. W. "Social Norms and the Prevention of Alcohol Misuse in Collegiate Contexts." *Journal of Studies on Alcohol,* 2002, Supplement no. 14, 164–172.

CHAPTER THIRTEEN

MOST OF US ARE TOBACCO FREE

An Eight-Month Social Norms Campaign Reducing Youth Initiation of Smoking in Montana

Jeffrey W. Linkenbach, Ed.D.; H. Wesley Perkins, Ph.D.

Common sense as well as research suggest that primary prevention—educating people before they start to engage in a high-risk behavior—is a wise use of prevention money that can reap a substantial return. Thus demonstrating effective primary prevention strategies using science-based theory and evaluation is an important objective of the Montana Social Norms Project, which developed the MOST of Us Are Tobacco Free campaign. This project, based at Montana State University, was contracted by the Montana Department of Public Health and Human Services, Montana Tobacco Use Prevention Project, to pilot test a social norms approach to tobacco prevention among adolescents. In 1999, several Montana agencies and the U.S. Centers for Disease Control and Prevention identified as a priority the importance of reducing the number of Montana teens who become first-time smokers.

Clearly, it is much more effective to prevent people from becoming smokers than to try to intervene to cease such behavior after an addiction has taken hold. Thus the purpose of this innovative project was to test and evaluate the effectiveness of a social norms media campaign in reducing the number of youths who begin to smoke cigarettes. The specific goals of the campaign were:

- A measured increase in awareness of the MOST of Us campaign message in the target population of twelve-through-seventeen-year-olds from pretest to posttest results

- A measured change in perception of tobacco-use norms by the target population to more accurately reflect actual tobacco-use norms
- A measured decrease in actual tobacco-use behavior of twelve-through-seventeen-year-olds in the campaign area, with a particular emphasis on the primary prevention goal of reducing the number of teens who use tobacco for the first time

How the MOST of Us Campaign Works

The Montana MOST of Us Are Tobacco Free campaign is based on social norms theory, which maintains that much of our behavior is influenced by our perception of how members of our social groups behave. Perceptions are often incorrect. For example, research consistently demonstrates that young people do not accurately perceive the substance use norms of their peers. Specifically, they overestimate the prevalence of all types of drug use including tobacco (Hancock and Henry, Chapter Eight of this volume; Perkins and others, 1999; Perkins and Craig, Chapter Twelve). Such misperception creates a false sense of peer pressure that is reinforced throughout the fabric of our social environment, including the media. Even health education programs that continue to focus on problem behavior may unwittingly lead youths to believe most peers are engaged in unhealthy lifestyles. Since all of us (especially teens) have a strong desire to fit in and belong to peer groups, the premise of social norms theory is that teens adopt behaviors they think are "normal" so that they are accepted and fit in with others. Thus, according to social norms theory, many youths begin smoking because they believe that it is normal and that most of their peers smoke. Fortunately, these perceptions are often incorrect. The MOST of Us Are Tobacco Free campaign works to prevent teenage tobacco use by informing young people of the actual norm of nonuse through advertising and education efforts that target teenagers.

As part of the social norms marketing strategy, a positive and inclusive message was developed to promote the healthy norm in a manner that was appealing and credible to the target group. The campaign's primary message, "MOST of Us, 70 percent of Montana teens, are tobacco free," was derived using data from the two leading health surveys administered in Montana public schools, the Youth Risk Behavior Survey and the Prevention Needs Assessment. The "70 percent are tobacco free" statistic represents an average of Montana youth aged twelve through seventeen who reported not using tobacco in the past thirty days on these surveys, as well as an initial phone survey conducted by the Montana Social Norms Project.

Selecting the Campaign Target Area

Prior to the 2000–01 campaign outlined in this report, an initial four-month pilot study was implemented during 1999–2000 for the purpose of conducting formative research and testing campaign materials in a three-county region of southwest Montana. In 1999, the director of the MSNP met with officials in the Montana Department of Public Health and Human Services to plan the media and research designs. Because of the increased importance of providing evidence of program effectiveness to state legislators and health administrators, a quasi-experimental design was chosen that would allow comparison of the initial four-month pilot project with a similarly matched control site that did not receive the media intervention.

One of the contributing factors directing selection of pilot and control sites was the importance of isolating media channels, so that television and radio message exposure could be provided to teens in one part of the state and not in others. To meet such a criterion, similar metropolitan areas on opposite sides of the state were chosen, those encompassing the cities of Missoula and Billings. Both of these metro areas allow independent purchase and placement of media and have other similarly matched demographic variables. The Missoula market area, consisting of the area of Lake, Ravalli, and Missoula counties, was chosen as the intervention site for the four-month 1999–2000 pilot project. The Billings market area served as the control site.

Phone surveys were conducted before and after the four-month campaign in both the pilot and control areas. A higher level of campaign awareness and significant changes in perception of tobacco use were documented in the pilot area after the campaign. These findings justified further expansion and development of the MOST of Us campaign into a seven-county intervention area.

The 2000–01 research study expanded from the original three-county pilot area to include all seven counties of the Missoula designated market area, which is home to approximately 28 percent (21,300) of Montana's teens aged twelve through seventeen. This expansion continued to allow the project to purchase and place media solely in these seven western counties while excluding such coverage in the remainder of the state. For the seven-county 2000–01 campaign, the control area consisted of the remaining forty-nine counties in the state.

Delivering the Message

The campaign message was delivered to the target audience using a variety of mechanisms. Radio and television advertising time was purchased. Six television ads and six radio ads aired during three eight-week media flights. The television ads appeared on cable and broadcast stations. The broadcast television exposure was approximately 1,500 gross rating points per flight; because cable audience share is measured on a national level, there are no accurate methods to determine the local cable exposure of the campaign commercials. In addition to radio and television ads, seventy-eight thousand print and promotional items containing the campaign message were distributed to schools in the campaign area. Four theater slides were developed and run during a one-month period at two movie theaters, and one billboard design appeared in four locations for a one-month period. Figures 13.1 and 13.2 are examples of some of the print messages.

Measuring the Results

To evaluate the 2000–01 campaign in the seven-county area, phone surveys were conducted before and after the campaign in both the intervention counties and the control area (all other counties). For the campaign pretest phone surveys, Montana households were randomly selected within the designated intervention and control areas and initial screening phone calls were made to parents to obtain permission for their teenagers to have privacy for participating in the phone interview.

Sample Characteristics

At time 1 (July and August 2000), the phone survey sample obtained 409 responses from the counties targeted for the intervention and 419 responses from the rest of the counties in the state serving as a control comparison. Respondents in the initial intervention and control groups represented grade levels across junior and senior high school years in the state. The two groups were similar on all demographic background data collected in the initial survey. As reported in Table 13.1, there were no statistically significant differences between the intervention and control samples for age, gender, or racial composition. Equally important, there was no statistically significant difference between the groups in terms of the percentage of participants who had any experience with tobacco use at the time (see Table 13.1).

When the time 2 posttest sampling was completed (July 2001), a total of 303 respondents from the intervention counties (74 percent response from time 1) and 338 respondents from the control counties (81 percent response from time 1) had been successfully contacted for follow-up interviews. As with the larger time 1 samples, there were no significant demographic differences between the intervention and control groups when only the subsets of respondents who persisted in the research were examined separately at either time 1 or time 2. Thus, any time 2 differences in smoking are not likely to be indicative of a sampling bias.

FIGURE 13.1. CAMPAIGN POSTER: MOST MONTANA TEENS A.

Source: Used by permission of Montana Social Norms Project, Montana State University.

FIGURE 13.2. CAMPAIGN POSTER: MOST MONTANA TEENS B.

Source: Used by permission of Montana Social Norms Project, Montana State University.

TABLE 13.1. SAMPLE CHARACTERISTICS AT TIME 1 (2000).

Characteristic	Intervention Counties	Control Counties
Mean age	14.6	14.6
Gender (percentage female)	49	50
Race (percentage minority)	4	5
Percentage have tried smoking	27	25
(n of cases)	(409)	(419)

Note: There are no statistically significant differences (*p* > .05) between intervention and control county samples.

Media Exposure Intervention

The social norms intervention consisted of exposing youth in the seven intervention counties to multiple media messages intended to communicate that the majority of youth do not use tobacco. Table 13.2 presents the data collected at time 2 on the degree of campaign exposure reported among youth residing in the intervention counties as compared with reported exposure by youth in the control counties. Statistically significant differences were found for all forms of media exposure itemized in the survey, including television, radio, and newsprint. In each instance, when asked if they had seen or heard any prevention ads and asked to recall what kind of content was included without specific prompting on content, adolescent respondents in the intervention sample were much more likely to report having seen a tobacco prevention message specifically communicating that the majority do not use tobacco.

In the interview section on media exposure, respondents were subsequently asked if they recalled a message specifically stating that "most of us, 70 percent of Montana teens, are tobacco free." Table 13.3 presents the percentage of students saying they saw or heard this message, broken down by intervention and control groups. Here again, the statistically significant differences make clear that the intervention counties got a comparatively larger dose of the social norms message.

Intervention Impact on Perceived Norms

The next question we examined was the degree to which such a clear difference in media message exposure might have been translated into greater accuracy in perceived norms in the intervention counties. Table 13.4 presents data on the adolescent respondents' perception regarding tobacco use and the behavior of the

TABLE 13.2. PERCENTAGE OF YOUTHS SPONTANEOUSLY RECALLING TOBACCO PREVENTION MESSAGE EXPOSURE DURING PAST THIRTY DAYS AT TIME 2 (2001) FOR INTERVENTION/CONTROL COUNTIES BY MEDIA TYPE AND TYPE OF CONTENT.

Media Type	Intervention Counties	Control Counties
Television advertisement** (percentage)		
Most teenagers do not use	25	5
Other prevention message	30	40
Uncertain or no recall	44	55
Radio advertisement** (percentage)		
Most teenagers do not use	22	3
Other prevention message	12	16
Uncertain or no recall	66	81
Newspaper story or advertisement* (percentage)		
Most teenagers do not use	5	1
Other prevention message	3	4
Uncertain or no recall	92	96

Note: Percentages within media category do not always add to 100 because of rounding error.

* Differences between intervention and control group categories are significant at $p < .01$; ** $p < .001$.

TABLE 13.3. PERCENTAGE RECALLING CAMPAIGN ADVERTISEMENT AT TIME 2 (2001) WHEN TOLD THE AD STATED "MOST OF US, 70% OF MONTANA TEENS, ARE TOBACCO FREE" FOR INTERVENTION/CONTROL COUNTIES BY MEDIA TYPE.

	Intervention Counties	Control Counties
On television*	82	33
On radio*	65	21
In newspaper*	26	7
On billboard*	80	37
At school*	79	32
On posters or frisbees*	78	29

Note: * Difference between intervention and control group categories is significant at $p < .001$.

TABLE 13.4. PERCEIVED PEER TOBACCO USE NORMS AT TIME 1 (2000) AND TIME 2 (2001) BY INTERVENTION/CONTROL COUNTIES (PERCENTAGE WITH ERRONEOUS PERCEPTION OF PEER NORM).

	Intervention Counties	Control Counties
Time 1 (2000)		
Think majority their same age have tried smoking	54	60
Think majority three years older have tried smoking	70	73
Think majority their same age have smoked in past thirty days	26	30
Think majority three years older have smoked in past thirty days	46	47
Time 2 (2001)		
Think majority their same age have tried smoking	53*	61
Think majority three years older have tried smoking	65**	75
Think majority their same age have smoked in past thirty days	22*	30
Think majority three years older have smoked in past thirty days	34**	45

Note: * Percentage misperceiving norm in intervention counties is significantly different from percentage in control counties at $p < .05$; ** $p < .01$.

majority of peers their age and of slightly older peers. These data are broken down by intervention and control groups at time 1 and time 2 for the respondents who participated at both time points. At the beginning of this experiment there were no statistically significant differences in perceived norms. By various measures, a large percentage of respondents in the intervention and control groups erroneously thought the majority of their same-age and older peers had tried and were currently using tobacco.

Perhaps it might be noted that, though statistically insignificant, the intervention group at time 1 did reveal some higher level of accurate perception that may be reflective of some social norms campaigning begun in a few of the intervention counties during the 1999–2000 four-month pilot project prior to the time 1 sampling in 2000. But clearly there had not been enough campaigning at that point to make a significant difference in perception, nor was it enough to produce a difference between the intervention and control counties in the incidence of tobacco use at time 1 (already reported in Table 13.1).

Intervention Impact on Initiation of Smoking

With the data having demonstrated a positive impact of the media intervention on perceived norms, we addressed the final question about initiation of tobacco use. This analysis excluded the minority of survey respondents who indicated at time 1 having tried smoking cigarettes already. Figure 13.3 presents the data on smoking initiation among respondents in the intervention and control counties for the 2000 and 2001 surveys. A marked and statistically significant difference is apparent. In the control group, 17 percent of adolescents who had never used tobacco previously at least tried smoking during the year. In contrast, in the intervention counties only 10 percent did so. The latter percentage in the campaign area represents a 41 percent lower rate of teens initiating smoking during the year compared to the rest of the state.

Implications for Future Prevention Initiatives

We have presented systematically collected data evaluating an eight-month experiment applying a social norms intervention strategy to reduce the onset of tobacco use among teens. It appears that the MOST of Us Are Tobacco Free campaign was successful in exposing many adolescents in the intervention area to the message that the majority of youths do not smoke. The evidence further suggests that this media exposure did translate into more realistic and positive perceptions about peer norms, and ultimately that creating more realistic perception was beneficial in reducing the initial incidence of tobacco use among young people. A substantial dosage of the campaign message was delivered to the target audience, thereby producing an important positive effect on their behavior.

FIGURE 13.3. MONTANA YOUTH TRYING SMOKING FOR THE FIRST TIME BETWEEN 2000 AND 2001, BY EXPOSURE TO SOCIAL NORMS CAMPAIGN.

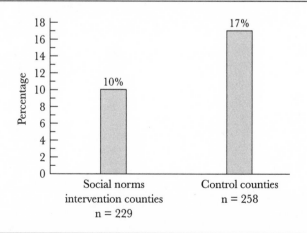

Note: * Significant difference between intervention and control groups at *p* < .05.

This initiative is among the first programs in the nation to be able to demonstrate widespread effectiveness using a social norms approach in reducing youth tobacco use. It is an important result for other programs that want to use this approach and are simultaneously charged with employing strategies that have already demonstrated effectiveness. After an eight-month campaign, significantly fewer teens in the intervention area of Montana reported first-time smoking than in the control area. Specifically, compared to control counties, the initiation rate during the year was cut by more than one-third (41 percent) in Montana counties where the social norms campaign was conducted. Our team of researchers is quite encouraged by this result, as it illustrates the positive impact of exposure to our message on Montana teens' lives. Finally, the data also indicated that, although many teens in the experimental counties had heard and, at least to some degree, internalized the campaign message, many other teens in the campaign area were still not sufficiently exposed to the campaign. Thus, with additional time and resources to broadcast the actual teen norms of nonuse, such a campaign could prevent even more teens from smoking.

Reference

Perkins, H. W., and others. "Misperceptions of the Norms for the Frequency of Alcohol and Other Drug Use on College Campuses." *Journal of American College Health*, 1999, *47*, 253–258.

CHAPTER FOURTEEN

USING SOCIAL NORMS TO REDUCE ALCOHOL AND TOBACCO USE IN TWO MIDWESTERN HIGH SCHOOLS

Michael P. Haines, M.S.; Gregory P. Barker, Ph.D.; Richard Rice, M.A.

It is well documented that the use of alcohol and cigarettes by adolescents remains widespread despite efforts to eliminate it (Johnston, O'Malley, and Bachman, 2000). Consequently, funding agencies increasingly require that the interventions they support be research-based and have a history of effectiveness. The results of a growing number of studies strongly suggest that the social norms approach is an effective method for reducing alcohol use and related harm among college students (Glider and others, 2001; Haines, 1996; Johannessen, Collins, Mills-Novoa, and Glider, 1999; Perkins and Craig, 2002). Various research findings suggest that the social norms approach might also be effective in targeting high school students in a communitywide setting. A number of studies have shown that overestimation of alcohol and cigarette use is widespread among adolescents of middle and high school age (Perkins and Craig, Chapter Twelve of this volume; Sussman and others, 1988; Thombs, Wolcott, and Farkash, 1997). Furthermore, such overestimation of peer use has been found to be a significant predictor of adolescent alcohol and cigarette use (Graham, Marks, and Hansen, 1991). In addition, it has been demonstrated that adolescent onset of use can be significantly delayed by correcting overestimation of alcohol and cigarette use among peers (Hansen and Graham, 1991). Finally, other research has repeatedly shown that media campaigns can be an effective component of prevention interventions targeting youthful populations (Flynn and others, 1992, 1994, 1997; Worden and others, 1988).

Introducing Social Norms to High School Constituencies

In 1998, a Midwestern community group applied for and received a grant from its state Department of Human Services to reduce alcohol and cigarette use by students at two local high schools using a social norms media campaign. The funding agency required that all proposed interventions be research-based, and that data collection and analysis be conducted by the Center for Research and Prevention Development (CPRD) in Champaign, Illinois, an independent agency specifically contracted by the funder for this purpose. Three measures among tenth grade students were selected for the purpose of evaluating project success: alcohol use in the last thirty days, five or more drinks consumed at an occasion in the last two weeks, and cigarette use in the last thirty days.

The intervention strategy was based largely on the social norm campaign implemented at Northern Illinois University (NIU), which achieved significant reductions in alcohol consumption and related harm among its students. However, the design and implementation of this project differed from the university-based intervention in two significant ways. First, it was important that nonuse was the norm for all three measures among the high school students targeted for evaluation in this project. Therefore all of the normative messages reinforced the norm of nonuse (that is, no messages about safe or moderate alcohol use were employed). Second, parents and teachers, in addition to students, were targeted as recipients of the messages reflecting the actual norms of nonuse. Unlike college students who leave home and enter a new social environment, high school students must remain in their community and are presumably subject to the community sphere of influence. Research suggests that parents remain influential in the lives of their adolescent children, in general with regard to having parental standards and expectations (Youniss and Smollar, 1985), and specifically regarding issues of alcohol use (Keefe, 1994). It was expected that teachers might exercise a comparable measure of influence as well.

This intervention was therefore intended to test the social norms approach in a communitywide setting. Specifically, the goal was to reduce parents', teachers', and students' overestimations of student alcohol and cigarette use, and to determine whether this resulted in actual reduction in student alcohol and cigarette use.

The Method of Intervention

As mentioned earlier, the intervention was modeled on the social norm campaign conducted at Northern Illinois University and followed the same four general stages of project development (Haines, 1996). The first stage, data collection, involves gathering data about the target population (patterns of use, perceptions of use, protective behaviors, and so on) and identifying protective, healthy behaviors that are in fact the norm in the target population.

The second stage, development of intervention strategies, involves several steps. First, marketing research is conducted to determine which media channels are currently used, which sources of information about alcohol use and smoking are deemed credible, and when this information is accessed by the target population. Next, media are selected for message delivery and a marketing plan is developed. Part of this marketing plan is to devise a prototype message that is simple, positive, truthful, and consistent. Finally, sample media to deliver the normative message(s) are developed and tested.

During the third stage, implementation, the marketing campaign is launched to deliver the message frequently and consistently during the campaign and data are collected to measure the extent to which the normative messages actually reach, elicit a reaction from, and are recalled by the target population(s). Finally, during the fourth stage, evaluation, outcome data are gathered and analyzed to assess the effectiveness of the media campaign.

Data Collection

Because this project included parents, teachers, and students as integral components of the intervention, data were collected for each population.

The funder required use of the Communities CAN! School Youth Survey, an instrument designed to gather from students a range of information related to demographics, drug and alcohol use and related behavior, and family-related issues. A supplemental forty-nine-question survey was included to assess student perceptions of peer alcohol use, source and frequency of statements related to alcohol, tobacco, and other drugs (ATOD), protective behaviors employed, and source credibility for ATOD-related information. These surveys were administered in April 1999 at the two high schools, to a combined total of 570 tenth grade students. A total of 319 surveys were completed and returned with parental permission, for a response rate of 56 percent.

Parent data were gathered using a thirty-five-question survey assessing perception of student use, sources of ATOD information, use of various community media channels, and the frequency with which sample ATOD-related statements were communicated to children. This survey was administered by mail to a randomly selected sample of two hundred parents of tenth grade students. A total of ninety-one surveys were completed and returned, for a response rate of 46 percent. A similar thirty-six-question survey was administered to a combined total of eighty-five teachers at both high schools during faculty meetings in April 1999. All eighty-five surveys were completed and returned.

In April 2001, the same Communities CAN! School Youth Survey with a supplemental forty-nine-question insert was administered again at the two high schools to a combined total of 571 tenth grade students. A total of 382 surveys were completed and returned with parental permission, for a response rate of 67 percent. Follow-up parent data were gathered using the same parent survey, administered again by mail to a randomly selected sample of two hundred parents of tenth grade students. A total of seventy-two surveys were completed and returned by the parents, for a response rate of 36 percent. All teachers were again surveyed during faculty meetings using the same thirty-six-question survey previously administered. A total of one hundred surveys were completed and returned.

Development of Intervention Strategies

The strategy called for a social norm campaign using various media to correct overestimations of student alcohol and cigarette use held by parents, teachers, and the students themselves identified in the initial surveys. Quantitative data regarding ATOD information sources and their credibility for all three population segments, as well as qualitative data gathered from focus groups, helped to determine which media channels to use for each audience. Messages stating that most students do not drink alcohol or smoke cigarettes, as well as messages modeling the protective behaviors that students employ to avoid alcohol and cigarettes, were then prepared and a plan to disseminate these messages frequently during the school year through the selected channels was put into place.

Implementation

Parents were targeted with display ads placed in both daily and weekly community newspapers, as well as in direct mailings printed on school letterhead. Teachers received detailed information about the campaign in presentations during staff meetings and in-service training (Teacher Institute Days), as well as through interoffice mail. In addition, teachers were exposed to the display ads placed in local newspapers and to the posters mounted throughout the schools. Students were targeted with posters (see Figure 14.1 for an example), pamphlets and flyers, advertisements on two local radio stations, and direct mailings sent to their homes. Given that peers were found to be an important source of ATOD information, it is pertinent to note that the normative messages were directed to students at all grade levels, even though only tenth grade students were selected for the purpose of project evaluation.

FIGURE 14.1. CAMPAIGN POSTER FOR STUDENTS: 8 OUT OF 10 DON'T SMOKE!

8 out of 10 don't smoke!

Health tools to share:
1. Leave places where people are smoking
2. Say "No thanks" if someone offers you tobacco
3. Avoid places where people are smoking

Source: Used by permission.

Evaluation

Parents and teachers were asked to indicate the *percentage* of students at their child's school or the school in which they taught who they believed had more than a few sips of alcohol in the last thirty days and the percentage of students who had five or more drinks in a row in the last two weeks. Parents were asked to estimate, as closely as possible, their beliefs in 10 percent increments (0 percent, 10 percent, 20 percent, and so on).

Parents and teachers were also presented with a thirty-day smoking perception item. Specifically, they were asked to indicate what they thought was characteristic of *most* students at their school in terms of how often students smoked in the last thirty days. These data were dichotomized so that all of the respondents were classified as having perceived smoking as occurring for most students or as not occurring for most students in the time frame described by the survey item.

All student respondents were asked to indicate how many out of one hundred students at their age, in their school, they believed had gotten drunk in the last thirty days, and the number out of one hundred who they believed had smoked cigarettes in the last thirty days. The response categories to these questions were none (0 percent), few (25 percent), some (50 percent), many (75 percent), or all (100 percent). These data were dichotomized so students were classified as having perceived the behavior as normative (meaning, *most* students engaged in the behavior described by the question) or not normative in the time frame described by the survey item.

Students were also asked to report their own alcohol and cigarette use. Specifically, students were asked to indicate the frequency of their alcohol use in the last thirty days, the number of occasions when five or more drinks were consumed in the last two weeks, the frequency of having gotten drunk in the last thirty days, and their thirty-day cigarette use. These data were dichotomized so that students were classified as having engaged in the behavior or not, as described by the survey item.

Initial analyses of the survey data found little difference in the response patterns of the two school districts. Therefore, response data for the two school districts were combined into an aggregate data set. All subsequent analyses used the aggregate data set.

Perceived Student Alcohol and Cigarette Use. Table 14.1 shows the parents' and teachers' perceived alcohol and cigarette use by tenth graders as reported for the 1999 and 2001 survey years. T-tests were used to compare the mean perceived percentage of students who had more than a few sips of alcohol in the last thirty days and who had five or more drinks in a row in the last two weeks. A chi-square was used to compare the percentage of parents and teachers who believed that most students at their child's school smoked a cigarette in the last thirty days.

As Table 14.1 indicates, there was a decline in the mean perceived percentage of students who had more than a few sips of alcohol in the last thirty days for parents (from 49 percent in 1999 to 44 percent in 2001) and a statistically significant decline for teachers (from 55 percent in 1999 to 44 percent in 2001). A similar decline occurred in the mean perceived percentage of students who had five or more drinks in a row in the last two weeks. This decline was significant for both the parents (32 percent in 1999 and 23 percent in 2001) and the teachers (34 percent in 1999 and 26 percent in 2001).

Table 14.1 also shows the percentage of parents and teachers who believed that most students at their child's school smoked in the last thirty days for the 1999

TABLE 14.1. PARENT AND TEACHER PERCEPTION OF TENTH GRADE STUDENT ALCOHOL AND CIGARETTE USE.

Group and Year	Mean Perceived Percentage of Student Thirty Day Alcohol Use		Mean Perceived Percentage of Students Having Five or More Drinks in Row in Last Two Weeks		Percentage Misperceiving Cigarette Use in Last Thirty Days as Typical of Most Students	
	Percentage	n	Percentage	n	Percentage	n
Parents, 1999	49	87	32	87	55	83
Parents, 2001	44	72	23*	72	44	72
Teachers, 1999	55	84	34	84	71	79
Teachers, 2001	44*	95	26*	96	67	91

Note: * significant decrease ($p < .05$) from the 1999 survey year.

and 2001 survey years. The misperception of thirty-day cigarette use as normative showed a similar decline in the 2001 survey year for both the parents (from 55 percent in 1999 to 44 percent in 2001) and the teachers (from 71 percent in 1999 to 67 percent in 2001), but these declines did not reach statistical significance given the limited sample sizes. In general, however, these findings suggest the media campaign led to reductions in the parents' and teachers' overestimation of alcohol and cigarette use.

The Center for Research and Prevention Development, the external evaluator, found a similar decline in student misperception that the majority of peers were getting drunk in the last thirty days (38 percent in 1999, 31 percent in 2001), and in the students' misperception that the majority of peers were smoking cigarettes in the last thirty days (39 percent in 1999, 24 percent in 2001). Both of these declines were significant ($p < .05$).

Actual Student Use of Alcohol and Cigarettes. Table 14.2 shows the students' self-reported alcohol and cigarette use for the 1999 and 2001 survey years. There was a reduction in the percentage of students having more than a few sips of alcohol in the last thirty days (45 percent in 1999, 33 percent in 2001), the percentage of students having five or more drinks in the last two weeks (from 27 percent in 1999 to 19 percent in 2001), the percentage of students having gotten drunk in the last thirty days (32 percent in 1999 and 26 percent in 2001), and the percentage of students smoking in the last 30 days (27 percent in 1999; 19 percent in 2001). All of these reductions were significant.

**TABLE 14.2. SELF-REPORTED ALCOHOL
AND CIGARETTE USE BY TENTH GRADE STUDENTS.**

	Year	Percentage	n
More than a few sips of alcohol in the last thirty days	1999	45	317
	2001	33*	379
Five or more drinks in a row in the last two weeks	1999	27	318
	2001	19*	382
Got drunk in the last thirty days	1999	32	319
	2001	26*	382
Smoked cigarettes in the last thirty days	1999	27	319
	2001	19*	380

Note: * significant decrease ($p < .05$) from the 1999 survey year.

New Insights from This Work

Together, these data indicate the media campaign led to reduction in parents', teachers', and students' overestimation of peer alcohol and cigarette use and, most important, to reduction in actual alcohol and cigarette use among students. This project represents the first attempt to use the social norms approach to achieve widespread reduction of alcohol and cigarette use among adolescents in a community setting by addressing the combination of student, parent, and teacher misperceptions. The fact that it achieved significant reduction of actual use in all of the measures selected for evaluation is an important advance for the field.

It is important to note that no new ATOD prevention programs were introduced into the schools once the social norm campaign was implemented. Also notable is the fact that the statistically significant reduction in alcohol and cigarette use was accompanied by exciting findings in other measures as well. For example, as part of the survey, students were presented with a series of potential sources of alcohol and cigarette information and asked to indicate the frequency with which they saw or heard information from these sources, on a five-point scale. They were also asked to indicate the believability of these sources. These data were analyzed to determine which of the sources were rated by students as having both a high degree of frequency and high believability as a source of ATOD information. Sources that were rated as highly credible but infrequently used were felt to be less desirable for use in the social norm campaign. For example, although the category "doctor or other health professional" was rated as a believable source of

ATOD information by the highest percentage of students (72 percent), the percentage of students who indicated that they frequently saw or heard information from this source was less (21 percent) than the percentage of students who frequently received ATOD information from peers, teachers, and parents (42 percent, 31 percent, and 25 percent respectively). The fact that parents, teachers, and peers were also rated as *believable* sources of ATOD information by a high percentage of students (63 percent, 56 percent, and 56 percent respectively) suggests they are an appropriate domain to target with messages that communicate the actual norms of nonuse. Interestingly, both parents and teachers were increasingly credible sources of ATOD information for students from the 1999 to 2001 survey years. The various media channels through which socially normative messages were delivered to students showed a substantial increase as a believable source of ATOD information as well.

National trend data indicate that adolescent alcohol and cigarette use continues to be a problem requiring solution (Johnston, O'Malley, and Bachman, 2000). Indeed, prior to implementation of the social norm campaign described here, a number of traditional prevention programs (D.A.R.E., peer-based efforts, curricula such as "Here's Looking at You 2000") had been instituted at each of the schools in this study but showed no demonstrable positive impact. Interestingly, this repeats the pattern of contrasting outcomes that first became apparent at a number of universities achieving a significant reduction of alcohol use and related harm among students only after abandoning traditional prevention strategies and adopting the social norms approach (Haines, 1996; Johannessen, Collins, Mills-Novoa, and Glider, 1999; Perkins and Craig, 2002).

As a model of effective, science-based prevention in a community setting, this project presents a number of exciting implications for the field. It is currently being replicated in two other Midwestern communities, while similar projects are now under consideration in various parts of the country as well. Further, its effectiveness in this domain suggests that it may be a promising approach for dealing with other issues of importance to adolescents, such as traffic safety, violence prevention, literacy, and bullying.

References

Flynn, B., and others. "Prevention of Cigarette Smoking Through Mass Media Intervention and School Programs." *American Journal of Public Health*, 1992, *82*, 827–834.

Flynn, B., and others. "Mass Media and School Interventions for Cigarette Smoking Prevention: Effects Two Years After Completion." *American Journal of Public Health*, 1994, *84*, 1148–1150.

Flynn, B., and others. "Long-Term Responses of Higher and Lower Risk Youths to Smoking Prevention Interventions." *Preventive Medicine,* 1997, *26,* 389–394.

Glider, P., and others. "Challenging the Collegiate Rite of Passage: A Campus-wide Social Marketing Media Campaign to Reduce Binge Drinking." *Journal of Drug Education,* 2001, *31*(2), 207–220.

Graham, J., Marks G., and Hansen W. "Social Influence Processes Affecting Adolescent Substance Use." *Journal of Applied Psychology,* 1991, *76*(2), 291–298.

Haines, M. P. *A Social Norms Approach to Preventing Binge Drinking at Colleges and Universities.* Newton, Mass.: Higher Education Center for Alcohol and Other Drug Prevention, 1996.

Hansen, W. B., and Graham J. W. "Preventing Alcohol, Marijuana, and Cigarette Use Among Adolescents: Peer Pressure Resistance Training Versus Establishing Conservative Norms." *Preventive Medicine,* 1991, *20,* 414–430.

Johannessen, K., Collins, C., Mills-Novoa, B., and Glider, P. *A Practical Guide to Alcohol Abuse Prevention: A Campus Case Study in Implementing Social Norms and Environmental Management Approaches.* Newton, Mass.: Higher Education Center for Alcohol and Other Drug Prevention, 1999.

Johnston, L., O'Malley, P., and Bachman, J. *Monitoring the Future: National Survey Results on Drug Use, 1975–1999.* Vol. 1: *Secondary School Students.* (NIH publication 00–4802.) Bethesda, Md.: National Institute on Drug Abuse, 2000.

Keefe, K. "Perceptions of Normative Social Pressure and Attitudes Toward Alcohol Use: Changes During Adolescence." *Journal of Studies on Alcohol,* 1994, *55,* 46–54.

Perkins, H. W., and Craig, D. *A Multi-Faceted Social Norms Approach to Reduce High-Risk Drinking: Lessons from Hobart and William Smith Colleges.* Newton, Mass.: Higher Education Center for Alcohol and Other Drug Prevention, 2002.

Sussman, S., and others. "Adolescent Nonsmokers, Triers, and Regular Smokers' Estimates of Cigarette Smoking Prevalence: When Do Overestimations Occur and by Whom?" *Journal of Applied Social Psychology,* 1988, *18,* 537–555.

Thombs, D. L., Wolcott, B. J., and Farkash, L. G. "Social Context, Perceived Norms and Drinking Behavior in Young People." *Journal of Substance Abuse,* 1997, *9,* 257–267.

Worden, J. K., and others. "Development of a Smoking Prevention Mass Media Program Using Diagnostic and Formative Research." *Preventive Medicine,* 1988, *17,* 531–558.

Youniss, J., and Smollar, J. *Adolescent Relations with Mothers, Fathers and Friends.* Chicago: University of Chicago, 1985.

PART SIX

FURTHER APPLICATIONS AND CHALLENGES FOR THE SOCIAL NORMS MODEL IN PROMOTING HEALTH AND WELL-BEING

CHAPTER FIFTEEN

PARENTS' PERCEPTIONS
OF PARENTING NORMS

Using the Social Norms Approach
to Reinforce Effective Parenting

Jeffrey W. Linkenbach, Ed.D.; H. Wesley Perkins, Ph.D.;
William DeJong, Ph.D.

Parents can feel overwhelmed by the challenge of preventing their adolescent children from using alcohol, tobacco, and other drugs. Movies, television, and popular music frequently glorify substance use while ignoring its negative consequences (Roberts, Henriksen, Christenson, and Kelly, 1999). Peer pressure can also lead to temptation, especially as children get older and spend more time with friends and less time with parents and other adult family members (Kimmel and Weiner, 1985). Neighborhoods where substance use is prevalent and highly visible present still more risk. How should parents respond?

Data for this chapter were drawn from the Montana Parent Norms Survey, produced and conducted by the Montana Social Norms Project (MSNP) at Montana State University in conjunction with Shannon Taylor of Montana State University and Jana Staton of Staton and Associates. We are grateful to Jamie Cornish of the MSNP for her advice on this work, to Alison Govi of the MSNP for making graphics available, and to Shari Kessel Schneider of the Education Development Center (EDC) in Newton, Massachusetts, for providing supplemental data analysis. Funding to support this project was through grants from the Office of Juvenile Justice and Delinquency Prevention, U.S. Department of Justice; and the Center for Substance Abuse Prevention, U.S. Department of Health and Human Services. Preparation of this report was supported in part by U.S. Department of Education contract ED-99-CO-0094 to EDC for operation of the Higher Education Center for Alcohol and Other Drug Prevention, directed by William DeJong. The views expressed in this chapter are those of the authors and do not necessarily reflect the official position of the U.S. Department of Education.

Seeking to assert an independent identity, teenagers frequently push against the rules their parents establish. For parents, whether to yield or stay firm is a complicated and difficult judgment call. Leniency may be harmful, but being too strict also may have negative consequences. This is a situation that invites social comparison. Quite naturally, parents judge the adequacy of their own parenting by looking at what other parents say and do. Teenagers understand this intuitively. What parent hasn't had the supposed leniency of other parents held up as a guide?

The good news for parents is that certain parenting strategies, when applied consistently, can prevent youth substance use, even in an environment where other risk factors are present (Resnick and others, 1997; Spoth, Yoo, Kahn, and Redmond, 1996). Indeed, there is no substitute for parents taking an active role in their teenage children's lives: declaring a clear expectation of no substance use; establishing firm family rules; monitoring their children's activities; getting to know their children's friends; and listening to their children, trying to understand their problems, and helping them figure out constructive solutions (Simpson, 2001).

Investing the time and energy it takes to be a good parent pays off. Research shows that teens who report spending a great deal of time with their family are far less likely to drink, smoke, or use other drugs compared to teens who report spending very little time with their family. Likewise, teens whose parents always know their whereabouts are at lowest risk for substance use, while those whose parents never know their children's whereabouts are at highest risk. Importantly, these factors are far more critical than type of family structure or household income in predicting youth substance use (Abdelrahman and others, 1998; Adlaf and Ivis, 1996; Center for Alcohol and Substance Abuse, 1999).

Teens themselves say that their parents have enormous influence on the decisions they make about substance use, both as positive role models and as a source of information about the danger of drugs (Office of National Drug Control Policy, 1998). According to a study conducted by the Partnership for a Drug-Free America (1999), teens say that "disappointing their parents" is the top risk associated with using drugs.

In this context, what do parents report doing to protect their teenage children from substance use? Do they believe they are doing more or less than other parents? To explore these issues, we conducted a mail survey to ask parents in Montana about their relationship with their teenage children, discussions they have had about substance use, and family rules and limits. We also asked a companion set of questions about what the typical parent in Montana does. To our knowledge, this is the first survey to explore social norms concerning protective parenting behaviors and misperception of those norms.

In general, we found that the vast majority of the surveyed parents reported taking several constructive steps to protect their children from substance use. They were far less likely to say that typical parents in Montana were taking these same steps. In this chapter, we review these survey findings in the context of social norms theory and then explore their implications for a statewide media campaign that encourages parental involvement and action. We conclude by outlining future directions for research.

Parenting Behavior: A Social Norms Analysis

Several studies have demonstrated that most young people tend to overestimate the percentage of their peers who smoke, use illicit drugs, and drink heavily (Perkins and others, 1999; Perkins, 2002; Perkins and Craig, Chapter Twelve of this volume). The behavioral choices that people make are guided in part by their perception of peer norms, whether they are accurate or not. Hence, a primary consequence of overestimation is the potential for even greater substance use (Perkins, 1997; Perkins and Wechsler, 1996).

According to social norms theory, misperceptions of substance-use norms arise from a combination of cultural, social, and psychological factors (Perkins, 1991, 1997): (1) media portrayal of substance use, including news reports that highlight substance-use problems while ignoring healthier and far more common behaviors; (2) conversation in which young people boast or joke about dangerous substance use; (3) the perceptual salience of substance use and its consequences, which can make these occurrences more memorable than normal and less remarkable events; and (4) a general tendency to think that observed behavior is predictive of what people normally do, rather than an aberration arising from a particular set of circumstances.

Parents have fewer direct opportunities than youths themselves to observe youth substance use, but otherwise they rely on similar cultural information when trying to gauge adolescent norms and are subject to the same biasing factors as their teenage children. In turn, if parents share the misperception that youth substance use is more prevalent than it is, then they are also more likely to underestimate the extent to which other parents are involved with their children or have taken a firm and consistent stand against alcohol, tobacco, and other drugs.

As noted previously, parents of teenagers often seek guidance from other parents on how to negotiate between wanting to grant their children increasing independence and protecting them from harm. Thus, if parents underestimate how frequently other parents are using certain protective strategies, this misperception may serve to undermine their own resolve to adopt those strategies or apply them consistently. Stated simply, it is harder for parents to uphold firm rules and standards when they believe they are among the few parents who are trying to do so.

Clearly, there is a need to assess what is really going on when it comes to what parents are doing to protect their teenage children from substance abuse, and then to communicate this positive information back to parents to counteract the mixed and negative messages they take in from the media and their own biased and distorted observation of other parents.

Montana Parent Norms Survey

To investigate these issues, the Montana Social Norms Project, which is based in the Department of Health and Human Development at Montana State University, was contracted by the Montana Department of Public Health and Human Services to conduct a statewide survey on parenting norms, and then to develop a media campaign to counteract misperceptions of those norms that were identified.

The Montana Parent Norms Survey was mailed to a randomly selected statewide sample of Montana households with teenagers between the ages of twelve and seventeen. A list of three thousand qualified households was purchased from GENESYS Sampling Systems in Fort Washington, Pennsylvania. The U.S. Postal Service confirmed that 2,973 addresses were valid locations where mail could be delivered. The survey was mailed with a cover letter and a postage-paid return envelope. A second questionnaire with a reminder notice was sent two weeks later.

The initial cover letter stated that the purpose of the study was to learn more about the role parents play "in guiding their teens away from the use of alcohol, marijuana, and tobacco." Either the father or mother was identified by name as the respondent, but the cover letter explained that if this individual were unavailable then the other parent could complete the survey. The cover letter also informed recipients that their responses would remain confidential.

A total of 787 completed surveys were received, a response rate of 27 percent of the total valid addresses. The actual response rate from potential parents in the sampling frame is likely much higher, though it cannot be calculated precisely. On the basis of experience, GENESYS Sampling Systems estimated that approximately 30 percent of the provided mailing addresses would not be for current residents or for homes with a teenager between the ages of twelve and seventeen. Taking this into account, the effective response rate may be on the order of 38 percent. Importantly, preliminary analysis showed no significant difference between early and late responders.

Nearly equal numbers of fathers and mothers completed the survey. Fully 98 percent of the respondents were Caucasian, with 1 percent categorized as Hispanic/Latino and 1 percent as Native American.

More than half of the respondents (55 percent) reported having only one child in the home between twelve and seventeen. The survey instructions asked parents having two or more children in this age range to answer the questions with the older or oldest of these children in mind. Genders of the referent teens were boys 52 percent and girls 48 percent. Their average age was 14.6 years (SD = 1.6).

Comparing Actual and Perceived Parenting Norms

The survey instrument asked parents about several important issues related to their parenting role, among them their policies on alcohol use, monitoring of their children's activities, and other family rules and limits. A parallel set of questions to most of these items asked the respondents to report on the attitudes and behaviors of the "typical" Montana parent, which allowed direct comparison of actual parenting norms with perceived norms.

Rules About Alcohol Use. Three-fourths of the parents surveyed (75 percent) reported that during the past three months they had discussed family rules about not drinking or using other drugs with their teen. Yet at the same time, more than half of these parents (53 percent) estimated that at most 40 percent of Montana parents typically had done so.

During the thirty days prior to the survey, 47 percent of the parents told their teenage child that they expect no underage drinking. Another 7 percent told their children they should never drink. In addition, 2 percent told their teen that a few drinks on special occasions would be all right, and 1 percent said that how much to drink was their teen's decision. Just over one-third (35 percent) had not talked about alcohol-related rules in the previous month. (The total exceeds 100 percent because of rounding error.) Thus most parents said they had communicated to their teenage children that they expected them not to drink. When asked what they thought was most typical of other parents, however, only 38 percent of the respondents correctly identified the actual norm, while 43 percent erroneously believed that not talking about drinking was the norm.

Truancy. A clear majority of respondents (60 percent) said they would be extremely concerned if their teen skipped school one or two times during the semester. In contrast, only 15 percent thought that typical Montana parents of teens would be extremely concerned. Although only 7 percent of the parents said they would be either not concerned at all or only a little concerned, more than one-quarter of parents (27 percent) thought that this response was most typical of other parents. Likewise, 62 percent of the parents indicated they would always know if their teen skipped school, but only 13 percent said parents of a typical Montana teenager would always know if their child were truant.

Parental Monitoring. Regarding schoolwork, 79 percent of the parents said they usually or always monitor their teen's homework and generally know if it is getting done. In contrast, only half (50 percent) said that this level of knowledge was the norm among parents.

When asked about times when their teenage children are not at home, the majority (57 percent) of the parents said they always know where their children are and whom they are with. In comparison, only 1 percent of the respondents thought that this high level of monitoring was typical of Montana parents. At the other end of the continuum, 2 percent of the parents said they only sometimes, seldom, or never know their children's whereabouts, yet almost half of parents (46 percent) thought this was the norm.

Similarly, while 86 percent of the respondents said they always know when their teenage children do not come home on time, just 6 percent said that it was typical of Montana parents always to know. Only 2 percent said they only sometimes, seldom, or never know when their children are late, but almost one-quarter believed that this limited monitoring was the norm among parents.

Use of Curfew. Regarding curfew, 48 percent of the parents said they had a set time for their teen to come home, while another 47 percent said they establish a curfew each night depending on the circumstances. Only 3 percent said their teen has a lot of latitude, and 2 percent said they impose no time constraints. In contrast, 19 percent of the parents said they believe that typical Montana parents give their teenage children a lot of latitude. Another 9 percent thought the typical parent imposes no time constraints.

Additional Parenting Norms

Other survey questions revealed further evidence of strong parenting norms among the majority of parents. For these items, the survey did not include parallel questions on perception of norms. These data emphasize the fact that the majority of parents report taking several preventive measures to protect their children from substance use.

Parents expressed high levels of concern regarding substance use. Nine out of ten parents (93 percent) said they would be extremely concerned if they found out their child were drinking alcohol, while 86 percent said they would have this level of concern if their child were smoking cigarettes. With marijuana use, 96 percent of the parents said they would be extremely concerned.

The survey asked respondents if they and their teen's other parent had discussed strategies for helping their child understand and avoid the risks of alcohol, tobacco, and other drug use. Four out of ten parents (41 percent) reported they had done this frequently, while an additional 43 percent said they had done so a few times. Only 3 percent said they had done it just once; 7 percent said they had not really talked about this issue. The remaining 6 percent said there was no other active parent.

The survey asked parents their opinion about allowing teenage children to drink at home to avoid unsafe behaviors such as driving under the influence. In response, 86 percent said this would send the wrong message and that parents should not allow teens to drink at home. When asked if they allow their teenage child to drink at home (even a small glass of wine or beer with dinner), 75 percent said they never did, while 24 percent said they occasionally allow drinking and 1 percent said they regularly allow it.

A Social Norms Approach to Improving Parenting Behaviors

Parents participating in the Montana survey said they have solid, trusting relationships with their teenage children and are informed about their activities. The majority of parents also said they have set out clear rules and report using curfew. At the same time, however, most of the surveyed parents did not accurately perceive the positive parenting norms of other parents.

Of course, we cannot know for sure from these data what parents are actually doing, as opposed to what they say they are doing. The mailed surveys were completed anonymously, so we have little reason to believe that the respondents were deliberately deceptive. Still, there remains the possibility that some parents overreported the extent to which they actually practice effective parenting strategies, from a combination of faulty memory and a tendency to report what they truly believe in, even if they do not follow their standards in all instances. A possible cause of such inconsistency, it should be noted, may be the misperception of the actual parenting norms, which may inhibit parents from holding to their normal strict standards on some occasions.

Even allowing for the possibility of overreporting, the discrepancy between what parents say they are doing and what they think other parents are doing is far too large to be written off as a measurement artifact. If parents somehow came to know themselves perfectly, or if they otherwise came to report their actions with total accuracy, we would still expect—because of the cultural, social, and psychological factors that lead to normative misperceptions—to find a widespread and erroneous belief that typical parents are considerably less conscientious than is actually the case.

Consistent with this argument, recall that 60 percent of the surveyed parents said they would be extremely concerned if their teen skipped school one or two times during the semester. This is an attitudinal statement, not a behavioral report subject to possible overreporting of frequency or consistency. Here as well, we find an enormous misperception of the norm: only 15 percent of the surveyed parents thought that typical Montana parents would be extremely concerned about their teen's truancy.

Social norms theory predicts that if parents believe that other parents of teenagers do not consistently communicate their values, set out clear rules, or impose curfew and other limits, then they are more vulnerable to social pressure to conform to that misperceived norm and become more lax in their own parenting. Conversely, if parents are given accurate and credible information about what typical parents are doing to protect their teenage children from substance use, then they are more likely to maintain or even raise their standards and to enforce them consistently. We turn next to a statewide media campaign in Montana designed to accomplish this objective.

The Montana Parents Campaign

The Montana Parents Campaign was part of a comprehensive, statewide substance abuse program operated by the Addictive and Mental Disorders Division of the Montana Department of Public Health and Human Services, with funding from the federal Center for Substance Abuse Prevention (CSAP). This media campaign sought to make it easier for parents of teenagers to establish clear expectations, set and maintain firm rules, and monitor their children by highlighting the positive parenting strategies already practiced by the majority of Montana parents.

From its inception, the campaign was designed to be one facet of a much larger statewide effort and not to be operated as a stand-alone intervention. For this reason, we are unable to tease out the effect of this campaign from that of the program as a whole. Despite this limitation, the decision was made to conduct the campaign, knowing many parents would likely benefit from learning that the vast majority of Montana parents are doing things right when it comes to steering their teenage children away from the dangers of substance use. Clearly, there is a need for future research to gauge the impact of this type of campaign independently of other prevention programs.

The process of establishing a communications strategy and developing the campaign message was shaped by (1) findings from the survey of Montana parents; (2) the results of focus groups, also conducted with parents; and (3) the overall goals of the Montana Department of Pubic Health and Human Services (MDPHHS).

The survey results revealed that parents greatly underestimated how frequently other parents engage in a range of parenting behaviors. The media campaign, needing to present a simple and memorable message, could not highlight all of these behaviors. Instead, the decision was made to focus on a single behavior, one that is central to effective parenting, but also one for which there is a very large misperception, believing that this creates the best opportunity for the campaign to have an impact. The behavior that stood out on both counts was parent-child communication. As reported before, 75 percent of the surveyed parents said that they had talked to their teens in the past three months about clear, family rules and expectations not to use alcohol or other drugs, but only 19 percent thought that this behavior was characteristic of typical Montana parents.

Focus groups of Montana parents, which were conducted in various regions of the state, showed that parents were receptive to the social norms message. Many participants even expressed relief to learn that the vast majority of Montana parents endorse what they are doing to guide their own teenage children. A theme that resonated favorably with focus group participants was to show appreciation to parents by thanking them for doing their job right. The consensus opinion was that the campaign materials should communicate both a strong sense of Montana's family values and the state's ethos as a caring community.

The campaign was sponsored under the aegis of the MDPHHS as part of its comprehensive substance abuse prevention program, which was built on the "Communities That Care" model (Hawkins, Catalano, and Associates, 1992). Key stakeholders in MDPHHS wanted that "brand identity" brought into the campaign. This request was consistent with the views of parents who participated in the focus groups, which made it easy to incorporate this concept into the campaign messages.

The campaign featured two thirty-second television commercials. Audio from those advertisements was lifted and modified for radio spots. Both the television and radio advertisements were placed in a free rotation for public service announcements, as the state did not have financial resources for media buys.

One of the television advertisements offered a general message about how Montanans care about children. The second advertisement was a social norms message about the high frequency of communication between parents and their children regarding not using alcohol, tobacco, or other drugs. The spot showed a diverse group of parents engaging in various activities with their children (gardening, reading a story, helping them study, and so on). Line by line, each parent in sequence added to the scripted message, which reinforced the basic idea that Montana is a good place to raise a family because most parents spend time with their children, talk to them, help them with homework, and set rules about not using alcohol or other drugs. The message concludes with the thought that this is the reason that "more Montana kids are drug and alcohol free." At the end of the commercial, there was the following text message: "75 percent of Montana parents regularly talk to our kids about not using alcohol, tobacco and other drugs. Thank you." The campaign's Website (www.MOSTOFUS.org) appeared at the bottom of the screen.

In addition, twenty-four camera-ready print advertisements (4" × 6") were developed for insertion into local newspapers (for one example, see Figure 15.1). The concept for these advertisements was based on the college student campaign Cam-

**FIGURE 15.1. MONTANA SOCIAL NORMS
PROJECT POSTER: MOST PARENTS.**

Source: Used by permission of Montana Social Norms Project, Montana State University.

pus Factoids™, which was developed by Perkins and Craig (see Chapter Three). Some advertisements reinforced the social norms message in the television and radio spots, while others communicated other positive norms messages derived from the parent survey. The advertisements were sent to community coalitions across the state, which then approached local newspapers about using them as public service announcements.

The campaign was well received. After a one-year broadcast flight, the television and radio spots continue to air in response to requests from local community members. Station scheduling managers stated that they appreciate the positive and affirming tone of the messages. Montana government officials and leaders of community coalitions across the state also commented positively on the campaign. Since the initial Montana campaign, government agencies in other states (such as the Pennsylvania Liquor Control Board) have inquired about replicating the campaign.

Through this campaign, parents and their teenage children learned that most Montana parents were doing the right thing when it comes to communicating clear expectations in opposition to substance use. Importantly, the campaign gave parents ammunition to counter the often-stated teen-to-parent complaint, "But everybody else's parents let them do it."

The essence of this campaign is to provide parents with hope. It is important to tell parents of teens that they can protect their children by spending time with them regularly, setting clear rules about substance use, and monitoring their activities—all steps that parents can take regardless of family structure or economic background. It is also important to tell parents that this is what the majority of parents do, a fact that should bolster their determination to continue to invest the time and energy it takes to be a good parent.

References

Abdelrahman, A. I., and others. "The Epidemiology of Substance Use Among Middle School Students: The Impact of School, Familial, Community and Individual Risk Factors." *Journal of Child and Adolescent Substance Abuse*, 1998, *8*(1), 55–75.

Adlaf, E. M., and Ivis, F. J. "Structure and Relations: The Influence of Familial Factors on Adolescent Substance Use and Delinquency." *Journal of Child and Adolescent Substance Abuse*, 1996, *5*(3), 1–18.

Center for Alcohol and Substance Abuse. *Back to School 1999: National Survey of American Attitudes on Substance Abuse*. Vol. 5: *Teens and Their Parents*. New York: CASA, Columbia University, 1999.

Hawkins, J. D., Catalano, R. F., and Associates. *Communities That Care: Action for Drug Abuse Prevention*. San Francisco: Jossey-Bass, 1992.

Kimmel, D. C., and Weiner, I. B. *Adolescence: A Developmental Transition*. Hillsdale, N.J.: Erlbaum, 1985.

Office of National Drug Control Policy. *The National Youth Anti-Drug Media Campaign: Communication Strategy Statement.* Washington, D.C.: ONDCP, 1998.

Partnership for a Drug-Free America (PDFA). *Partnership Attitude Tracking Study, 1999.* New York: PDFA, 1999.

Perkins, H. W. "Confronting Misperceptions of Peer Drug Use Norms Among College Students: An Alternative Approach for Alcohol and Other Drug Education Programs." In *Peer Prevention Program Resource Manual.* Fort Worth: Higher Education Leaders/Peers Network, Texas Christian University, 1991.

Perkins, H. W. "College Student Misperceptions of Alcohol and Other Drug Norms Among Peers: Exploring Causes, Consequences, and Implications for Prevention Programs." In *Designing Alcohol and Other Drug Prevention Programs in Higher Education: Bringing Theory into Practice.* Newton, Mass.: Higher Education Center for Alcohol and Other Drug Prevention, U.S. Department of Education, 1997.

Perkins, H. W. "Social Norms and the Prevention of Alcohol Misuse in Collegiate Contexts." *Journal of Studies on Alcohol,* 2002, Supplement no. 14, 164–172.

Perkins, H. W., and Wechsler, H. "Variation in Perceived College Drinking Norms and Its Impact on Alcohol Abuse: A Nationwide Study." *Journal of Drug Issues,* 1996, *26*(4), 961–974.

Perkins, H. W., and others. "Misperceptions of the Norms for the Frequency of Alcohol and Other Drug Use on College Campuses." *Journal of American College Health,* 1999, *47*(6), 253–258.

Resnick, M. D., and others. "Protecting Adolescents from Harm: Findings from the National Longitudinal Study on Adolescent Health." *Journal of the American Medical Association,* 1997, *278,* 823–832.

Roberts, D. F., Henriksen, L., Christenson, P. G., and Kelly, M. *Substance Use in Popular Movies and Music.* Washington, D.C.: Office of National Drug Control Policy and Substance Abuse and Mental Health Services Administration, U.S. Department of Health and Human Services, 1999.

Simpson, A. R. *Raising Teens: A Synthesis of Research and a Foundation for Action.* Boston: Center for Health Communication, Harvard School of Public Health, 2001.

Spoth, R., Yoo, S., Kahn, J., and Redmond, C. "A Model of the Effects of Protective Parent and Peer Factors on Young Adolescent Alcohol Refusal Skills." *Journal of Primary Prevention,* 1996, *16,* 373–394.

CHAPTER SIXTEEN

APPLICATIONS OF SOCIAL NORMS THEORY TO OTHER HEALTH AND SOCIAL JUSTICE ISSUES

Alan David Berkowitz, Ph.D.

There is growing interest in applying social norms theory to issues of social justice and to health problems other than alcohol abuse, along with funding on the part of a number of federal agencies of social norms interventions to address sexual assault and violence prevention. In light of this interest, this chapter reviews the theoretical assumptions of the social norms approach; assesses the relevance of the theory to other health and social justice issues; and presents examples of social norms interventions for sexual assault prevention for men, eating problems among women, second-hand effects of high-risk drinking, and antibias programs.

Social norms theory describes situations in which individuals incorrectly perceive the attitudes or behaviors of peers and other community members to be different from their own. This phenomenon has also been called "pluralistic ignorance" (Miller and McFarland, 1987, 1991). Misperception occurs in relation to problem or risk behavior (which is usually overestimated) and in relation to healthy or protective behavior (which is usually underestimated), and it may cause individuals to change their own behavior to approximate the misperceived norm

The comments and editorial assistance of Myra Berkowitz, and comments by Cornelia Lee, Chris Kilmartin, and Julie White on an earlier draft of this chapter, are greatly appreciated. Additional thanks to Jan Kusch for her insightful comments on the etiology of eating disorders and for suggesting the possibility of using social norms theory for eating disorder prevention.

(Prentice and Miller, 1993). This in turn can cause expression or rationalization of problem behavior and inhibition or suppression of healthy behavior. This pattern has been well documented for alcohol, with college students almost universally overestimating the frequency and quantity of their peers' consumption (Perkins and others, 1999). Such misperception can facilitate increased drinking and may be used by problem drinkers to justify their own abuse. Similar misperceptions have been documented for illegal drug use (Perkins, 1994; Perkins and others, 1999), cigarette smoking (Chassin and others, 1984; Grube, Morgan, and McGree, 1986; Sussman and others, 1988), and eating disorders (Kusch, 2002; Mann and others, 1997). The research documenting the existence of misperceptions and their role in predicting behavior has been reviewed by Berkowitz (2001).

Social norms theory predicts that interventions correcting misperception by revealing the actual, healthier norm have a beneficial effect on most individuals, who will either reduce their participation in potentially problematic behavior or be encouraged to engage in protective, healthy behaviors.

Social norms theory can also be extended to situations in which individuals refrain from confronting the problem behavior of others because they incorrectly believe the behavior is accepted by their peer group. That is, individuals who underestimate the extent of peer discomfort with problem behavior may act as "bystanders" by refraining from expressing their own discomfort with that behavior. However, if the actual discomfort level of peers is revealed, these individuals may be more willing to express their own discomfort to the perpetrator(s) of the behavior. Recent research on homophobia, for example, suggests that most college students underestimate the extent to which their peers are tolerant and supportive of gay, lesbian, and bisexual students (Bowen and Bourgeois, 2001).

Decreasing the climate of tolerance for problem behaviors is a goal of all prevention programs. Thus application of social norms theory to bystander behavior is an additional focus of this chapter.

Assumptions of Social Norms Theory

As noted, social norms theory predicts that people express or inhibit behavior in an attempt to conform to a perceived norm. This phenomenon of pluralistic ignorance can cause an individual to act in a way that is inconsistent with true beliefs and values (Miller and McFarland, 1991). Misperception of a norm discourages expression of opinions and behaviors that are falsely thought to be nonconforming, creating a negative cycle in which unhealthy behavior is expressed and healthy behavior is inhibited. It also allows abusers and perpetrators of problem behaviors to deny or justify their actions because of the (mis)perception that their behavior is normative (Baer, Stacy, and Larimer, 1991), a phenomenon called "false consensus" (Pollard and others, 2000). This cycle can be broken or reversed by giving individuals correct information about the actual norm. All individuals who misperceive the norm contribute to the climate that allows problem behavior to occur, whether or not they engage in the behavior. Perkins (1997) coined the term "carriers of the misperception" to describe these individuals. These are the assumptions of social norms theory (portions adapted from Miller and McFarland, 1991; and Toch and Klofas, 1984):

- Actions are often based on misinformation about, or misperception of, others' attitudes or behavior.
- When misperception is defined or perceived as real, it has real consequences.
- Individuals passively accept misperception rather than actively intervene to change it, hiding from others their true perceptions, feelings, or beliefs.
- The effects of misperception are self-perpetuating, because it discourages expression of opinions and actions that are falsely believed to be nonconforming, while encouraging problem behaviors that are falsely believed to be normative.
- Appropriate information about the actual norm encourages individuals to express those beliefs that are consistent with the true, healthier norm, and inhibit problem behaviors that are inconsistent with it.
- Individuals who do not personally engage in the problematic behavior may contribute to the problem by the way in which they talk about the behavior. Misperception thus functions to strengthen beliefs and values that the carriers of the misperception do not themselves hold and contribute to the climate that encourages problem behavior.
- For a norm to be perpetuated, it is not necessary for the majority to believe it, but only for the majority to believe that the majority believes it.

The assumptions of social norms theory have been supported by empirical research (Baer, Stacy, and Larimer, 1991; Miller and McFarland, 1987; Perkins and Berkowitz, 1986; Perkins and others, 1999; Prentice and Miller, 1993) and interventions (Haines and Spear, 1996; Haines, 1996; Johannessen, Collins, Mills-Novoa, and Glider, 1999; see also other chapters in this volume) with respect to college student alcohol use (for a recent literature review, see Berkowitz, 2000). These assumptions lead to a number of questions that can be used to determine the applicability of the theory to other health issues, such as eating disorders, sexual health, and sexual assault, or to bystander behavior. Thus, the following questions assess whether a particular health or social justice behavior issue is amenable to a social norms intervention:

- What misperceptions exist with respect to the behavior in question?
- What is the meaning and function of misperceptions for individuals and groups?
- Do the majority of individuals in a group or community hold these misperceptions?
- Does the target group function as a group with respect to the behavior in question (that is, do the individuals in the group exert an influence on each other's behavior)?
- What is the hypothesized effect of misperceptions?
- What changes are predicted if misperceptions are corrected?
- What healthy behaviors already exist in the population that should be strengthened or increased?

These questions establish the parameters or conditions for health promotion interventions based on social norms theory. If these questions are not adequately addressed, a social norms intervention may not be appropriate. Keeling (1999) has noted that uncritical application of the model can lead to failed interventions because of incorrect assumptions about students and their behavior. Thus, a critical first step is to determine if a social norms intervention is appropriate for a particular problem.

If a particular problem does meet the criteria I have just outlined, an intervention can be designed that is appropriate to the target population for the issue in question, taking into account three "cultures": the culture of the issue, the culture of the message delivery system, and the culture of the target population (Berkowitz, 1999a). For example, health problems may carry different meanings for specific groups, and these meanings must be addressed when designing an intervention. Native Americans have a unique relationship to the issue of alcohol abuse because of the way alcohol was used as a tool of genocide. Similarly, the meaning of sexual assault among African Americans has been shaped by how sexual assault was a feature of slavery. In addition, groups may have their own cultural practices regarding acquisition and dissemination of information. Thus, for a social norms intervention to be effective, one must take into account the culture of the issue, the culture of the message delivery system, and the culture of the target group, and adapt the intervention to all three.

Enthusiasm about the success of the social norms approach in reducing alcohol use and its negative consequences may also result in the naïve assumption that the same approach can be applied to other issues without change or adjustment. This would be possible if the etiology and dynamics of other problems were identical to those of substance use and abuse. However, as I have noted, each problem has its own history, meaning, and associated culture, and although the social norms approach may help address other issues, it cannot be applied indiscriminately or simplistically. The case studies that follow illustrate some of the complexity and limitations of the model as they apply to other issues.

Sexual Assault Prevention for Men

Sexual assault is an acknowledged problem on college campuses and in communities. Interventions designed to reduce its prevalence either focus on teaching women risk awareness and deterrence strategies to decrease the chances of an assault, or they emphasize men's responsibility for ending violence against women (Berkowitz, 1998a, 2002). Because men are responsible for the overwhelming majority of sexual assaults perpetrated against children, other men, and women, it is reasonable to expect that men should take responsibility for prevention (Berkowitz, 1992, 2002). In the past decade, a variety of strategies for working with men have been developed from this assumption. These programs may focus on empathy induction (Foubert and Marriott, 1997; Foubert and McEwen, 1998; Schewe and O'Donohue, 1993), on defining and understanding consent (Berkowitz, 1994a), on discouraging bystander behavior (Mahlstedt and Corcoran, 1999; Katz, 1995; Berkowitz, 1994a), and on resocialization of men (a theme common to most programs). I have previously recommended a social norms approach to sexual assault prevention for men, suggesting that it would complement these other approaches while addressing many of the dynamics of male socialization and peer influence that cause sexual assault to occur (Berkowitz, 1998a, 1998b, 1999b, 2002).

My own experiences as an adolescent inform my thinking about this issue:

As a teenager I was frequently uncomfortable with the language my friends used to describe women's bodies, or the sexual relations they claimed to have had with women. Often in all-male groups someone would use language that objectified or put down women, or describe alleged sexual exploits in graphic detail. In some cases, I knew from private conversation that what was being described had not happened at all, or that it was being exaggerated. In each one of these situations, I kept my discomfort to myself, assuming that others enjoyed or at least did not mind the conversation, and that I was in the minority.

Research on men's discomfort with other men's language suggests that this experience is common for most men. Berkowitz (1994b), Bruce (2002), and Kilmartin and others (1999), in separate studies, documented that most college men underestimate the extent to which other men feel uncomfortable with language or behavior that objectifies or degrades women. In addition, other misperceptions have been documented that may enable sexual assault to occur. Berkowitz and Perkins (cited by Berkowitz, 1993; Morgan, 1997; and White, 2002), for example, found that college men and women commonly believe that other students are more sexually active than themselves. Misperception has also been documented with respect to rape myths, with most students assuming that other students are more likely to believe in rape myths than themselves (Boulter, 1997; Caruso, 1996; and Ray Schwarz, personal communication, Fall 1993). Finally, Paul A. Schewe (personal communication, Sept. 9, 1999) found that most college men would not enjoy forcing a woman to be sexually intimate but thought that most other men would. All of these misperceptions encourage men to suppress their discomfort with other men's behavior and may result in men feeling pressure to be sexually active whether or not they want to. Muehlenhard and Cook (1988), for example, found that more than two-thirds of men engaged in unwanted sex with women at some point in their lives as a result of pressure they felt from other men. More recently, Kilmartin and others (1999) found that men overestimated the extent to which other men engaged in unwanted sex in comparison with themselves.

Miller and McFarland (1991) have suggested that pluralistic ignorance is strongest when fear of social disapproval motivates behavior. For men, the need to fit into a masculine ideal and be accepted by other men may result in suppression of behavior inconsistent with this ideal and foster the assumption that other men, unlike oneself, actually live up to it. As a result, men operate under what Jackson Katz has referred to as the "tough guise" syndrome, pretending in most cases to be something they are not (Katz and Jhally, 1999). Heterosexual sex, in particular, is seen as a way of proving one's "manhood" and accomplishing the ideal of masculinity. Consider, for example,

> . . . how this process might operate in the development of gender-typed beliefs among males. Initially, young boys may act or speak in a sexist manner around their peers because they do not wish to be embarrassed by not appearing appropriately masculine. They may not understand why a boy should not play girls' games or like girls' activities but they may act as though they do so as not to seem deviant. Over time, however, they may internalize the gender-typed rhetoric to which they originally just paid lip service because they thought everyone believed it [Miller and McFarland, 1991, pp. 305–306].

This in turn unintentionally encourages the more hypermasculine men who engage in inappropriate behaviors, giving them the belief (that is, false consensus) that their actions are normative and condoned by others.

This understanding of male behavior is consistent with integrative models of sexual assault proposed by Berkowitz (1992) and Schwartz and DeKeseredy (1997), which emphasize the role of male peer support as a facilitator of coercive sexuality. If male peer pressure is based on pluralistic ignorance rather than actual behavior, then a social norms approach might be effective in reducing men's proclivity to sexual assault and encouraging men to express their discomfort with other men's behavior.

Revealing the true norm of intolerance among men can occur informally or formally. Berkowitz (1994a) has described a peer-facilitated rape prevention program in which men are given permission to share their true feelings about the issue in the presence of older, respected students who model honesty and willingness to confront inappropriate behavior. Creating a safe space for men to discuss the issue fosters an opportunity for the true norm to surface and encourages men to speak honestly about their disapproval of opportunistic and coercive sexuality. This is perhaps the most important component of rape prevention programs for men (Berkowitz, 2002).

This type of traditional workshop intervention can incorporate social norms information and be reinforced and supplemented by a social norms marketing campaign through residential and campus-based media presenting the true norm for men. A number of studies suggest that small group applications of the social norms model can be effective (Berkowitz, 2001). Far (2001) has presented a prototype for a small group norms-challenging intervention for alcohol that can be adapted to issues of sexual assault. It can be implemented with relevant data in fraternities, athletic teams, and other groups of men.

Examples of information on men's pluralistic ignorance that can be included in workshop presentations or social norms marketing media are (1) men's misperception of other men's sexual activity, (2) incorrect beliefs about other men's support of rape myths, and (3) false assumptions about other men's comfort with degrading language toward women. In an exploratory study described in more detail later in this chapter, Kilmartin and others (1999) used a poster and media campaign that documented the majority of men's discomfort with inappropriate language about women. Following the campaign, men reported a reduction in their misperception of other men's level of comfort with such language. Future studies are needed to determine if this reduction can be replicated and if it translates into an increase in men's willingness to confront other men's behavior and in the likelihood to rape.

Using a survey based on the College Date Rape Attitudes and Behavior Scale (Lanier and Elliot, 1997) and Kilmartin's research (Kilmartin and others, 1999), Bruce (2002) implemented a social norms media campaign at James Madison University to change men's intimate behavior toward women. Data was collected revealing positive attitudinal and behavioral norms among men regarding sexual intimacy, and a poster campaign was developed to advertise these norms. Three messages were developed:

1. A man always prevents manipulation. Three out of four JMU men think it's *not* OK to pressure a date to drink alcohol in order to increase the chances of getting their date to have sex.
2. A man talks before romance. Most JMU men believe that talking about sex doesn't ruin the romance of the moment.
3. A man respects a woman. Nine out of ten JMU men stop the first time their date says no to sexual activity.

This campaign was successful in improving behavior in a positive direction among the treatment group for two of the ten outcome variables, including a significant increase in the percentage of men who indicated they "stop the first time a date says no to sexual activity," and a significant decrease in the percentage of men who agree that "when I want to touch someone sexually, I try and see how they react." Results were in the predicted direction but not significant for four of the remaining eight outcome variables. This campaign suggests that a social norms media campaign can be successful in changing heterosexual men's attitudes and behaviors regarding sexual intimacy with women.

Disordered Eating Among Women

For women, concern about physical appearance and eating may serve to affirm femininity just as men's concern with sexual activity is a way of proving masculinity. Striegel-Moore and Cachelin, for example, noted that "by being concerned with her appearance and making efforts to achieve our culture's beauty ideal, a girl affirms for herself and for others that she is feminine" (1999, p. 86). Some studies have suggested that up to two-thirds of college women may have disordered eating patterns, with a smaller percentage (approximately 7 percent) meeting the clinical criteria for an eating disorder (Mazzeo, 1999). In this chapter, the term *disordered eating* is used as inclusive of both disordered eating patterns and clinically definable eating disorders.

Most of the strategies for primary prevention of disordered eating have been concerned with risk factors, with little attention to possible protective factors (Striegel-Moore and Cachelin, 1999). These focus on individual, familial, social, or cultural issues thought to be etiologically significant in creating risk. However, none of the strategies designed to eliminate or reduce disordered eating among college women have been demonstrated to be successful (Martz and Bazzini, 1999). As a result, many professionals have wondered if a social norms approach might be effective, especially in addressing cultural, interpersonal, or social causes of the problem. Any attempt in this direction remains speculative, however, because of the lack of relevant data. In addition, since the etiology of disordered eating is complex and multifaceted, the impact of an intervention based on social norms theory is uncertain.

What misperception of protective or risk behaviors exists that may encourage disordered eating? In a summary of research on body size, Fallon concluded that women "tend to overestimate their own body size and underestimate what others find attractive," thereby creating pressure to diet (1987, p. 79). Women may thus believe that they need to be thinner than is necessary if they are to be seen as attractive to others. This conclusion is consistent with research reported by Martz and Bazzini (1999) suggesting that appearance (as defined by body weight) is a more important determinant of dating behavior for women than it is for men. Women also overestimate the percentage of their peers who have eating disorders (Mann and others, 1997). Results from two studies suggest that prevention programs on eating disorders may actually exacerbate the misperception (Carter, Stewart, Dunn, and Fairburn, 1997; Mann and others, 1997). Such an increase in pluralistic ignorance regarding the prevalence of eating disorders (that is, unintentionally teaching women that eating disorders are more common then they really are) could potentially normalize the behavior—a clearly undesirable result.

One of the first studies to apply the social norms model to issues of body size and disordered eating confirms predictions that are based on the theory. Kusch (2002) had a sample of 163 college women and 136 college men identify ideal female body size using Stunkard silhouettes ranging from extreme thinness to obesity. Subjects answered a second set of questions about actual and ideal female height and weight. Female participants used both of these measures to identify their own actual size, their self-ideal, the size they believed their female peers would select as ideal, and the size they believed their male peers would select as ideal. The study determined that women significantly overestimated the degree of thinness that their female and male peers selected as ideal. These overestimations were found to positively correlate with measures of body dissatisfaction, disturbed eating, and concern with appearance.

Another recent study found that adult men and women both misperceive their own weight and attractiveness, with men likely to be overweight but misperceive themselves as more underweight, and women likely to be underweight or normal weight but misperceive themselves as more overweight (McCreary and Sadava, 2001).

These studies suggest that a social norms intervention for eating disorder prevention could be developed. It would require documentation of misperceptions of body size and attractiveness, healthy norms and behaviors of the majority of women, and protective behaviors that women engage in to prevent overconcern with attractiveness and eating problems. If women were found to underestimate the prevalence of healthy or protective behaviors, a social norms media campaign could be used to correct the misperception, and information on protective behaviors could be included in workshops as well, thus fostering health and resilience among women.

Understanding the issues involved in designing an intervention to address concerns about body image can illustrate the complexities and difficulties of adapting the model to this topic. For example, concern about attractiveness is one of the many factors contributing to development of eating problems. How do women make judgments about what is physically attractive? As I have noted, women are taught that attractiveness is associated with thinness and is a sign of femininity. In addition to the media, there seem to be two possible pathways for this influence: what women believe other women define as attractive, and what heterosexual women believe men define as attractive. Thus, women may try to achieve a standard of feminine beauty that is based on what they think is attractive to women or men, engaging in disordered eating if they are not able to accomplish this by healthier means. The fact that women misperceive what male or female peers find attractive suggests that a social norms intervention could focus on reducing pressure to diet by giving women accurate information about what is actually attractive to their peers. This is an empirical question that can be tested in future studies.

However, this social norms intervention—teaching women to correctly perceive what men think about body size—could have unintended consequences. Carol Gilligan and her colleagues (Gilligan, Rogers, and Tolman, 1991) have noted that our culture teaches girls to devalue themselves and to overvalue boys' opinions as they get older, which contributes to many mental health problems, including eating disorders in later life. Thus a proposed social norms intervention focusing on women's misperception of what men find attractive could exacerbate a fundamental problem for women by reinforcing women's privileging of men's opinions. This speculative example suggests that correcting misperception alone may not be desirable for all health problems and could even be detrimental.

A more effective workshop using social norms theory could be designed to incorporate both of these components, including information on healthy, protective behaviors and information on what men and women perceive to be attractive to women. The first half of the workshop would focus on women's perceptions of what other women and men find attractive, encourage discussion of the pressures women feel to be seen as attractive by women and men, and present campus data on misperceptions. This would be followed by discussion of the reasons women are encouraged to place importance on men's opinions and the role of peer pressure among women to be thin. The workshop could conclude with discussion of healthy, protective behaviors actually employed by women that reduce the risk of eating disorders. The data on protective behaviors presented in the workshop could also be disseminated as part of a social norms marketing campaign.

In this intervention, a social norms analysis can be used to illustrate a negative cultural dynamic (women's overvaluing of men's opinions) relevant to the etiology of disordered eating, but once this dynamic is revealed it is critiqued and deconstructed and replaced by information about healthy, protective norms among women. A social norms intervention regarding perception of attractiveness here serves as a means to an end but is not the final step. This example reminds us that the form and process of social norms interventions differ with the issue.

Responding to the Problem Behavior of Others

When problem behaviors occur in the college environment, students often witness them directly or know about them from other students. Yet even when students experience the negative effects of others' drinking-related actions they may not speak up or confront these behaviors. Wechsler and others (1995), for example, coined the term "second-hand effects of binge drinking" to describe how frequent heavy drinkers cause problems that interfere with the lives of other students. Similarly, students who observe prejudicial comments may be bothered but not say anything.

In these examples, individuals take a public position that is in conflict with their private opinion. How can students be taught to express their discomfort with problematic behavior? This section summarizes relevant research, reviews some of the causes and stages of bystander behavior, and uses results from four experimental interventions to speculate on the design of a social norms intervention to reduce bystander behavior.

The literature on bystander behavior suggests that most people want to respond but may not do so do for three reasons (Latane and Nida, 1981). Individuals may see that others are not doing anything and assume that there isn't a problem (social influence), may fear doing something that could cause embarrassment (audience inhibition), or may assume that if they don't do anything someone else will (diffusion of responsibility). Social norms theory predicts a fourth factor contributing to bystander behavior: the belief that others, unlike oneself, are not bothered or concerned about the problem behavior. Thus pluralistic ignorance is an additional cause of bystander behavior.

For all of these motivations, the presence of other people inhibits the desire to help because of potentially false assumptions about others' positions. In studies of individuals witnessing an emergency, for example, 55 percent of individuals offered help when alone, while only 22 percent did so in a group (Latane and Nida, 1981). Thus incorrect beliefs about how others view the situation and whether they define it as a problem may cause individuals to inhibit healthy behavior, as predicted by social norms theory.

Is there evidence that individuals underestimate others' concern about problem behavior? A number of studies of pluralistic ignorance suggest that this is a widespread phenomenon. O'Gorman (1975) found that in 1968 most white Americans grossly exaggerated the support among other white Americans for racial segregation, and that this misperception reduced their willingness to act on behalf of integration. Matza (1964) observed that gang members engaged in action they personally disapproved of because they incorrectly believed that others supported the behavior. In one of the first studies on pluralistic ignorance, Katz and Allport (1931) found that although most fraternity members favored greater diversity in their houses, they excluded those who were different because they believed their brothers were less tolerant than they were. In each of these examples, healthy behavior was inhibited as a result of pluralistic ignorance, while intolerant, problematic, or unhealthy behavior was expressed or overlooked.

A more recent study of attitudes toward lesbian, gay, and bisexual students found that most students incorrectly perceived their friends and the average student on campus to be less accepting of LGB students than they actually were (Bowen and Bourgeois, 2001). This misperception was greater and more influential for students in general than friends.

Not acting on personal beliefs can prevent accomplishing normal developmental tasks such as achieving congruence between values and behavior (Chickering, 1978). Social norms interventions to reduce bystander behavior may thus contribute to emotional well-being and enhance psychological growth by helping individuals resolve the cognitive dissonance associated with acting against their beliefs.

The first step in a social norms intervention to reduce bystander behavior is to document the true norm of intolerance for the behavior in question. This would be followed by dissemination of this information to the target population with the hope that revealing the norm of intolerance will increase the number of individuals confronting the perpetrator(s) of the behavior.

In a review of the literature on bystander behavior, Latane and Darley (1970) identified five stages in the transition of individuals from passivity to action: (1) notice the event, (2) interpret it as a problem, (3) feel responsible for finding a solution, (4) possess the necessary skills to act, and (5) intervene. Particular interventions could be designed for each stage to remove the causes of bystander behavior and help individuals move on to the next stage. Encouraging individuals to feel responsible for the solution should be accomplished without exacerbating or exaggerating the misperception regarding the problem to be corrected. Here are possible social norms interventions appropriate for reducing the causes, at each stage, of bystander behavior (adapted from Berkowitz, 1998a):

1. *Notice the event.* Offer examples or call attention to the problem behavior of the minority or to positive attitudes of the majority. Document the actual and perceived incidence of problem behaviors and healthy attitudes and behaviors.

2. *Interpret it as a problem.* Design a survey to obtain data about how respondents feel about types of problem behavior and determine if they have been a victim of these behaviors or observed others experiencing their effects. Educate participants that the behavior in question occurs and is upsetting to most people by presenting responses informally in workshops or through a social norms marketing campaign. Give workshop participants blank cards and ask them to describe how they would feel if they observed an incident. Collect the responses and read them aloud. Ask students or student leaders to interview bystanders when they learn of an incident of problem behavior and assess the bystanders' feelings about what happened. Collect a number of examples and discuss them with students to show that many other peers are uncomfortable with such behaviors.

3. *Feel responsible for the solution.* Help participants understand how they are personally hurt by problem behaviors and how they can intervene to prevent these effects. For example, document how secondhand effects of high-risk drinking interfere with their lives, how men are hurt by sexual assault, or how prejudice can hurt them personally. Understanding how we are personally hurt by others behavior can promote the motivation to intervene.

4. *Possess the necessary skills to act.* Offer training in intervention skills, including how to talk to others who are present; how to approach and talk to the perpetrator; and how to defuse the situation through humor, exaggeration, or appeal to a positive standard of behavior.

5. *Intervene.* Respond when incidents occur.

Recently, Berkowitz (2002) suggested that these stages of bystander behavior fit well with the stages of change theory developed by Prochaska (Prochaska and Velicer, 1997).

Monto, Newcomb, Rabow, and Hernandez (1994) studied these stages in an analysis of bystander behavior with respect to driving while intoxicated (DWI). They determined that passing through each stage significantly increased the likelihood that a student would intervene with a drunk driver. For example, although 51 percent of students in general reported trying to intervene in a DWI situation in the last year, 65 percent of those who noticed the event intervened, 73 percent of those who thought the situation was serious intervened, and 82 percent of those who felt they had the skills to act intervened with a drunk driver, thus empirically supporting the stages of the model. The authors also found that students were more likely to intervene if they reported having a conversation with others about the problem.

Individuals and communities may begin at different places in the model. For example, most individuals are already uncomfortable with problem behavior and need to begin working at a later stage. Others may be motivated to act by discovering through informal conversation that friends share their concerns. Because some students already possess intervention skills, it may be necessary only to impart the information that they are not alone to motivate action. This encouragement could come from respected peers who model appropriate use of intervention skills and who share information about the true norm, or from social norms media. If, on the other hand, students do not have the skills necessary to intervene appropriately, an additional skill-building step would have to be incorporated. The National Coalition Building Institute has an excellent model for teaching individuals to interrupt prejudicial remarks (Brown and Mazza, 1991, 1997) that can be adapted to stage four of the bystander model.

A trial intervention to reduce bystander behavior with respect to secondhand effects of high-risk drinking has been conducted by the Student Health Service at the University of Iowa. The "Say Something" campaign was designed to complement a social norms media campaign already in place in first-year residence halls that had successfully prevented an increase in drinking during the first year of college (Pat Ketcham, personal communication, December 1, 1999). The intent of the campaign was to empower students to act on their discomfort about secondhand effects of other students' drinking. The campaign had two components: a social norms marketing campaign and intensive training of residence life staff in support of the effort. Media developed for the campaign included posters with these messages:

- If you've been babysitting a friend who drinks too much, maybe it's time you said something. Think about it: if you and the rest of the 54 percent who babysat this weekend speak up, maybe you'll only have to say something once. After all, you're adults, *right?* SPEAK UP.

- Sixty-seven percent of UI students have had their studying or sleep interrupted by a loud, obnoxious, drunken student. Say Something!
- Tired of losing sleep after a friend's night out? SAY SOMETHING . . . the next day . . . nonjudgmental . . . and clear the air. (You'll all sleep better.)

In its second year, this campaign focused on teaching residence hall staff, residents, and off-campus students skills to provide feedback to problem drinkers. One poster said, "When your friend goes out and you end up with a headache . . . say something . . . the next day, be objective, clear the air."

Although the program was not formally evaluated, anecdotal information in comments from students indicated that they felt support for engaging in conversation with their roommates or friends about the secondhand effects they were experiencing. Students informed staff they hadn't really thought of themselves as having the right to speak out.

In any attempt to address secondhand effects, it is important to emphasize that, even when most individuals experience the secondhand effects of high-risk drinking or other behaviors, the problems are caused by a minority. Otherwise there is a danger of exacerbating the misperception that causes bystander behavior in the first place.

Kilmartin and others (1999), as noted earlier, designed an intervention to reduce bystander behavior among men who observe sexist language about women. It was based on the assumption that men's silence about sexist language serves to enable violence toward women, as noted by Thorne-Finch: "A large number of men continue to be silent about male violence against women. Men need to recognize that by not criticizing their sexist and abusive male peers, they help to perpetuate the tradition of male violence . . . it would appear that many men are afraid to risk suspicion among their peers that they are not hegemonically masculine men. Speaking out against male violence demands a critical approach to one's real and mythical peer group" (1992, pp. 217–218).

As part of a course at Mary Washington College (MWC), students designed a survey containing twelve scenarios in which sexist behavior was exhibited within an all-male peer group, including examples of sexual objectification of women, coercive sexuality, and sexist stereotypes. Participants were asked to rate the level of discomfort for themselves, for a close male friend, and for the average male student on campus. Results were consistent with social norms theory: all men underestimated their friend's and other men's discomfort with sexist language in an all-male peer group. In the next phase of the intervention, a social norms marketing campaign was conducted to publicize the true norm of discomfort among men. Messages incorporated into a variety of campus advertisements and posters included:

- All men feel some level of discomfort with men's sexist behavior.
- Over half (60 percent) overestimate the "typical male" MWC student's level of comfort with men's behavior.

- Over half (60 percent) overestimate a male friend's level of comfort with men's sexist behavior.
- Sexist behavior feeds the attitude behind sexual assault. Challenge this attitude with your male friends—they may be as uncomfortable as you.
- Eighty-one percent of MWC male students report some level of discomfort when men use terms like "bitch" and "slut" to refer to women.
- Most MWC male students report some level of discomfort with sexist attitudes towards women.

A survey conducted one month after the social norms marketing campaign revealed a reduction in the misperception of the average male student's discomfort with sexist language and behavior, although there was no reduction in the misperception of a friend's discomfort. A future phase of this project will assess whether a reduction in misperception can increase men's ability to confront other men's problematic language and behavior.

At Western Washington University, this model is being used to help students take action as "allies" to end the oppression of other groups (Fabiano, 2000). Focus groups conducted as part of the Ally Building Project indicate that most students are concerned about intolerance on campus. However, students also assume that peers are less concerned than themselves and that friends may disapprove if they act to end prejudice. The project acknowledges the egalitarian yearnings of the majority of students; alleviates their belief that other students do not share similar concerns; and teaches ally-building skills through posters, a Website, and a series of three workshops. The workshops are sequenced to advance ally building. The skills are taught in four steps: (1) awareness, (2) information, (3) intervention skills, and (4) action. The workshops are titled "Flash Judgments: Acknowledging Learned Stereotypes," "Speaking Up: Awareness into Action," and (the National Coalition Building Institute's workshop) "Building Community and Reducing Prejudice" (Brown and Mazza, 1991, 1997). The project has been met with great enthusiasm and interest from students.

The Gay Alliance of the Genesee Valley, New York (Smolinsky, 2002) has used the small group norms-challenging model in a workshop to increase heterosexual ally behavior. The goals of the workshop are:

- To give people accurate information about their peers' attitudes toward lesbian, gay, bisexual, and transgendered (LGBT) people
- To empower people to act as allies toward LGBT individuals by correcting misperceptions
- To encourage people to see themselves as allies
- To reduce people's shame and guilt about not speaking up as an ally for fear of social ostracism or being perceived as LGBT themselves

Workshop participants fill out a survey assessing perception and misperception of attitudes toward LGBT people and then discuss the results in the workshop. A stage model of heterosexual ally behavior is presented and discussed.

These examples from University of Iowa, Mary Washington College, Western Washington University, and the Gay Alliance of the Genesee Valley present models and preliminary data supporting prediction of social norms theory with respect to bystander behavior. Although none of the interventions evaluated the effect on actual bystander behavior, anecdotal data from all four interventions indicate that a bystander intervention would need to take place in stages. First, information about the true norm would be offered. This encourages students to share their discomfort with peers (validating the feelings of discomfort). Second, those students who have the skills to respond could then do so on their own, but others may need an opportunity to learn those skills.

In summary, both theory and research suggest that social norms interventions can be designed to address secondhand effects of high-risk drinking and expression of prejudicial behavior. Preliminary data indicate that the adequacy of a social norms intervention to reduce bystander behavior may depend on the skill level of the student population. For some individuals, a social norms intervention may be adequate, but for others further skill-building steps may be needed to accomplish the desired outcome.

This chapter has extended social norms theory to prevention of sexual assault among men; disordered eating among women; and bystander behavior in relation to secondhand effects of binge drinking, sexist language by men, homophobia, and ally behavior. Predictions from the theory are supported by data on misperception and by results from preliminary interventions, suggesting that the social norms approach holds promise for other health issues in addition to alcohol. Further confirmation awaits development of carefully designed interventions that can be more fully evaluated.

Much has been learned from successful application of social norms theory to alcohol abuse prevention. Adjustments are necessary, however, when interventions are designed for other health and social justice issues. First, the problem must be assessed to determine if a social norms intervention is appropriate, because interventions that have been successful in reducing alcohol abuse cannot simply be transferred to other issues. Second, each intervention must be adapted to the culture, etiology, and context of the problem in question. Thus interventions developed on one campus cannot be adopted elsewhere with the expectation of similar results, because of the unique culture and history of each educational institution. Interventions must be tailored to the target population in a way that is comprehensive and relevant, using survey data from questions that are carefully designed to reveal healthy norms and protective behaviors (Berkowitz, 1997).

Finally, research and interventions described in other chapters of this volume suggest that the social norms approach alone can be successful in reducing alcohol abuse and related problems. Applications discussed in this chapter, however, indicate that for some issues or communities a social norms intervention may not be adequate by itself and should be complemented by parallel interventions, such as skills training for interrupting oppressive remarks.

In conclusion, social norms interventions hold considerable promise for addressing a variety of health and social justice issues. It is hoped that this chapter will stimulate thinking in this direction and encouragement for designing these interventions.

References

Baer, J. S., Stacy, A., and Larimer, M. "Biases in the Perception of Drinking Norms Among College Students." *Journal of Studies on Alcohol,* 1991, *52*(6), 580–586.

Berkowitz, A. D. "College Men as Perpetrators of Acquaintance Rape and Sexual Assault." *Journal of American College Health,* 1992, *40,* 175–181.

Berkowitz, A. D. "Innovative Approaches to Behavioral Health and Social Justice Issues on Campus." Proceedings of the Annual Conference of the Association of College and University College Counseling Center Directors, Keystone, Colo., Oct. 16–20, 1993.

Berkowitz, A. D. "A Model Acquaintance Rape Prevention Program for Men." In A. Berkowitz (ed.), *Men and Rape: Theory, Research, and Prevention Programs in Higher Education.* San Francisco: Jossey-Bass, 1994a.

Berkowitz, A. D. "The Role of Coaches in Rape Prevention Programs for Athletes." In A. Parrot, N. Cummings, and T. Marchell (eds.), *Rape 101: Sexual Assault Prevention for College Athletes.* Holmes Beach, Fla.: Learning Publications, 1994b.

Berkowitz, A. D. "From Reactive to Proactive Prevention: Promoting an Ecology of Health on Campus." In P. C. Rivers and E. Shore (eds.), *A Handbook on Substance Abuse for College and University Personnel.* Westport, Conn.: Greenwood Press, 1997.

Berkowitz, A. D. "How We Can Prevent Sexual Harassment and Sexual Assault." *Educators Guide to Controlling Sexual Harassment,* 1998a, *6*(1), 1–4.

Berkowitz, A. D. "The Proactive Prevention Model: Helping Students Translate Healthy Beliefs into Healthy Actions." *About Campus,* Sept.–Oct. 1998b, pp. 26–27.

Berkowitz, A. D. "Applications of Social Norms Theory to Other Issues." Presented at Second National Conference on the Social Norms Model: Science Based Prevention, Big Sky, Mont., July 28–30, 1999a.

Berkowitz, A. D. "Questions About Social Norms Theory and Its Applications." (Special issue.) *Alcohol Issues and Solutions.* Garfield, N.J.: PaperClip Communications, 1999b.

Berkowitz, A. D. *The Social Norms Approach: Theory, Research and Annotated Bibliography.* Newton, Mass.: Higher Education Center for Alcohol and Other Drug Prevention, 2000. (www.edc.org/hec/socialnorms/)

Berkowitz, A. D. "Social Norms Interventions with Small Groups." *Report on Social Norms,* 2001, *1*(1), 1, 7.

Berkowitz, A. D. "Fostering Men's Responsibility for Preventing Sexual Assault. In P. A. Schewe (ed.), *Preventing Intimate Violence in Relationships: Interventions Across the Life Span.* Washington, D.C.: American Psychological Association, 2002.

Boulter, C. *Effects of an Acquaintance Rape Prevention Program on Male College Students' Endorsements of Rape Myth Beliefs and Sexually Coercive Behaviors.* Doctoral thesis, Washington State University, Pullman, 1997.

Bowen, A. M., and Bourgeois, M. J. "Attitudes Towards Lesbian, Gay and Bisexual College Students: The Contribution of Pluralistic Ignorance, Dynamic Social Impact, and Contact Theories." *Journal of American College Health,* 2001, *50*(2), 91–96.

Brown, C. R., and Mazza, G. J. "Peer Training Strategies for Welcoming Diversity." In J. Dalton (ed.), *Racism on Campus: Confronting Racial Bias Through Peer Interventions.* San Francisco: Jossey-Bass, 1991.

Brown, C. R., and Mazza, G. J. *Healing into Action: A Leadership Guide for Creating Diverse Communities.* Washington, D.C.: National Coalition Building Institute, 1997.

Bruce, S. "The 'A Man' Campaign: Marketing Social Norms to Men to Prevent Sexual Assault." *The Report on Social Norms.* (Working paper #5.) Little Falls, N.J.: PaperClip Communications, 2002.

Carter, J. C., Stewart, D. A., Dunn, V. J., and Fairburn, C. G. "Primary Prevention of Eating Disorders: Might It Do More Harm Than Good?" *International Journal of Eating Disorders,* 1997, *22*, 167–172.

Caruso, M. E. "An Extension of Misperception Theory to Rape Myths." Dissertation submitted to faculty of Mississippi State University, 1996.

Chassin, L., and others. "Predicting the Onset of Cigarette Smoking in Adolescents: A Longitudinal Study." *Journal of Applied Social Psychology,* 1984, *14*(3), 224–243.

Chickering, A. W. *Education and Identity.* San Francisco: Jossey-Bass, 1978.

Fabiano, P. "Using a Social Norms Approach for Building Just and Non-Violent Communities." Paper presented at the Third Annual Conference on the Social Norms Model: Science-Based Prevention from Theory to Practice, Denver, Colo.: July 26–28, 2000.

Fallon, A. "Standards of Attractiveness: Their Relationship Toward Body Image Perceptions and Eating Disorders." *Food and Nutrition News,* 1987, *59*(5), 79–81.

Far, J. "The Small Group Norms Challenging Model." *Report on Social Norms,* 2001, *1*(1), 1–5.

Foubert, J. D., and Marriott, K. A. "Effects of a Sexual Assault Peer Education Program on Men's Beliefs in Rape Myths." *Sex Roles,* 1997, *36*(3/4), 259–268.

Foubert, J. D., and McEwen, M. K. "An All-Male Rape Prevention Peer Education Program: Decreasing Fraternity Men's Behavioral Intent to Rape." *Journal of College Student Development,* 1998, *39*(6), 548–556.

Gilligan, C., Rogers, A. G., and Tolman, D. L. *Women, Girls and Psychotherapy: Reframing Resistance.* New York: Haworth Press, 1991.

Grube, J. W., Morgan, M., and McGree, S. T. "Attitudes and Normative Beliefs as Predictors of Smoking Intentions and Behaviors: A Test of Three Models." *British Journal of Social Psychology,* 1986, *25*, 81–93.

Haines, M. P. *A Social Norms Approach to Preventing Binge Drinking at Colleges and Universities.* Newton, Mass.: Higher Education Center for Alcohol and Other Drug Prevention, 1996.

Haines, M. P., and Spear, S. F. "Changing the Perception of the Norm: A Strategy to Decrease Binge Drinking Among College Students." *Journal of American College Health,* 1996, *45*, 134–140.

Johannessen, K., Collins, C., Mills-Novoa, B., and Glider, P. *A Practical Guide to Alcohol Abuse Prevention: A Campus Case Study in Implementing Social Norms and Environmental Management Approaches.* Tucson: Campus Health Service, University of Arizona, 1999.

Katz, D., and Allport, F. H. *Student Attitudes.* Syracuse, N.Y.: Craftsmen Press, 1931.

Katz, J. "Reconstructing Masculinity in the Locker Room: The Mentors in Violence Prevention Project." *Harvard Educational Review,* 1995, *65*(2), 163–174.

Katz, J., and Jhally, S. "Tough Guise: Violence, Media and the Crisis in Masculinity." (Video.) Northampton, Mass.: Media Education Foundation, 1999.

Keeling, R. P. "Proceed with Caution: Understanding and Changing Norms." *Journal of American College Health,* 1999, *47,* 243–246.

Kilmartin, C. T., and others. "Using the Social Norms Model to Encourage Male College Students to Challenge Rape-Supportive Attitudes in Male Peers." Paper presented at Virginia Psychological Association Spring Conference, Virginia Beach, Va., April 1999.

Kusch, J. M. "Test of a Social Norms Approach to Understanding Disordered Eating Practices in College Women." Unpublished master's thesis, Washington State University, Pullman, 2002.

Lanier, C. A., and Elliot, M. N. "A New Instrument for the Evaluation of a Date Rape Prevention Program." *Journal of College Student Development,* 1997, *38*(6), 673–676.

Latane, B., and Darley, J. M. *The Unresponsive Bystander: Why Doesn't He Help?* Englewood Cliffs, N.J.: Appleton-Century-Crofts, 1970.

Latane, B., and Nida, S. "Ten Years of Research on Group Size and Helping." *Psychological Bulletin,* 1981, *89*(2), 308–324.

Mahlstedt, D., and Corcoran, C. "Preventing Dating Violence." In C. Crawford, S. David, and J. Sebrechts (eds.), *Coming into Her Own.* San Francisco: Jossey-Bass, 1999.

Mann, T., and others. "Are Two Interventions Worse Than None? Joint Primary and Secondary Prevention of Eating Disorders in College Females." *Health Psychology,* 1997, *16*(3), 215–225.

Martz, D., and Bazzini, D. G. "Eating Disorders Prevention Programming May Be Failing: Evaluation of Two One-Shot Programs." *Journal of College Student Development,* 1999, *40*(1), 32–42.

Matza, D. *Delinquency and Draft.* New York: Wiley, 1964.

Mazzeo, S. E. "Modification of an Existing Measure of Body Image Preoccupation and Its Relationship to Disordered Eating in Female College Students." *Journal of Counseling Psychology,* 1999, *46*(1), 42–50.

McCreary, D. R., and Sadava, S. W. "Gender Differences in Relationships Among Perceived Attractiveness, Life Satisfaction, and Health in Adults as a Function of Body Mass Index and Perceived Weight." *Psychology of Men and Masculinity,* 2001, *2*(2), 108–116.

Miller, D. T., and McFarland, C. "Pluralistic Ignorance: When Similarity Is Interpreted as Dissimilarity." *Journal of Personality and Social Psychology,* 1987, *53*(2), 298–305.

Miller, D. T., and McFarland, C. "When Social Comparison Goes Awry: The Case of Pluralistic Ignorance." In J. Suls and T. Wills (eds.), *Social Comparison: Contemporary Theory and Research.* Hillsdale, N.J.: Erlbaum, 1991.

Monto, M. A., Newcomb, M. D., Rabow, J., and Hernandez, A.C.R. "Do Friends Let Friends Drive Drunk? Decreasing Drunk Driving Through Informal Peer Intervention." In P. J. Venturelli (ed.), *Drug Use in America: Social, Cultural and Political Perspectives.* Boston: Jones and Bartlett, 1994.

Morgan, S. "How Much Sex? How Much Alcohol? A Study of Perceived Norms." Paper presented at Annual Meeting of the Eastern Sociological Society, Baltimore, March 1997.

Muehlenhard, C. L., and Cook, S. W. "Men's Reports of Unwanted Sexual Activity." *Sex Research,* 1988, *24,* 58–72.

O'Gorman, H. J. "Pluralistic Ignorance and White Estimates of White Support for Racial Segregation." *Public Opinion Quarterly,* 1975, *39*(3), 313–330.

Perkins, H. W. "The Contextual Effect of Secular Norms on Religiosity as Moderator of Student Alcohol and Other Drug Use." In M. Lynn and D. Moberg (eds.), *Research in the Social Scientific Study of Religion.* Greenwich, Conn.: JAI Press, 1994.

Perkins, H. W. "College Student Misperceptions of Alcohol and Other Drug Use Norms Among Peers: Exploring Causes, Consequences and Implications for Prevention Programs." In *Designing Alcohol and Other Drug Prevention Programs in Higher Education: Bringing Theory into Practice.* Newton, Mass.: Higher Education Center for Alcohol and Other Drug Prevention, 1997.

Perkins, H. W., and Berkowitz, A. D. "Perceiving the Community Norms of Alcohol Use Among Students: Some Research Implications for Campus Alcohol Education Programming." *International Journal of the Addictions,* 1986, *21,* 961–976.

Perkins, H. W., and others. "Misperceptions of the Norms for the Frequency of Alcohol and Other Drug Use on College Campuses." *Journal of American College Health,* 1999, *47,* 253–258.

Pollard, J. W., and others. "Predictions of Normative Drug Use by College Students: False Consensus, False Uniqueness, or Just Plain Accuracy?" *Journal of College Student Psychotherapy,* 2000, *14*(3), 5–12.

Prentice, D. A., and Miller, D. T. "Pluralistic Ignorance and Alcohol Use on Campus: Some Consequences of Misperceiving the Social Norm." *Journal of Personality and Social Psychology,* 1993, *64*(2), 243–256.

Prochaska, J. O., and Velicer, W. F. "Transtheoretical Model of Health Behavior Change." *American Journal of Health Promotion,* 1997, *12,* 38–48.

Schewe, P. A., and O'Donohue, W. "Sexual Abuse Prevention with High-Risk Males: The Role of Victim Empathy and Rape Myths." *Violence and Victims,* 1993, *8,* 339–351.

Schwartz, M. D., and DeKeseredy, W. S. *Sexual Assault on Campus: The Role of Male Peer Support.* Thousand Oaks, Calif.: Sage, 1997.

Smolinsky, T. "What Do We Really Think: A Group Exercise to Increase Heterosexual Ally Behavior." *The Report on Social Norms.* (Working paper #4.) Little Falls, N.J.: PaperClip Communications, 2002.

Striegel-Moore, R. H., and Cachelin, F. M. "Body Image Concerns and Disordered Eating in Adolescent Girls: Risk and Protective Factors." In N. G. Johnson, M. C. Roberts, and J. Worell (eds.), *Beyond Appearance: A New Look at Adolescent Girls.* Washington, D.C.: American Psychological Association, 1999.

Sussman, S., and others. "Adolescent Nonsmokers, Triers, and Regular Smokers' Estimates of Cigarette Smoking Prevalence: When Do Overestimations Occur and by Whom?" *Journal of Applied Psychology,* 1988, *18*(7), 537–551.

Thorne-Finch, R. *Ending the Silence: The Origin and Treatment of Male Violence Against Women.* Toronto: University of Toronto Press, 1992.

Toch, H., and Klofas, J. "Pluralistic Ignorance, Revisited." In G. M. Stephenson and J. H. David (eds.), *Progress in Applied Social Psychology, Vol. 2.* New York: Wiley, 1984.

Wechsler, H., and others. "The Adverse Impact of Heavy Episodic Drinkers on Other College Students." *Journal of Studies on Alcohol,* 1995, *56*(6), 628–634.

White, J. "New Ideas to Prevent Violence Against Women: A Social Norms Approach." Presented at Annual Meeting of the American College Health Association, Washington, D.C., May–June 2002.

CHAPTER SEVENTEEN

THE PROMISE AND CHALLENGE OF FUTURE WORK USING THE SOCIAL NORMS MODEL

H. Wesley Perkins, Ph.D.

The research on social norms presented in this book clearly makes the case suggested by previous studies that norms regarding alcohol, tobacco, and illicit drug use and related behavior are grossly misperceived in ways that are detrimental for youth and young adults. Likewise, this compendium offers substantial evidence demonstrating the positive effect of a range of practical interventions reducing harmful misperceptions, and in turn harmful behaviors. As suggested by these chapters, there are many opportunities to apply the social norms approach in secondary schools, college populations, and community initiatives; the potential benefits for youth and young adults have been clearly demonstrated.

As the approach has grown in popularity, we see intervention projects create new techniques to communicate social norms, incorporate social norms material within more traditional programs, and even rename traditional prevention activities as social norms approaches. This has all led to the emergence of studies under the rubric of social norms work that range dramatically in the degree of effect they achieve. As more prevention programs and research projects construct initiatives that ostensibly use this approach, this expansion is likely to exacerbate the problem of maintaining the fidelity of the model. It has already begun to create such questions and challenges as why the approach might appear to be ineffective in some instances. This concluding chapter considers these and other emerging questions that will, no doubt, continue to challenge the model.

When Is a Social Norms Intervention Most Effective?

The degree of success one might experience using this approach varies according to many local factors and how the approach is implemented. On the basis of my experience with projects reported in this book as well as many other projects that have begun to introduce social norms, I have found that there are a few conditions that serve to maximize the positive impact of this approach.

Clear Positive Messages About Actual Norms

Students need to receive clear messages about the actual norms that exist among their peers. Prevention programs should include unambiguous factual statements about peer norms that have a basis in current data collected in a fashion that gives credibility to the facts. If the message is delivered in print media, there may be limitations on how much information can be offered in any one communication. It is not important (and may be distracting) to incorporate data about misperception simultaneously. The latter information can be effective in helping communicate the contrasting reality if one has the time to explain the phenomenon of misperception, how it comes about, and its impact, along with the communication of actual norms. Workshop, group meeting, and classroom presentations are formats wherein such discussion of misperception might take place. In brief media communications, however, simultaneous presentation of data on perceptions along with actual norms may be a confusing distraction.

Including in a media message attractive images of youths and young adults in positive activities may help catch the eye of students and reinforce the positive message, but care must be taken that the images do not clutter or overshadow the message and blur recall of the norm message being conveyed. In some projects, an advertising agency or students in mass media are brought in to help create attention-getting images to be included with the facts. Here again, however, a word of caution is in order if the media group does not really understand the fundamentals of the social norms approach. For example, I have seen advertising agency creations using an image of the aftermath of a heavy drinking party, or someone passed out, overlaid with the social norms message encompassing the facts about the majority percentage of students who drink only moderately or do not take risks. The image was chosen to grab the attention of students, but ironically it sends a message contrary to the facts and they become less interesting in the graphic display.

Although one can never completely control what is said and done by others concerned with prevention in a student population, it is also crucial to limit or eliminate, if possible, any concerted efforts by others to publicize scare messages about problem behavior and negative consequences that are occurring among students. Besides the fact that "health terrorism" has not worked, it is likely to be counterproductive in inflating misperception about normative behavior and present a confusing distraction juxtaposed against a message of actual positive norms.

High Doses of True Norms

When asked what are the three most important factors in real estate sales, the familiar anecdotal reply is "location, location, location." Similarly, I believe "dosage, dosage, dosage" is most important for improving the effect of social norms campaigns. We cannot simply put out the message once about actual norms, even with the best of data drawn from a large representative and recent sample, and expect a conversion in perceptions. It is probably not seen or heard by most youths in the population, and among those who do take notice it is likely to be dismissed by most of them as not true, a fluke or a distortion, because of their solid belief that the misperceived norm is the actuality. Even among youths who do not approve of or behave in accordance with what they perceive as the norm (still "carriers" of the misperception), it is common to observe outright rejection of the message of the actual norm as being impossible on account of what they themselves have observed. No one likes to be challenged that his or her view of the world is incorrect. Even if one does not like the landscape, it is unsettling to be presented with a map of one's surroundings that does not fit with the expectation of what will be encountered.

So the first point about dosage is that students need to see and hear the message multiple times if they are to recall and wrestle with it, and ultimately to consider the possibility that their notions of what is normative may not be entirely accurate. The message should be presented not only multiple times but also in a sustained campaign throughout the year. One cannot simply display several posters about actual norms regarding alcohol during an alcohol awareness week and assume that this does the job. The forces that produce misperception—the mind assuming that the observed behavior of others is typical, memory and conversation focusing on the sensationalized activities of the few, and media attention to substance abuse—are all in play every day of the year.

Second, adequate or increased dosage means going beyond a message based on data drawn from one specific measure or from one time point. A campaign should use positive normative data collected on a variety of attitudes as well as risk behaviors and protective behaviors associated with substance use. Information about one particular behavior collected one time can only go so far in reaching students before it becomes a media jingle or is simply ignored as uninteresting.

A variety of measurements collected at each continuing time point are most useful. Results of each measure at each time can be introduced over the course of a social norms intervention, all pointing to the overarching positive norm of moderation or abstinence (depending on the age group and substance), thus serving to reinforce the fundamental point.

Third, achieving adequate or increased dosage requires using synergistic strategies. Not all students are exposed to or pay attention to the same media. Some read the student newspaper or see posters in a residence hall or the cafeteria, while others are more likely to see information on a computer screen or to hear about actual norms in a classroom, orientation program, or team workshop or on a radio program. Thus to get the widest coverage, a variety of venues should be employed. Furthermore, using multiple means to get the word out not only widens the coverage in the population but intensifies the exposure to individuals as they encounter the message and discussion of actual norms in multiple contexts. In this way, conversation about actual norms and responsible behavior is cross-fertilized among students, faculty, counselors, administrators, and parents in a school environment.

Delivery of Accurate Norms Beyond Risk Groups

It is quite understandable that occasionally social norms initiatives channel most of their time and resources into messages about accurate peer norms for a selected high-risk group of students. Targeting athletes, entering students, Greek organization members, or policy violators with social norms messages about college alcohol use, or giving accurate messages about normative abstinence rates for tobacco use to certain age strata where initiation of smoking is most likely to occur in a secondary school population, makes sense on the one hand because those students' behavior may be of greatest concern. Reducing their misperception about substance use can be a direct constraint upon their behavior as they internalize a more realistic view of what is normative and deemed appropriate among peers.

Targeting a high-risk group with accurate messages, on the other hand, may yield only modest benefit, or perhaps none at all, if misperceptions of substance-use norms in the larger student population go unattended. This is because misperceived (as well as accurately perceived) norms have both a psychological and sociological effect. At the psychological level, exaggerated perception of risky behavior creates internal psychological pressure or permission for the individual to act out the behavior. But the majority of students who are not problematic in their own behavior are most often "carriers" of the misperception as well, and they are detrimental in a contextual or sociological sense. Their misperception psychologically inhibits them from socially speaking out against risky actions or intervening to stop the behaviors of problem students. Thus, the carriers cannot serve well as agents of social control for their high-risk peers. In contrast, if the carriers' own misperceptions are reduced, thereby giving them the confidence of normative support to intervene, they can more easily help restrict the behavior of problem peers.

Moreover, as carriers, the majority of students help perpetuate misperceived norms among risk groups simply by reinforcing the misperceptions as they are passed along in conversation. Thus, carriers perversely help the risk-taking students maintain their erroneous notions of permissive norms, which, as I have already stated, contribute to their risky personal behavior. As a result, reducing misperceptions among the majority of students becomes a sociological intervention strategy to help reduce misperceptions among the high-risk groups. This type of intervention uses the broader population of peers to help communicate accurate norms to potential risk takers, while using direct delivery strategies of media and workshops for these particular groups. We cannot say at this point what degree of intervention delivered to a target group relative to that delivered to the wider population produces the maximum effect—just that attention to each level is an important consideration. Future research has to identify the right balance of targeted versus populationwide social norms interventions.

Does the Approach Always Work?

Occasionally, one hears or reads about a social norms project that did not reduce substance abuse. A natural response to this outcome is to ask why the approach did not work, or to uncritically assume that the theory must be flawed. In my experience, failure—or apparent failure—can be accounted for by a few basic factors already articulated in the model. Recall that the theory holds that misperceptions are pervasive and must be significantly reduced to more accurate level so that students can in turn act in accordance with the more responsible norms that are better seen as a result of the intervention. So the intervention must produce a correction in the misperception, which then produces more responsible behavior. If one finds that a project has not reduced substance abuse, in almost all instances the project has not reduced misperceptions of the norms regarding substance use. Thus the theory and the model have not failed; the intervention simply did not succeed in getting any correction to the misperceived norms.

The lack of impact on perceived norms may occur for a variety of reasons. The intervention message may be confusing, there may be competing scare messages appearing simultaneously, the dosage may be too little to affect misperception, or it may not be delivered for an adequate length of time. In any of these cases, the point still remains that the project is not able to change misperceptions with its limited or confounded intervention message and strategy. Again, this circumstance by no means violates the social norms theory and model of intervention. The model is sequential; reducing misperception of exaggerated norms is what in turn reduces problems and positively influences personal behaviors.

Although it is quite rare, I have encountered the circumstance where a social norms project is able to get some intervention effect in terms of reduced misperception but without a significant decline in problem behavior in a target group or the student population as a whole. Here, one of two factors is likely to be the culprit. First, the project may be reporting results from the first few months of intervention. It may have begun making inroads on the misperceptions that students typically hold; students may have started adjusting, at least to some degree, their view of the peer norm as the campaign communicates reality. But the evaluation of effect may be premature, not allowing enough time for correction of misperceptions to grow or enough time for this correction to filter down to individual behavior. Most projects reported in this book required at least one year, if not two, before the positive benefit to behavior could be fully demonstrated. Another explanation might be that only the risk group was the target of perceived norms correction. As previously discussed, even when the target group's highly exaggerated perceived norms are attenuated to some extent, if the larger population of students still continues to hold a perception that is exaggerated, then the modest but notable correction in the target group may not translate to moderated behavior. Here the larger peer group is still reinforcing the problematic actions of the risk group as (erroneously) normative.

Skeptics and Critics of the Social Norms Approach

Any new strategy for substance abuse prevention that grows in popularity is subject to honest skepticism and naïve criticism about the claims of the approach. The social norms approach is no exception in this regard. As more prevention specialists and school professionals working with youth pay attention to claims and example applications of the social norms model, there are going to be more questions. It is also likely for certain constituencies to feel threatened by the suggestion of a new way of doing things, even if the old familiar way is not producing the desired results. In my experience presenting research and practical examples about this approach at conferences and schools across the country, and in observing the commentary of skeptics over several years, critical voices have changed in terms of professional background.

In the earliest stages of the development of this approach, the most vocal skeptics were usually counselors and therapists working in health centers, counseling offices, and clinics where daily work was focused upon getting the problem user or addict to acknowledge his or her problem and to control or change behavior. Not only did their individualistic or family systems orientation seem to run counter to the social norms approach on peers as a critical element, but also what seemed to be emphasis on the lack of a problem in the population at large in this new approach did not fit well with their experience in the trenches. How could one be talking about positive norms and the predominance of healthy youth when so many individuals needed counseling and often exhibited obvious addictions? Would not promotion of the fact that most students did not have a problem hurt efforts to get the problem students into counseling?

Over time, however, most counselors' fears of this approach have subsided as they have begun to more clearly understand the model and see its benefits. The model has never denied the importance of addressing dysfunctional personalities and family dynamics in the case of addiction. The fundamental emphasis of the social norms approach has focused on primary prevention, reducing substance abuse and related risky behaviors in the general population before these problems reach a repetitive crisis point for individuals; it has never claimed that substance abuse is not a crucial problem in our society. Furthermore, experiments incorporating normative feedback in counseling contexts have produced positive results in reduced problem behavior. Thus, the approach has begun to be successfully integrated in counseling models. Rather than allowing substance abusers to ignore their problem behavior by thinking that their actions are normal, the social norms approach, when applied both in the general population of youth and in the counseling setting, helps break down the denial of problem youths. They can no longer say that they are simply "like everybody else."

A second stage of skepticism has come from some prevention specialists working from a framework that advocates policy implementation and enforcement to reduce problems. Some groups promoting the policy approach have been fearful that the social norms approach might be a diversion from creating and strictly enforcing rules. There may be debate in the general prevention field about which policies are effective and how and when enforcement can most positively contribute to reduction in substance abuse problems, but the social norms approach is not antithetical to policy initiatives. It simply concentrates on peer norms and perceived norms as a primary arena neglected by most research and prevention practice where there may be the greatest potential to achieve positive change in youth populations.

Some of the skepticism among policy advocates about the social norms approach has begun to erode, however, in the face of several important observations. There is growing evidence of more support among youth for many desired or already instituted policies than is actually perceived. So misperception about the extent of support for policies weakens their effect. This phenomenon is another aspect of norm misperception and suggests that social norms efforts to communicate actual norms where policies are supported by the majority could be beneficial to policy advocates' strategies (see Chapter Nine). Moreover, riots and backlash from students, and the failure to observe positive change in instances where policies have been introduced without attention to student norms, are leading some policy advocates to take a more sympathetic look at the norms approach.

Finally, skepticism and naïve criticism are voiced by a few other researchers working on problems of student substance abuse who have had little or no involvement with the social norms approach, not because the social norms strategy runs counter to a prevention technique they are promoting but because their research and publications routinely concentrate on the problem, thus bringing them the attention of the media and the public. Most perversely, if funding for their research and their employment depends on a continued statement of the problem and public attention to that work, then an alternative paradigm that demonstrates (with similar research or even the same data) that the majority are not a problem becomes a direct threat to their work rather than an approach that can be potentially integrated. Thus, "health" research institutes and media production organizations that gain their livelihood through continued publicity about youth problems rather than youth resilience have little or no interest in confronting the truth about the positive norms that exist if they want to maintain their funding and position in the spotlight. Consequently, this last group of skeptics have little motivation to carefully consider the theory or evidence from the social norms approach. They are likely to continue, and even increase, their critical commentary without serious consideration of the approach as they follow their organizational or individual self-interest.

Responses to Questions and Criticisms

It is important to review the naïve criticism sometimes voiced about social norms work in substance abuse prevention, assuming this criticism is likely to continue, so that educators, counselors, and clinicians considering or already using this approach in their school and community environments will be equipped with responses to these challenges.

Is the Approach "Sugar Coating" the Problem?

Some critics suggest that the social norms approach is "sugar coating" the problem by emphasizing talk about a positive majority in the student population and not really pointing out the significant number of students who exhibit alcohol or other substance abuse problems doing significant harm to themselves and others.

This is a simplistic notion, of course. Prevention specialists conducting research and designing interventions to correct misperception are not doing so because they think there is nothing to worry about. Rather, social norms advocates are just being clear about the distinction between the problem as a motivation for prevention work and the need for funding support on the one hand, and the most effective strategies to reduce the problem on the other hand. Those who voice this naïve criticism somehow think that if one keeps stating the problem over and over and ever more loudly it will go away, which is, of course, ludicrous. Noting a substantial problem may be useful for getting a larger team of people involved in working on the problem or in getting funding to address it, but dwelling on the problem publicly with students is not productive and may actually increase the problematic misperception of an exaggerated peer norm. Identifying the problem must be understood as a different task from prevention. Talking about the problem does not inherently reduce it; while acknowledging that problematic behavior exists, the social norms approach focuses on truthful presentation of the healthy majority as a way to combat the very real problem that exists among a portion of youth.

Are Misperceptions of Norms Overstated?

Although increasingly uncommon, as social norms research has progressed there is still an occasional individual voicing skepticism about whether misperceptions actually exist in such a consistent and massive way to justify designing a whole prevention strategy around reducing them. The review of the literature in Chapter One of this book as well as many of the empirical studies presented in this volume demonstrating pervasive misperceptions speak to the question. In the rare instance when a study appears to show no difference between the actual and perceived norm in a student population, I have always found it was because the measures being used to identify actual norms were not directly comparable to those used to measure perceived norms. In contrast, whenever the actual norm has been compared with perceived norms using identical measures for personal and other student behavior or attitudes in a student population, clearly exaggerated norms have been identified for a substantial portion of students in every study published to date on the topic.

A variety of survey instruments used throughout the United States have designed and incorporated parallel personal questions (to establish actual norms) and perceived norm questions. For example, the Campus Survey of Alcohol and Other Drug Norms, from the Core Institute (Southern Illinois University), and the National College Health Assessment Survey, produced by the American College Health Association, both intended for use by colleges and universities nationally;

and the Survey of College Alcohol Norms and Behavior, developed by the Education Development Center (Newton, Massachusetts) for a thirty-two-site controlled study of the social norms approach funded by the National Institute on Alcoholism and Alcohol Abuse, all include scores of parallel questions and have been conducted at hundreds of colleges and universities. Likewise, the HWS Alcohol Education Project Surveys Online for secondary schools include scores of parallel questions to assess actual and perceived norms (see Chapter Twelve). Results from the use of all of these surveys routinely document substantial misperceptions.

Will Normative Messages About Moderate Alcohol Use Encourage Abstainers to Drink?

Sometimes the question is raised about whether telling college students how much, on average, their peers actually drink is harmful to those individuals who want to abstain from alcohol use. The notion is that the message encourages them to drink because it is normative. This naïve assumption neglects a fundamental point about the intervention. Students who abstain in college do not currently believe that abstinence is the norm, so telling them most students drink does not put some new normative pressure on them to start doing so. Not only do they already know that drinking is the norm, but like their other peers many of them tend to misperceive more frequent consumption, a greater amount of alcohol being consumed, and a more permissive attitude among peers than is the reality. So putting the truth out publicly about the actual drinking rate does not put more pressure on them to drink just because they are told most other college students consume some level of alcohol. Communicating the truth either reduces their misperception, thereby lessening pressure on them to begin drinking, or it simply confirms their already accurate perception, having no effect on them.

Furthermore, there is no empirical research suggesting that abstinence declines in response to a social norms campaign. For example, the evidence from each case study in this book where abstinence was measured in addition to heavy alcohol consumption reported no change or an increase in the abstinence rate overall after introduction of this approach.

Was the Social Norms Approach Invented by the Alcohol Beverage Industry to Promote Sales and Avert Criticism?

Some people believe that the alcohol beverage industry should be highly involved in supporting prevention work, given that misuse of its product is the point of concern. Others think the industry should be kept out of prevention efforts entirely for reasons of conflict of interest. For the latter group, any industry involvement in prevention is a wolf in sheep's clothing. The belief is that the industry will only support prevention work that is ineffective as a way to keep sales high while looking concerned. From a cynical viewpoint, one might suggest that the social norms approach is growing thanks to promotion by alcohol beverage organizations who find the message compatible as it acknowledges alcohol use as normative among young adults. An even more cynical conspiracy theory has it that the whole approach was somehow the brainchild of the industry to keep sales high. Though absurd, this criticism of social norms has been trumpeted by a few individuals who are either completely ignorant of the history of intervention research using social norms or are perversely trying to discredit the approach in any way possible so as to bring greater interest and support to their own work, which may be threatened by the social norms movement.

Setting aside any debate about the appropriateness of industry involvement in prevention efforts, I maintain that this cynical view of the development of the social norms approach could not be farther from the truth. The simple fact is that all of the social norms projects serving as primary examples of the development and success of this approach in colleges and universities over the last decade (all of the schools and projects represented in the chapters of this book included) as well as the initial research on misperception and the initial theoretical development of the model were supported solely by federal government grants through the U.S. Department of Education and the Center for Substance Abuse Prevention and by local academic institutions' prevention funds, with no support from the alcohol beverage industry. It is true that in recent years beverage industry organizations have given some promotional attention to the approach and some funding support to a few colleges and universities experimenting with a social norms strategy, but many schools are implementing it without industry funding. So at this point, industry funding cannot be connected in any way with the creation, success, or dramatic spread of this approach over the last several years, even if late-blooming industry support is assisting some programs today. Furthermore, it is just nonsense to assume that the approach does not work, without considering the previous scientific evidence collected in the field showing a positive impact using social norms, simply because the industry is now interested in the approach, especially when other strategies have not been able to produce such reduction in problem drinking in college.

Moreover, the social norms approach and its evidence of effectiveness go well beyond the issue of college alcohol use. Research presented in this book and elsewhere showing increased abstinence in primary and secondary school age populations surely does not support the cynical notion that publicizing information about accurate norms (of abstinence, in this case) is expanding an alcohol consumer base. We see too the growth of social norms implementation and success with regard to prevention of tobacco use across age groups. Clearly, this approach is not the brainchild of a secret plot supported by the tobacco industry. Thus the warning that really needs to go out to prevention practitioners is against any accusations that the social norms approach is just an alcohol industry product or plot.

Does the Social Norms Approach Breed Conformity?

Yet another curious position argued by a few (usually the same) detractors of the social norms model is the notion that the strategy breeds conformity and is anti-intellectual, thus not in keeping with the mission of education. There are at least two responses to this naïve criticism. First, one must acknowledge that the strategy indeed recognizes that humans do conform to group norms most of the time. It is a reality that we are social animals directed not by instinct but by cultural practices and learned expectations from symbolic interaction with our family and peer groups. Following the group norm is not inherently bad or good; it depends on what the norm is. In the case of substance use in secondary schools, the norm is typically abstinence, as it is in college—with the exception of alcohol use, where moderate use prevails as normative. So in these cases we might as well take advantage of our tendency to follow the norm. Moreover, if students are going to conform by following peer norms in large part anyway (as most studies in social psychology suggest), then they should at least follow accurate norms, which are much better than the commonly misperceived ones. In other words, the approach does not breed conformity. It simply redirects the already occurring conformity to the more moderate actual norm.

Second, in making students more aware of a moderate and healthy or lower-risk norm, the approach actually frees students to act more responsibly by adhering more closely to their personal attitudes (which most often support abstinence or low-risk behavior). From this perspective, then, the approach helps most students act more closely to their personal preferences rather than a perceived group standard that is not their own.

Is There Really Such a Thing as a "Typical Student" in the Population?

This question is sometimes raised as a criticism of the social norms approach because questions about perceived norms in surveys often ask students what they think is the most "typical" attitude or behavior among students, and because intervention messages often say something about the "average" student. Diversity is justifiably celebrated in most educational contexts, and an empirical scan of most student bodies would indeed find considerable diversity, whether it be in terms of ethnicity, socioeconomic or geographic background, religious belief, sexual orientation, extracurricular interest, or academic ability. So the thought of amalgamating all students into an average in describing a population may not seem logical, or it may not be inherently pleasing to some educators and counselors who are simultaneously speaking about the importance of diversity.

If there is no one average or typical student, then how can measurement or discussion of what is typical for the population be relevant or even possible? Critical commentary from this perspective suggests that we can only talk about norms within smaller group categories that distinguish students of different types. Anyone offering this challenge fails to understand, however, that even though diversity exists in terms of sociocultural subgroups, there are certain widely shared values and actions that can be typical of most people in a cultural context regardless of subgroup diversity—whether it be walking on the right in pedestrian traffic, raising one's hand to speak in a class, or thinking that an unprovoked assault on another person is unacceptable. So even though perhaps we cannot identify a typical student in terms of many characteristics simultaneously, there is a typical student when we focus on a particular norm.

It is true that there may be few or even no students who exactly fit the description of what is normative across a variety of measures, but this does not really matter. What matters is that what is normative or most common for a peer group or student population in a particular school does exist as an empirical entity, and it also exists in the minds of students, be it accurate or not. Relatively few students have any difficulty answering survey questions about what is most common or what the typical student says or does at their school. Almost all students have some notion of this, even if they feel they cannot be absolutely precise. In the end, what matters most for the social norms approach is that this concept, as it resides in the minds of students—empirically accurate or not—influences their behavior and that changing their perception of what is most typical among peers at their school does make a difference in their own actions.

As people grow out of childhood, they begin to behave in accordance with what the famous social psychologist and theorist of human symbolic development George Herbert Mead called the internalization of a sense of "the generalized other" (Mead, 1934). Over time, humans expand their consciousness beyond thoughts of what "significant others" (parents, siblings, teachers, and so forth) think of them to begin thinking about how "people" will perceive them and what people expect of them. We do not have specific faces in mind as we have this mental conversation with ourselves. It is a generalized notion of our peers and society at large. It is a complex abstract concept internalized in the socialization process that has very concrete effects on how we behave in social interaction. We can observe it operating any time we are in an anonymous public situation and behave or ask a friend to behave in accordance with social customs even though there would be no legal or personal ramifications for behaving strangely. We do so all the time, wondering *What will others think about us?* Thus the concept of a typical student or the notion of other students in general is a social and psychological reality that is quite relevant to our work.

What If the Problem Is the Norm?

What if the majority of students in a population do exhibit problem behavior on a particular measure? Does this mean the social norms approach will not work in this situation? The answer is no, for two reasons. First, we should not be tied to any one measure as if it were a gold standard. If one measure of an actual norm is not as positive as we might like, we should consider whether or not the measure is constructed with some arbitrary parameter and what other measures might also be available that might give a different picture. Second, and more important for the rationale of using a social norms model, is the fact that even if the norm is not ideal, if it is a higher level of risk than we would want, students still believe that their peers are, on average, engaged in a still higher level of risk than this actual norm. Thus addressing misperceived norms is a potentially beneficial strategy even in these contexts.

This question is usually raised in reference to alcohol use in a college or university where survey data on a particular measure might reveal the majority falling in the high-risk category. The popular benchmark that sometimes produces a majority in this category is something like having four or more drinks (women) or five or more drinks (men) on at least one occasion in the last two weeks. Students who fall into this category are certainly more likely to experience more negative consequences as a result of their drinking for themselves and others, compared to students below this benchmark. If the benchmark is set at a higher level, however, students consuming above that point will also exhibit more consequences than those below the cut off point. When amount of time is considered, one can be in the curious position of drinking what is sometimes defined as a relatively safe amount and simultaneously still be in the high-risk group (such as having one drink per hour, which can be metabolized by most people without increasing blood alcohol level yet still being high risk by having had four drinks over the course of four or more hours in an evening). Indeed, when amount of time and body weight are simultaneously considered along with the number of drinks one consumes in the estimate of the likely blood alcohol concentration (and therefore risk) incurred by young adults on an occasion, one finds a substantial drop in the percentage (well below the majority) who would be classified as a problem (Perkins, DeJong, and Linkenbach, 2001).

Furthermore, the common measure asking about the last two weeks is in another sense arbitrary. If we asked whether one consumed the specified amount on an occasion at least once during the year, or perhaps ever during one's lifetime, the percentage falling into the category would obviously be much larger. If we restricted the measure to the previous week, one would be hard pressed to find a majority, even on a campus where consumption is heaviest. The point is not to suggest that there is no reason to be concerned with the extent of risky drinking on campus. Rather, the point is that we should not assume the majority are a problem and walk away from a social norms approach on the basis of a single simple measure without considering a larger set of data.

Still another consideration here is the assessment of "injunctive" norms—the most common attitudes—as well as behavioral norms. The majority of students always hold a relatively moderate attitude about drinking, even if they do not always behave in accordance with that attitude. Yet they misperceive the dominant attitude as being more permissive than it is, explaining much of the behavior that is riskier than would be predicted by actual personal attitudes. So we can start with attitudinal norms in a social norms campaign to make students aware of what the majority really values as responsible behavior. Thus we can get more students behaving in accordance with those attitudinal norms.

A Final Word About Comprehensive Prevention Efforts

When talking about designing substance abuse prevention strategies, one frequently encounters the remark, "There is no magic bullet. Any intervention approach must be part of a comprehensive strategy." The general point of this statement is clear. No single approach, however successful it is in reducing the problem of substance abuse among youth, can be relied upon to eliminate the problem entirely, and combining the force of multiple approaches with demonstrated positive effect is likely to achieve a greater desired outcome overall.

Thus even the most enthusiastic advocates of a social norms approach should consider integration of other models in their prevention work, so long as the additional approaches do not significantly contribute to misperceptions of norms (as with promotion of scare tactics). Offering traditional pharmacological education (usually not effective by itself) may produce a benefit when coupled with accurate social norms information. As previously discussed, normative feedback is being used effectively in brief counseling interventions to break down denial of problems. Holding more social activities that do not support alcohol and other drug use may be a more effective strategy to help avert substance abuse if one is simultaneously correcting the misperception that "nobody likes these activities," which, left unchallenged, produces the self-fulfilling prophecy where very few go because most individuals are thinking others will not be there. Also as previously mentioned, the social norms approach can be used to build support for and compliance with policy initiatives that are already supported by most students, though not always followed because of misperceptions of peers. I expect that more work in the future will explore how these linkages can produce greater benefit.

If one interprets the statement that "any approach must be part of a comprehensive strategy" as meaning simply *in order for it to work*, however, there would certainly be disagreement from those promoting a social norms approach. Programs introducing a social norms approach not necessarily linked to other intervention initiatives have certainly produced significant positive effects on their own, as demonstrated by several of the experiments reported in this book. This is not to say that professionals planning to use a social norms approach should go it alone, but neither should they think they must have other prevention activities up and in place before starting a social norms campaign. There is tremendous potential in just getting the truth out about youth and young adult norms, as the studies in this book reveal. Do not wait for other strategies to be put into action before considering a social norm intervention. If you are considering introducing multiple strategies, the social norms approach is likely to be the most useful starting point as it produces a benefit on its own and sets the stage for other interventions to be more effective.

Finally, if one must make practical decisions about which approaches to employ because of budget and personnel limitations, doing just a little bit of everything to be "comprehensive" and yet stay within the budget may be counterproductive. Any approach needs to be implemented with care and fidelity if it is to be given a true test of its effectiveness. Promoting variety in prevention programming with little depth may simply look good to outsiders when a program is described but ultimately not produce significant change. We have already noted that conducting an effective social norms intervention requires delivery of a substantial dosage of communication about the true norms throughout the year, and from a basis in carefully collected data. Even though social norms interventions can be quite cost-effective compared to other strategies, to skimp on this approach in order to keep other programs going that may not have demonstrated significant prevention potential is a recipe for a disappointing result.

As a closing comment for this chapter and the entire volume, I would add one more note of encouragement to anyone considering getting involved with social norms work in the field of substance abuse prevention. We know that burnout among professionals working in substance abuse prevention is generally quite high. Yet for educators, counselors, and clinicians who have adopted a social norms strategy, I have observed just the opposite: a growing excitement and continued commitment to work in this field. I believe the explanation for such a difference can be found in two basic points. First, it is difficult to sustain oneself in prevention activities that are constantly focused on problems and human failings. In contrast, the social norms approach allows one to concentrate on what is simultaneously normative and positive about youths and young adults. This does not drain the spirit of professionals; it enriches their spirit. Second, it is hard to continue working in a field where little or no progress is observed. The fact that the social norms approach has produced and continues to produce notable improvements among youths and young adults makes the work even more exciting for all of us involved in this effort.

References

Mead, G. H. *Mind, Self and Society: From the Standpoint of a Social Behaviorist* (C. W. Morris, ed.). Chicago: University of Chicago Press, 1934.

Perkins, H. W., DeJong, W., and Linkenbach, J. "Estimated Blood Alcohol Levels Reached by 'Binge' and 'Non-Binge' Drinkers: A Survey of Young Adults in Montana." *Psychology of Addictions*, 2001, *15*, 317–320.

ABOUT THE EDITOR

H. Wesley Perkins, Ph.D., is professor of sociology at Hobart and William Smith Colleges (HWS), where he has taught for more than twenty years and previously served as chair of the Department of Anthropology and Sociology as well as chair of the institutionwide Committee on the Faculty. He received his B.A. from Purdue University, the M.Div. degree from Yale Divinity School, and his M.A. and Ph.D. in Sociology from Yale University. In 1993, he was honored with the HWS faculty prize for outstanding scholarship, and in 1997 the HWS faculty prize for outstanding service to the college community for his work in reducing student alcohol abuse. He directs the Alcohol Education Project at HWS (with colleague David Craig), an initiative providing research, resources, and strategies to reduce substance abuse both locally and nationally. In 1999 the project received a Model Prevention Program award from the U.S. Department of Education.

Perkins has published extensive research in professional journals on alcohol and other drug problems among college students, adolescents, and young-to-middle-aged adults. He pioneered the work that uncovered peer misperception of alcohol and other drug norms and developed the theory underlying the social norms approach to prevention. He has delivered more than two hundred guest lectures; keynote addresses; and workshops for colleges, universities, secondary schools, and professional conferences nationwide. He frequently serves as a consultant to local schools and to state and federal drug abuse agencies. In 1999, he received the Outstanding Service Award from the Network of Colleges and Universities Committed to the Elimination of Alcohol and Other Drug Abuse for his career contribution to prevention work at the local and national levels. His work has been frequently cited in the press and in television news coverage, including the *New York Times,* the *Los Angeles Times,* CNN, *New York Times Magazine, Newsweek,* and *Time* magazine. Perkins is also currently conducting a project on forgiveness and its relation to health and well-being in the life course.

ABOUT THE CONTRIBUTORS

Gregory P. Barker, Ph.D., received his doctorate in cognitive/research psychology from Northern Illinois University in 1998 and immediately began work as the assistant director for psychometric services at NIU's Testing Services. Since that time, he has consulted for a variety of research projects using the social norms approach and social marketing methods to reduce heavy episodic drinking and related injuries. Barker has acted as a statistical consultant for NIU's Health Enhancement Services and as a research associate for Michael Haines of the National Social Norms Resource Center. He has also acted as a research and statistical consultant for numerous research projects at the state and local levels.

Alan David Berkowitz, Ph.D., is an independent consultant who helps colleges, universities, and communities design programs to address health and social justice issues. His expert opinion is frequently sought after by federal government and professional organizations, and he is highly regarded for his scholarship and innovative programs in the sexual assault prevention, drug prevention, and diversity fields. He has been a central figure in developing the social norms approach and is a leader in research and implementation strategies for the model. Berkowitz is the recipient of numerous awards and is a Fellow of the American College Health Association. He received his Ph.D. in psychology from Cornell University and is a licensed psychologist in New York State.

David W. Craig, Ph.D., Philip J. Moorad '28 and Margaret N. Moorad Professor of Science, is chair of chemistry at Hobart and William Smith Colleges. As a biochemist, he is a leader in interdisciplinary program development, particularly in integration of the sciences into programs focusing on health and wellness. He is the developer of electronic media resources for many social norms prevention campaigns and has promoted these strategies nationally at workshops for secondary schools and higher education. He has conducted extensive research in applying social norms strategies to substance abuse prevention in both college and middle school settings and has presented at universities, professional associations, and public health agencies throughout the nation; he is the recipient of numerous national grants. He directs (with colleague Wesley Perkins) the Hobart and William Smith Colleges Alcohol Education Project, which received a model program recognition award from the U.S. Department of Education in 1999.

William DeJong, Ph.D., is a professor of social and behavioral sciences at the Boston University School of Public Health, and director of the U.S. Department of Education's Higher Education Center for Alcohol and Other Drug Prevention, which is based at the Education Development Center (EDC) in Newton, Massachusetts. He is also the principal investigator of the Social Norms Marketing Research Project at EDC. In 2000, he received the College Leadership Award from the Alcohol, Tobacco, and Other Drugs section of the American Public Health Association. A graduate of Dartmouth College, he received his doctorate in social psychology from Stanford University in 1977.

Patricia M. Fabiano, Ph.D., is the program director of Prevention and Wellness Services at Western Washington University, where she has developed a model college health promotion program in her work there for more than eleven years. She has been in college student services for nearly twenty years (first at Southern Illinois University at Carbondale and then at Stanford University) and has made research and program development contributions to her profession throughout that time. She holds a doctorate in community health and is the author of numerous alcohol and other drug prevention and violence prevention grants.

Jeanne M. Far, Ph.D., has worked with prevention efforts at Washington State University (WSU) since 1989. She developed the counseling portion of the Substance Abuse Prevention Program at WSU. Far also has an extensive background and experience in substance abuse prevention research and the Small Groups Norms-Challenging Model intervention. She has been research director for the WSU Substance Abuse Prevention Program since 1991. She is currently director of Project Empowerment and codirector of Project Culture Change, prevention research projects at WSU funded by the U.S. Department of Education. Project

Culture Change recently received national recognition as a model program by the DOE and the Higher Education Center for Alcohol and Drug Prevention.

John D. Frisone, Ph.D., is an experimental psychologist who served as chair of the Psychology Department at Rowan University for more than a decade. He received his doctorate from the City University of New York and has specialized in applied psychology research in the areas of addiction and child abuse and neglect. He has served as a statistical consultant to the New Jersey Division on Youth and Family Services and that state's Department of Health and Senior Services. He has presented on the topic of the impact of domestic violence on children at international conferences and published in the *Journal of Psychology* and *Psychological Reports.* He served as a statistician on the New Jersey Consortium of Alcohol and Social Norms Projects, as well as the Rowan University Alcohol Social Norms Project.

Peggy Glider, Ph.D., is the coordinator of evaluation and research for the Campus Health Service at the University of Arizona. She holds a doctorate in educational psychology from UA, with emphasis on statistics, research design, and computer analysis. She is recognized nationally in evaluation and research of prevention and intervention strategies, having served as principal investigator or research director on multiple federal research and demonstration grants in the alcohol, other drug, and violence arenas. She has also participated in national panels and evaluation teams for the Public Health Service and the U.S. Department of Education. Over the past eight years, she has overseen evaluation of nine grants (eight federal and one state) dealing with university alcohol and other drug/violence issues at UA.

Michael P. Haines, M.S., is the director of the National Social Norms Resource Center and a senior research fellow at Northern Illinois University. He was a certified senior addiction counselor for seventeen years and executive director of a community-based substance abuse program. Until recently, he coordinated a campus health promotion office where he and his staff were the first to combine the social norms approach with social marketing methods to successfully reduce heavy episodic drinking and related injuries. Their effort was chosen as an exemplary program by the U.S. Office of Education. He is a fellow of the American College Health Association and cochairs a committee that oversees their National College Health Assessment.

Linda C. Hancock, M.S.N., F.N.P., Ph.D., is a family nurse practitioner who has provided health care to college students at Virginia Commonwealth University (VCU) since 1987. She also currently serves as the assistant director for the Office of Health Promotion at VCU. In the past several years, she has helped to create social norms campaigns related to both alcohol and tobacco. She has a B.S. in nursing from the University of Maryland and an M.S. in community health nursing from the Medical College of Virginia; she completed her Ph.D. in education at VCU in 2001. Hancock is the author of the *Tobacco Use Reduction Guide for Colleges and Universities*. She is the chair of the Virginia College Co-op for Tobacco Use Reduction.

Neil W. Henry, Ph.D., is associate professor of statistics at Virginia Commonwealth University, where he has held joint appointments in the Department of Sociology and Anthropology and the Department of Statistical Sciences and Operations Research since 1975. He earned his M.A. in mathematics from Dartmouth and his Ph.D. in mathematical statistics from Columbia University. At Columbia he also studied survey research methodology and the use of mathematical models in the social sciences. This led to collaboration with Paul F. Lazarsfeld in codifying the set of models that make up latent structure analysis, and later in teaching and writing about causal and structural equations modeling. He also taught at Cornell University and was statistician for the Gary Income Maintenance Experiment.

Linda R. Jeffrey, Ph.D., has been a faculty member at Rowan University for nearly thirty years. She is a professor of psychology and directs the Rowan University Center for Addiction Studies. She received her Ph.D. in psychology at Rutgers University and master's degrees in English and development and learning from the University of Chicago and Teachers College, Columbia University. She is a licensed New Jersey psychologist specializing in prevention and treatment of addiction, and child abuse and neglect. She was a founding member of the New Jersey Higher Education Consortium and has served as its grant project director for statewide alcohol and tobacco social norms projects, statewide projects in curriculum infusion, peer education, and party drug use prevention.

Koreen Johannessen, M.S.W., currently serves as senior advisor for prevention at the University of Arizona Campus Health Service, and was formerly the director of UA's Health Promotion and Preventive Services. She holds a B.S. in education from Long Island University and an M.S.W. from Florida State University. She currently serves as a consultant and trainer of social norms for the NIAAA Social Norms Marketing Research Project, the Kansas Health Foundation Social Norms Media Campaign to Prevent Binge Drinking, and the Higher Education Center. She was project director for the first Center for Substance Abuse Prevention project to address college drinking and other drug use. In 1999 she was recognized as the Arizona Public Health Association Health Educator of the Year.

Jeffrey W. Linkenbach, Ed.D., is an assistant professor in the Department of Health and Human Development at Montana State University and director of the Montana Social Norms Project (MSNP). He has more than seventeen years of experience working in the field of substance abuse, has authored several publications, and is a popular national-level trainer and keynote speaker on his innovative applications of the social norms model. He is known for pioneering work applying his MOST of Us® campaigns in macro-level settings and with emerging issues. Dr. Linkenbach is credited with developing and coordinating the first two years of the National Conference on the Social Norms Approach to Prevention and is on the editorial advisory board of the *Report on Social Norms*.

DeMond S. Miller, Ph.D., is an associate professor of sociology and director of the Liberal Arts and Sciences Institute at Rowan University. He has worked as an evaluator for alcohol and tobacco social norms projects and as principal investigator to facilitate research projects involving environmental issues and community satisfaction. His primary area of specialization is environmental sociology, with concentrations in qualitative and quantitative evaluation research methods, community development, and social impact assessment; he has also presented several professional papers. Recent examples of his work can be found in the *Researcher*, the *Qualitative Report*, the *Journal of Emotional Abuse*, and the *Southeastern Sociological Review*.

John A. Miller, M.S., M.Ed., is research administrator for Health and Wellness Services-Wellness Programs at Washington State University (WSU). He has coordinated substance abuse prevention efforts at WSU since 1986 and currently serves as codirector of Project Safe and Sound at WSU and Project Culture Change and Project Empowerment. He was involved in developing and implementing the Small Group Norms-Challenging Model at WSU, which received national recognition in 2000 as a model program. He has codirected research projects; coauthored papers, articles and an SGM training manual; and presented at state and national conferences. He is a certified alcohol/drug counselor and clinical supervisor.

Pamela Negro, M.S.W., received her master's degree from Rutgers University and is a certified alcohol/drug counselor and certified prevention specialist. She is the associate director of the Rowan University Center for Addiction Studies. She is a member of the New Jersey Governor's Council on Alcoholism and Drug Abuse, where she serves as chair of the Prevention Committee. She has served on the New Jersey Higher Education Consortium as project coordinator since 1993.

Richard Rice, M.A., is the coordinator of information and education at the National Social Norms Resource Center. He is currently a member of the editorial advisory board of the *Report on Social Norms*.

INDEX